THE
BLOOD
AND
GUTS

THE BLOOD AND GUTS

How TIGHT ENDS
Save Football

TYLER DUNNE

TWELVE

NEW YORK   BOSTON

Twelve
Hachette Book Group
1290 Avenue of the Americas, New York, NY 10104
twelvebooks.com
twitter.com/twelvebooks

First Edition: October 2022

Twelve is an imprint of Grand Central Publishing. The Twelve name and logo are
trademarks of Hachette Book Group, Inc.

The publisher is not responsible for websites (or their content) that are not owned by
the publisher.

The Hachette Speakers Bureau provides a wide range of authors for speaking events.
To find out more, go to www.hachettespeakersbureau.com or call (866) 376-6591.

Library of Congress Cataloging-in-Publication Data

Names: Dunne, Tyler, author.
Title: The blood and guts : how tight ends save football / Tyler Dunne.
Description: First edition | New York, N.Y. : Twelve, Hachette Book Group, 2022.
Identifiers: LCCN 2022019462 | ISBN 9781538723746 (hardcover) |
    ISBN 9781538723760 (ebook)
Subjects: LCSH: Tight ends (Football) | Football—Offense.
Classification: LCC GV951.25 .D96 2022 | DDC 796.332/2—dc23/eng/20220630
LC record available at https://lccn.loc.gov/2022019462

ISBN: 9781538723746 (hardcover), 9781538723760 (ebook)

Printed in the United States of America

LSC-C

Printing 1, 2022

For Mom and Dad, who love and support
and inspire beyond comprehension

CONTENTS

INTRODUCTION

The absurdity of the profession becomes clear to players once they're ejected into mainstream society.

As a player in the National Football League, you are contractually obligated to physically punish your coworkers. You strap on a helmet and take the field with bad intentions. The temperature will rise into the nineties during training camp, too, with livelihoods at stake every rep of every drill. That pales in comparison to your internal temp, of course, because the window of opportunity is small. With an endless supply of potential replacements, one mistake can quickly get you fired in this testosterone-fueled environment.

As coworkers beat the hell out of each other, tempers reach a breaking point. Fists are thrown. Helmets are pulled. *Manhood* is tested. And, moments later, those same two combatants are seated next to each other in a meeting watching film and talking X's and O's. No, this is not the scene at your local bank or neighborhood pharmacy. Imagine walking down the hallway at your job, picking up that brownnoser in sales by the collar and piledriving him into a desk, then walking back to your office and running more accounting numbers. It takes a special kind of person to play professional football and, by God, it's beautiful. This is as close as we have to modern-day gladiators.

No sport captivates America like football because football is the most primitive form of competition in human existence. And no position captures the essence of this all quite like the NFL tight end.

Remember Jeremy Shockey showing zero regard for human life in an exhibition game? Remember the night Jason Witten was sandwiched by two Philadelphia Eagles defenders, his helmet popped off, and he kept running? And Travis Kelce's walk-off touchdown in the playoffs? And Rob Gronkowski throwing Sergio Brown out of the club? And John Mackey treating the Detroit Lions' defense as a collection of bowling pins? This is the book for you.

As the men playing this sport get stronger and faster, the league has tried to curtail injuries. Rules overcorrect over time. Controversy threatens the league's brand just about every year. Yet the NFL plows through it all because what drew everyone to football to begin with— the violence, the fact that this sport is not for everyone—remains. Anyone can play a game of H-O-R-S-E in the driveway or gather at the neighborhood park for a baseball game. This requires something different from the pit of your stomach.

The tight end is the sport itself distilled to one position. You must possess the athleticism to burn a 190-pound defensive back downfield one play, the guts to stick your face into the chest of a 300-pound defensive end the next, and the toughness to wipe that blood away and play on. Brawn alone is not enough at tight end, either. You're required to tap into corners of your brain other players never do. The NFL can try to sanitize its product year to year, rule to rule. Everything we love about football will always be saved at the position Mike Ditka essentially founded sixty-plus years ago.

I traveled all over the country to get inside the minds of the players defining the sport you love. My hope is that *The Blood and Guts* veers a magnifying glass over the individuals who were uniquely qualified to ensure football is forever *football*. Maybe all that yellow laundry on the field has you ready to hurl your remote control directly through the television set. Rest assured. The sport will never become too soft for its own good...thanks to the tight end.

Down in Miami, I throw back drinks with Shockey, a man who brought the sport back to its eye-for-an-eye roots. In St. Louis, Jackie Smith relives a football life that took him to the highest of highs and lowest of lows. He proved just how powerful the mind can be in this sport. In Austin, Tony Gonzalez soul-searches for hours. He's the one who forced the league to reimagine this position's endless possibilities. As that revolutionary force, Gonzalez made friends and enemies and, above all, discovered exactly how playing tight end makes you a better person. The lessons Gonzalez learned are now being passed down to his kids. Same goes for Dallas Clark, a tight end miracle who's a direct product of his hardships. He lost his mother. He walked on at Iowa. He transformed from a walk-on mowing the grass at Kinnick Stadium to catching third-down passes in the playoffs from Peyton Manning. It wasn't an accident.

In North Carolina, Ben Coates struggles to walk around his house. He sacrificed his body and never thought twice about it. He'd do it all over again, too. No way did Jimmy Graham imagine a life in pro football when he feared for his life inside a group home. Now? He's a source of hope for both orphans and, of course, any basketball player trying to cross over to this ruthless sport.

Rob Gronkowski lived like there's no tomorrow, pounding booze and popping his top and ejecting defensive backs into another dimension. George Kittle turned moving another man against his will into a lifestyle. Together, they've driven the tight end into the next generation.

And down at his golf course, I kicked back with the man who started it all. It's hard to imagine where the sport would be without Mike Ditka. He grasped the cutthroat reality of the sport. Be it conscious or unconscious, tight ends forever take their cue from Iron Mike.

Maybe nobody could possibly relate to the nine-to-five that is professional football, but there's no need to panic. It's being preserved.

A funny thing happened the more I chatted with these tight ends, too. The tight end position doesn't only show us everything we need to know about football. It teaches us about life.

THE
BLOOD
AND
GUTS

Chapter 1

THE BLUEPRINT

Mike Ditka is exactly where he should be. A living legend in the heaven on earth he deserves. Enter the clubhouse of Olde Florida Golf Club in Naples, veer left, and of course Ditka's relaxing with a cigar in his hand. He stares off at his course through the window. Back when he cofounded it in 1992, Ditka had one simple request: "No bullshit." That is, no golfers can dillydally. Everyone must keep moving, hole to hole, because you're here to golf, dammit. Not screw around. Fast greens on rolling terrain reflect this vision.

He sets the cigar in an ashtray, and his friends migrate to a nearby table for another game of gin.

The patriarch of pain in football is obviously hurting at age eighty-two. There's a walker within arm's reach and, when he tries to scoot in his chair over to chat, it's a struggle. Forged in the steel town of Aliquippa, Pennsylvania, "Iron Mike" has been one of the sport's most indestructible forces from player to coach to commentator, and now this room serves as the twilight of his extraordinary life. Ditka brushes off help from others, notes that he's had "four or five" hip replacements and leaves it at that. "I can't complain," he says. No use listing all the permanent wounds this sport inflicted when these wounds, to him, were always part of the deal. Those legendary hands that caught 427 passes and mauled linebackers for twelve bruising pro seasons are weathered. Mounds have swollen over the knuckles on the index and middle fingers of his right hand.

I

This day, there's a Band-Aid about six inches above his left knee.

His voice crackles. His thoughts occasionally flicker.

Yet look closely and it's abundantly clear Ditka is still *Ditka*. The intimidating jowls. The brow that weighs heavy over soft blue eyes. The wavy hair slicked back. The iconic mustache that's so tightly groomed. This is still a man who can make a visitor sit up straight and half expect a whistle to be blown for a dozen up-downs. There's no Rob Gronkowski, no George Kittle—no modern NFL tight end, period—without the man sitting here. Before Ditka, the tight end was a blocker attached to the hip of the offensive tackle. He changed that forever. Most important, this position taught Ditka about life. So, no, don't interpret his tendency to repeat himself as a fading mind. It's a default. His tendency to heap praise upon everyone else, over and over, is more so an everlasting effect of the turning point in his life a half century ago.

So many memories remain preserved in the corners of his mind, and he brings them to life here. The NFL existed for forty-one years before Ditka was drafted with the fifth overall pick by the Chicago Bears in 1961, but the league was more of a footnote then. A regional attraction your milkmen and shoemakers mentioned on occasion. Ditka drove the sport directly into America's living room. It's no coincidence that over the course of his career, 1961 to 1972, the number of Americans who cited pro football as their favorite sport increased by 15 percent while baseball slid from 34 to 21 percent. The sport's inherent violence was intoxicating—ruthless, yet aesthetically beautiful. There was something special about football's attrition, the fact that this game is not for everyone. Swinging a baseball bat was quite different than bashing into another human being at full speed. Football weeded out the mentally and physically weak.

No one grasped this reality better than Ditka through the '60s. At tight end, he injected the sport with an unprecedented dose of toughness.

His sanctuary these days often resembles a nature exhibit. Deer tend to prance over those Olde Florida greens. Raccoons aren't nocturnal around here, either. They'll zigzag through the palm trees in the daytime. And watch out for the alligators strutting onto the fairways during mating season. They're particularly bold. Maybe because they're the ones lucky enough to be alive. As one employee here points out, birds love to swoop in and eat the babies. Which all makes this a fitting environment to relive Ditka's rise. He operated at the very top of the food chain in his kingdom.

"You have to understand," Ditka begins, "where I came from."

There isn't a cloud in the sky this eighty-one-degree day or one critter on the course as Ditka leans back.

He starts in Aliquippa, the town that made him. More specifically, he starts with the man who made him: Mike Sr.

One of his dad's beatings certainly stands out above the rest. Eyes fixated forward at nothing in particular, Mike Jr. relives that day. He was in third grade and wanted to give smoking a try, so he swiped a pack of his dad's Lucky Strike cigarettes and headed off into a wooded area outside their home. Mike Jr. found a nice spot to relax, lit the cigarette, and took a puff. The inhalation made him extremely dizzy and he dropped the cigarette. Here, Ditka turns to make eye contact.

"I burned the goddamn woods down."

When Dad came home from work, he looked out the back window, saw the damage, and asked his wife what happened. She said he should ask his son and, moments later, Mike Sr. retrieved his thick leather belt, which he'd kept from his time in the Marines.

"I got my ass beat so bad it was unbelievable. That's OK. I learned. And, listen, he was old-school. He was raised that way. He raised me that way. His other kids didn't get any hits. But I got 'em. I was the oldest, I was supposed to be the example, so I got them. When I got out of line, I got my ass whipped. I thank God I was raised the way I was."

Ditka holds his thumb and index finger a half inch apart. That's how thick his dad's belt was, and it made contact with his ass more times than he can count. As the oldest of four kids, he was made out to be that example.

He was perfectly fine with it all, too. The relationship was based on "respect," he adds. "Not fear. *Respect.*"

This was how Mike Sr. was raised by his father, who emigrated to the States from Ukraine, so Mike Jr. received the same upbringing. Simple as that. The family's last name was actually "Dyczko," and Mike Sr. changed it to what he thought the name sounded like: "Ditka." He was in the Marines until Mike Jr. was four years old. Never overseas, he spent a good amount of time across the country at a base in San Diego. In Aliquippa, the family lived in a housing project. "It wasn't a special life," Ditka says, "but it was a good life." When Dad came home for dinner, Mike knew to sit down immediately and wasn't allowed to leave until he washed and dried the dishes. At age nine, he had a paper route and, initially, didn't own a bike. That meant walking up and down the hills by foot. All money earned was given to his parents, who then gave him an allowance.

"We didn't have anything," Ditka says, "but we earned everything we had."

Aliquippa was a booming steel town through those '40s and '50s. America was at war with communism and refineries like J&L Steel manufactured steel for battleships and planes. J&L employed about half of the entire town. The richest families lived up on the hill in mansions while most families, like the Ditkas, lived down in the valley. Mike Jr. never saw color. To him, fathers of Black kids in his school worked at the mill just like his, so what was the difference? His family didn't own anything they lacked. Still, as Ditka wrote in his autobiography: "It was a very ethnic area, which was also very prejudiced. Whether you were a Polack or a Hunky or a Jew or a Dago or a Wop or a Cakeeater or Colored—we didn't use the other slang word for Blacks—it was prejudiced."

His dad worked on the railroad that serviced J&L Steel. He was also a welder and the president of a local union where, his son says, "he didn't take any shit from the workers or the management." When Mike Sr. returned home for dinner, his clothes were burnt and blackened, a daily reminder to all four kids of what a true work ethic entailed. Especially his oldest. "When he said, 'Jump,' I said, 'How high?'" All the way to eighth grade, Mike Jr. needed to be home by 7 p.m. He was close to his younger brother, Ashton, and the two fought constantly. During one youth baseball game, Mike was the losing pitcher because Ashton dropped a fly ball. Mike chased him home and beat him up. Dad promptly whipped them both.

"There was no sparing the rod. If you did something wrong, you got your ass whipped. But I don't regret it one bit. He raised me the right way, and because of that, I had a value system. I knew what was right and I knew what was wrong. And I tried to stay away from doing what was wrong."

He'd occasionally take a BB gun into the woods to shoot frogs, but Ditka quickly realized it was best to play sports as much as possible. His youth was a nonstop loop of football, baseball, basketball. The weather never mattered much. He and his buddies would shoot hoops until their fingers cracked in the cold. His temper would still get him in trouble. Even if his dad missed a baseball game, he'd hear about a tantrum his son threw and make sure there were consequences. Press Maravich, the father of future NBA star Pete Maravich, was his high school basketball coach, while the hard-driving Carl Aschman was his football coach. Ditka played fullback, linebacker, end, pretty much anywhere that allowed him to kick somebody's ass. As a junior, he even caught a touchdown in the state championship game.

What Ditka remembers most this day is Aschman teaching him how to block. For a good twenty minutes after practice, he'd have Ditka at the blocking sled.

"I was a better baseball player. I thought I'd be a baseball player and ended up being a football player. It was all because of Carl Aschman. It wasn't because of me. He took the time. He taught me how to block. He taught me how to receive. He took the time. He cared. I don't know what he saw, but he saw something."

Colleges passed through and Aschman told them about Ditka. That was the extent of football scouting in the '50s. With his choices down to the University of Pittsburgh or Penn State, Ditka chose Pitt...not that he envisioned pro football as a career. The thought never crossed his mind. Nor did Ditka have any desire to work in the steel mill.

His plan was to be a dentist. There was only one problem. "I had a little problem with chemistry," he says, smiling. It's not that Ditka didn't like the class. The class, he points out, didn't like him.

As it turned out, neither did anyone who got into his way on a football field. At Pitt, Ditka played end on both sides of the ball and didn't merely enjoy contact. This tree trunk in a crew cut *demanded* it. One teammate, Foge Fazio, later recalled Ditka looking "like a prizefighter in the ring" between plays because he couldn't wait to fight again. Ernie Hefferle, who coached the team's ends, said Ditka would plead for the team to hit more in practice. "All he wanted to do was hit, hit, hit." Teammates were on high alert in the locker room, too. After missing a tackle on Michigan State's Herb Adderley, Pitt's Chuck Reinhold was a tick too upbeat for Ditka's liking in saying, "We're only down 7-0." Ditka told Reinhold that he was the reason they were losing, then bounced him off a locker. Ditka always backed up his bark. In his last college game, he dislocated his shoulder trying to block a punt and still played the rest of the game.

Pitt hardly threw the ball—Ditka caught all of eleven passes for 229 yards as a senior—but his brutality on both sides of the ball was rare.

Opponents saw it. Future Pro Football Hall of Famer Dave Robinson faced Ditka in college (at Penn State) and the pros (with Green Bay) and remembers Ditka most as a menace of a defensive end. On film, Penn State noticed that every time a team tried to run a sweep to the left, Ditka sprinted right down the line to catch their halfback. Since the Penn State power sweep called for both guards to lead the way, they changed it up vs. Ditka. They had Robinson, the right guard, spin around to peel back on Ditka. Unfortunately, the left guard got confused and both guards blocked Ditka, thus nuking the play. Scouts saw it, too. As the Dallas Cowboys' VP of personnel, Gil Brandt remembers watching Ditka catch balls in a workout and sprinting right into a cement mixer that was the size of an oversized barbeque pit. The mixer wasn't even on the field of play, but when Ditka ran routes, he had a tendency to continue running. "If he caught the ball at the 20-yard line, he ran it into the end zone," Brandt says. "If he caught the ball at the 40-yard line, he ran it into the end zone." Ditka blasted into the mixer at the end of the field, put a large dent into it, yet hardly flinched. He acted like he casually bumped into a stranger at the grocery store.

A consensus All-American, Ditka was selected fifth overall by the Chicago Bears in the 1961 NFL Draft and given a deal worth $12,000 with a $6,000 signing bonus. Off to the big time he went. Mike Jr. showed the contract to Mike Sr., and his dad only grunted.

Most people, he told his son, work a long time to earn this amount of money.

To this day, Mike Ditka is dumbfounded. Pitt ran the ball nearly four times more than they passed it. He cannot fathom how his two hands would go on to catch 427 passes in professional football.

"I have no idea," says Ditka, pausing.

"Luke Johnsos. Without him. I wouldn't be talking to you today."

This isn't a name celebrated alongside the greatest innovators in the sport's history, but it should be. Johnsos played for the Bears from 1929 to 1936 before then coaching under founder-owner–head coach George Halas the next thirty-three seasons. As the team's offensive coordinator in '61, he recognized that Ditka owned a set of soft hands for his size and knew it'd be difficult for defensive backs to tackle him in open space. The birth of the tight end was rooted in simple strategy. Detached from the trenches, a large human could do serious damage against much smaller humans.

One vivid memory resurfaces. When Ditka was struggling to get off the line of scrimmage, Johnsos asked why and the rookie told him that the linebacker kept jamming him into the tackle. Johnsos instructed

Ditka to line up about three yards wider at the line of scrimmage and, voila, the tight end now had a "two-way release." He could go inside. He could go outside. The kid who lit the woods on fire then did the same thing to pro football with 56 receptions for 1,076 yards and 12 touchdowns as a rookie. Ditka credits Johnsos ("he revolutionized the position") and quarterback Bill Wade ("he loved to throw the football to me—thank God") and claims all he did was catch the ball and run ("I became an offensive weapon"), all while remaining baffled by his coach's vision.

"He used the tight end how no one else had ever thought about using him. He was the reason I had success. What made him have the vision to throw me the football that much? I don't know."

There were clobbering fullbacks before, like Marion Motley. There were prolific receivers, like Raymond Berry. Yet never were these skills blended into one package. The closest comparison was Pete Pihos, whom Brandt describes as a tight end playing wide receiver for the Philadelphia Eagles from 1947 to 1955. Running eight- and nine-yard routes, Pihos was awkward to defend and could box out linebackers with a broad-shouldered frame. He caught sixty-plus passes in three straight seasons. Pihos, however, was also twenty-five pounds lighter than Ditka, a man with bad intentions. A man who ushered in a level of cruelty foreign to offensive football.

Mike Ditka treated the field as primitive, eat-or-be-eaten terrain that 1961 season.

In his first game ever, a 37–13 loss, the rookie told guard Ted Karras to get the lead out of his ass and Karras threw a punch at him. "Was I right?" Ditka asks here. "Probably not. But I wasn't wrong, either." Ahead of a game against the Baltimore Colts, the Bears were well aware that their linebacker, Bill Pellington, had knocked out Detroit Lions tight end Jim Gibbons. Halas even alerted the commissioner of Pellington's dirty play and, the first play of the game, Pellington punched Ditka in the mouth. The next play, Ditka cocked an arm back and returned the favor. And that was that. Pellington didn't bother him the rest of the game. When San Francisco 49ers defensive back David Baker hit one of his teammates with a cheap shot later that season, Ditka teed off on him.

His code wasn't complicated. Accept getting bullied, you will be bullied. Stand up for yourself, you'll command respect. Instantly, the NFL knew where Mike Ditka stood. When the ball was in his hands, his mentality was to simply do everything in his power to prevent people from tackling him. If that meant lowering his shoulder? Fine. A stiff arm? Perfect. Linebackers started to clothesline Ditka before he had a chance to get a head of steam but they soon learned that this came with a consequence.

"If they clotheslined me and I had a chance to blindside him," Ditka says, "I was going to get him."

Most opponents retreated, never to test Ditka again. One, however, always came back for more.

Nobody pushed Ditka to his edge quite like linebacker Ray Nitschke. Ditka doesn't even consider clotheslines from the snarling, balding, savage heartbeat of the Green Bay Packers' defense dirty. Rather, Ditka insists Nitschke was "physically tough" and that he needed to match his toughness. The rivalry between the Packers and the Bears defined football through the 1960s, and central to it all were these two apex predators fighting for dominion. After Nitschke knocked him unconscious in a preseason game, Ditka got revenge in a regular-season game. His crackback block sent the linebacker to the locker room and Nitschke, he says, never forgot. That point forward, Nitschke took a run at Ditka every chance he could. "He tried to knock the shit out of me," says Ditka, "but I'd get him back." Nitschke even confronted Ditka outside of a Milwaukee restaurant once. The two didn't fight...but it was close. "I'm going to get you," Nitschke promised. To which Ditka replied, "If you're going to get me, you better get me good."

Then, they continued to face each other three games a season. Ditka runs the math in his head and estimates they broke even.

"Nitschke tried to kill me. He didn't take any prisoners. When you played the Packers, it was survival of the fittest. You had to play them a certain way if you wanted to survive. I played with the Cowboys. I played with the Eagles. There was never a rivalry like the Bears and the Packers. That was the epitome of what a rivalry was in the National Football League. I mean, we kicked the hell out of each other."

The Bears could lose every game, but beat Green Bay? Halas considered that a successful season. Robinson started alongside Nitschke for most of those battles. Whenever the two Hall of Famers shed other tight ends to the grass, he says, that's where they stayed. Ditka pounced to his feet and drilled them in the back while making a tackle.

"You knew he was going to knock you off the ball," Robinson says. "He was tougher than nails."

Ditka and Nitschke gained a mutual respect, of course. The two became friends and kept in touch up to Nitschke's death in 1998.

Football, to Ditka, was always a *Me vs. You* test of will. "You want to go head-to-head?" he says. "Fine. OK." No play epitomized this mentality more than when he returned for his first pro game back in Western Pennsylvania. On November 24, 1963, two days after President John F. Kennedy was assassinated, the NFL decided to play on and the Bears visited the Steelers in Pittsburgh. Dad, Mom, and so many relatives made the short twenty-mile trip to see Mike Jr. play. Trailing 17–14 with five minutes left, the Bears faced a second-and-thirty-six and Wade told his tight end to run a corner route. Exhausted, Ditka asked if he could run a short hook route instead. The NFL would label what happened next the sixty-ninth-best play ever. Ditka caught the short pass, Clendon Thomas whisked by him, and Ditka stormed upfield into a trio of Steelers defenders. First, he flattened Glenn Glass with the crown of his helmet. Myron Pottios dove and could only grasp his right foot for a split second. And poor Willie Daniel. All Daniel could do was helplessly lunge for any cloth possible in embarrassing fashion before being flicked away like a fly.

Ditka rumbled ahead for sixty-three yards to set up a game-tying field goal that helped catapult Chicago into the NFL Championship, where they'd beat the New York Giants, 14–10.

"He was the meanest, toughest rascal in the league, and I've got the dent in my head to prove it," Thomas told the *Pittsburgh Press*. "Anytime you came near Ditka, you had to expect forearms and fists. You came away bruised. He was mean, but he was also as talented as anyone I ever lined up against."

Practicing against an all-time defense helped, too. He shouldn't only be associated with the "85 Bears." The unit that won a title in 1963 was historic, too, in allowing a meager ten points per game. The best player Ditka ever faced might've been on his own team in the six-foot-eight, 285-pound Doug Atkins. Nobody—ever—gave Atkins shit in practice. He was big. He was mean. He was the nicest fella on the team until you pissed him off. As Ditka explains, Atkins was both lean and muscular, "so he just threw people around like rag dolls."

This was one player Ditka would never piss off.

"No! I'm not dumb."

Playing this violently meant doing serious damage to his own body, of course. Not that Ditka sat out. He couldn't shake the thought of how much money his dad made at the mill. That was real work. This was a game. He injected his body with novocaine and cortisone all the time to play on. In 1964, Ditka even played all season with a dislocated shoulder. He initially separated it in an exhibition game against the College All-Stars, which seemed innocent enough. When the darn thing kept popping out, Ditka strapped it into place with a harness and didn't miss a game. "Hey," he says, "you learn to play with pain." Here, he demonstrates how. His left arm was fine. He could stretch that all the way up, like so. His right arm? He couldn't even bend it to shoulder height. That season, he figured out a way to knock a pass with his good arm down into his chest to catch seventy-five passes, the most in his career, for 897 yards with five touchdowns.

Decades later, it still hurts to lift that arm.

The worst injury of them all struck the following season. In 1965, the arch in his foot "cracked" and he then felt it pop once more in its cast while fooling around at practice. Ditka played that entire season with a dislocated foot by numbing it up once before the game, then again at halftime. Life sure was good for Mike Ditka…until it wasn't. In 1966, he caught only 32 passes on a 5-7-2 Bears team, and his most memorable moment was decking a drunken fan on the field. The more he challenged authority and flirted with the AFL's Houston Oilers, the more he agitated Halas. Finally, in 1967, the Bears boss traded his star tight end to the Philadelphia Eagles and Ditka's life unraveled. He has since described his two seasons with the Eagles as "purgatory on earth."

He was depressed. He hated football. He'd later admit he almost killed himself drinking. Toiling at rock bottom is burnt into Mike Ditka's memory as much as any touchdown. That second year in Philly, he nearly self-destructed.

Living by himself, in a downtown apartment, Ditka would go out every single night, and the alcohol had a way of whipping him into a strange haze. He'd often wake up in "strange places" with zero recollection how he got there or who he was with. The next day, his hangover would be more of a severe fog in which Ditka was unable to comprehend what was real and what wasn't. He drank so much that the complexion of his skin started to change. His playing time decreased. The Eagles went 2-12. It all spiraled the five-time Pro Bowler deeper and deeper and deeper into depression. At work, he'd spar often with new head coach Joe Kuharich and, late in a 47–13 loss in Cleveland, the mess Ditka created for himself clubbed him harder than any Nitschke clothesline. With his parents sitting in the stands—when he explicitly told them not to come—Ditka sat on the bench and wept.

Three weeks later, after a season-finale loss to the Vikings, he didn't say goodbye to anyone. Ditka got into his car and drove straight through a blizzard back to his home in Chicago. He did not care that there was still one year left on his contract.

"I was going to quit," Ditka says. "I lost my love of the game, but what else was I going to do? I wasn't a rocket scientist."

As the decades pass, this low point of Ditka's life only vanishes from the minds of football fans but, here, it's clear that Ditka has not forgotten.

"It seemed to be the thing to do. You think you're a big-time football player—'I'm going to go get drunk.' It could've been the end of it, really."

He stares at the ground. "I was a mess."

Ditka was the first tight end to lose himself, to enter such a darkness, and he wouldn't be the last. This position tends to attract the wildest personalities in football, and those personalities tend to push themselves to the brink. It's a fine line. When all hell-raising is funneled into stiff-arms and crackbacks, the tight end is one of the most entertaining athletes in all of sports. Yet it's not easy to confine all belligerence to three hours on a Sunday. Years later, Tony Gonzalez would face the same moment of truth.

Tight ends find a way of digging themselves out of the abyss, too. Starting with Ditka.

Three days after deciding he was finished with football—devoid of any Plan B in life—Ditka received a phone call from Tom Landry. The Dallas Cowboys head coach told Ditka he had traded for him and, while he had no clue if Ditka could still play, he wanted to give this a try. Ditka had no clue why any team would want him. His best guess is that one of his only good games that wretched season came against Dallas.

That phone call, however, saved his career. And, honestly, his life.

"The best thing that happened to me was when I met Tom Landry. He really made me. He made me understand what it was to be a team player. He was fantastic. He was just absolutely the best. I went there and cleaned up my act and became a pretty good football player. A team player."

Granted, Ditka got off to a rocky start. After a night out, he got into a car accident with Walt Garrison that sent him through the windshield and knocked his teeth out. As Garrison later recalled, the dentist gave Ditka two options. He could wire his teeth shut (and not play the next day) or pull his teeth. Ditka told him to "pull the son of a bitches," but soon learned he didn't have a choice because, it turned out, his jaw was also broken. Said Garrison: "You could hear him out on the field breathing through his teeth. 'Hiss-haw, hiss-haw, hiss-haw,'" Garrison recalled in *Cowboys Have Always Been My Heroes*. "Sounded like a rabid hound. And you could hear that mad dog Ditka cussin' even with his mouth wired shut." As legend has it, he didn't even use an anesthetic.

Ditka soon cleaned up his act and supplied the Cowboys exactly what they needed: toughness. As a receiver, he couldn't get separation anymore. But he was crafty enough to get open, he could still catch with his hands and, Brandt adds, he was still a competitor. In Dallas, Ditka worked out more than he ever did in Chicago, trimming down to 215 pounds.

"What happens is people get down on people too quickly," Brandt says. "A guy might have a bad year. Mike played when he could hardly walk. You always hear that Mike played when other people would've sat. He played when other people did sit. He was tougher than heck."

As a twenty-two-year-old rookie, Cliff Harris had no problems covering Ditka in practice. The tight end's speed was obviously shot. But right when you'd be up on him as a DB, ready to break where he broke at the top of a route, he'd blast you with a forearm. "Boom!" Harris says. "I learned to stay a forearm distance away." That's how Ditka still managed to catch 72 balls for 924 yards with 5 touchdowns through four seasons as a Cowboy. Four seasons that helped define the tight end position as much as anything because Ditka overcame his demons. Ditka embraced the altruism of the profession. Landry was a man of faith who pulled no punches, and he loved it. Landry made it clear that Ditka was here to block and lead, a responsibility he took to heart.

At the time, the Cowboys were known as chokers. This was the team that lost two NFL Championships to the Green Bay Packers, including the "Ice Bowl" in 1967, and then Super Bowl V to the Baltimore Colts, 16–13. Expectations were high into 1971. After a sluggish

4-3 start, Ditka was the one who spoke up. He told the team that when everyone works together "miracles happen."

"All of a sudden," quarterback Roger Staubach later said, "these same human beings won ten games in a row."

In Super Bowl VI, Dallas romped the Miami Dolphins, 24–3. Ditka caught a touchdown pass for old time's sake, too.

The Cowboys would go on to make the playoffs in eleven of their next twelve seasons with one more Super Bowl title, and Staubach credited Ditka as the player who made this a team that refused to back down. To anybody. Of course, the long-term effect was greater for Ditka. He retired after the 1972 season and seamlessly transitioned into coaching on Landry's staff as the special teams coordinator. Harris returned kicks then and, every week, Ditka coached like he played. His face was red. His voice was hoarse. He stormed around the practice field like a man ten coffees deep and warned everyone that *this* was the best special teams unit the Cowboys had faced yet, so "You guys really gotta get after 'em!" Harris would never object, lest he piss Ditka off, but he could not help but ask himself, "Didn't he say that last week?" Either way, the enthusiasm was contagious.

In 1981, Ditka buried the hatchet with Halas by writing the Bears' founder a letter. He said he wanted to renew their friendship and asked if Halas would one day consider him for the head coaching job.

Halas asked Landry if Ditka was ready. He was. And, in 1982, Ditka shuffled back to Chicago, where his name became synonymous with football itself. On a team loaded with characters, Ditka was larger than life in winning six division titles over ten years. The '85 Bears remain one of the greatest teams of all time. All along, one principle guided Ditka. He played as hard as he could for as long as he could so, as a coach, demanded the same thing from every player.

Ron Rivera lived it. He spent his entire nine-year career as a linebacker playing for Ditka and, as the team's union rep, says the two developed a "unique relationship." They'd meet one-on-one every two weeks. Training camps under Ditka were as ruthless as one could imagine from a disciple of both Halas and Landry. The Bears were in pads twice a day for a good eight weeks.

After one merciless practice, Rivera felt compelled to speak up.

"He just ripped our ass," Rivera says. "It was a hot, tough day and we were dragging ass. He had this thing: 'Fatigue makes cowards out of all of us.' That's one of the things he'd always grind on us about. So afterwards, it was one of those days I had to go in and talk to him about some general stuff and I said to him, 'Coach, I've got to ask you something. Why are you so hard on us? I mean goddamn. What the fuck, Coach? What's that all about?' He looked at me and said, 'Ronnie, I would never ask you guys to do anything I couldn't do as a player because I believe you guys can do it.'"

The words hit home. This was two years after Ditka was inducted into the Pro Football Hall of Fame and the Bears were playing an exhibition game in Canton. On the team bus, Ditka made a point to sign and hand one of his Hall of Fame portrait cards to Rivera. Three decades later, as an NFL coach himself, Rivera still hung onto that card, too.

"The whole point was the dude had a standard and he believed that if he could do it, we could do it."

Ditka coached the New Orleans Saints for three disappointing seasons (1997–1999), wearing a dreadlock wig in his press conference after trading his entire draft for Texas running back Ricky Williams. And, hey, why not pose in a bride-and-groom photoshoot with the Heisman Trophy winner for a magazine cover? Ditka was himself. Always. It didn't matter if a reporter asked him why he was in a bad mood after a loss. "What do you care?" he once sniped back. "If you were 2-7, you'd be in a bad mood, too." Or if he was starring in the 2005 movie *Kicking and Screaming* with Will Ferrell. Or if he was dishing unfiltered takes as an unofficial narrator of the sport for various TV networks.

This raw authenticity endeared the man to people of all ages from all backgrounds. If the NFL ever did create a silhouette logo for its league, like the NBA did with Jerry West, it'd sure be hard to top *Ditka*. Two syllables that ooze grit. And the tipping point for this all was '68. Only by looking himself in the mirror—and admitting he had a problem—was Ditka able to rediscover his true self. Landry threw him a life raft, and Ditka was once again that yes-sir, no-sir kid from Aliquippa.

Those principles instilled by his father years ago would serve as the compass for the rest of his life.

"Hard work. Effort. Don't be a complainer," Ditka says. "Don't be a whiner. That's the way I tried to play the game and coach the game. If you were willing to work your ass off and do the right thing—even if you didn't—then I would care about you. It was a great run. You don't know why things happen. If I had to change something, I don't know what I'd change. You have setbacks, so you can move forward again.

"It's been a hell of a run. I have no complaints."

His wife, Diana, leans in with a quick story to share. Back when they first started dating, in the early '70s, she'd tell people her new boyfriend played football and when they asked what position he played, she was stumped. "I think he's a 'tight ass' or something," she'd reply. In fairness to her, a tight end really wasn't a *tight end* until Ditka made it so. Not surprisingly, when he flips on the TV today, Ditka sees a sport that's getting softer. All this showboating irritates him, too. "I think you respect your opponent. If you beat him, fine. Don't try to make him look bad." Even the coverage of the sport, the talk show fodder, can be too much to stomach. "All bullshit."

Ditka does enjoy watching modern tight ends. All are a heck of a lot more athletic than he was at his peak.

"But," he adds, "it doesn't mean they were tougher or smarter or hit harder. They do things I could never do. But I know one thing: They couldn't play any harder than I played."

Good luck finding any tight ends post-Ditka that'd ever argue this.

Now, Ditka is perfectly content watching the sun slowly set surrounded by the people he loves. At one point, his daughter arrives from out of town, gives her dad a kiss on the cheek and shows him a football card one of her coworkers' husbands recently dug up. Right there, is the iconic mean mug—the cheeks, the crew cut, the eyes. "Handsome man!" she says. Ditka can credit Mike Sr. and Aschman and Johnsos and Landry all he wants, but he is the true godfather of the tight end position.

And, if history is any guide, there's no need for Ditka to worry. The position he created will protect this sport's bludgeoning violence forever.

Chapter 2

"SUPERMAN"

The stare was intimidating and nobody was off-limits. His eyebrows would first tilt at forty-five-degree angles. Next, his pupils met yours for an uncomfortable one…two…three seconds that sent a shiver down your spine.

Conversation was brief. Always brief. All John Mackey needed to do was shoot you this glare.

"You didn't want to see it," says former Baltimore Colts center Bill Curry, one of Mackey's best friends. "He didn't contort his face. It didn't change at all. It was very fixed. What it was saying was, 'How are you going to respond?'"

One day in the middle of the Colts locker room, a teammate simply would not stop bitching about his playing time. Curry won't say who it was, only that it was quite melodramatic. After hearing enough pontification, Mackey spoke up. Always a team leader, the tight end rarely followed up his icy stare with many words. This time, he made an exception. "The reason you're not playing is because you're fat," Mackey said. "Get yourself in shape and you'll get to play."

That player did not complain about his playing time ever again. He whipped himself into shape and played a critical role on the Colts.

Such was the power of Mackey. Nobody else in the Colts locker room would've been able to get away with this.

"Not without having at least one fistfight," Curry says. "But no one was going to challenge him."

Two years after the Chicago Bears drafted Mike Ditka, another brahma bull of a football player revealed to the masses everything a tight end ought to be. Mackey was a one-man work hazard for the eleven players across the line of scrimmage. Defenders were not avoided. They were *trampled*. Once the ball was in his hands, Mackey ran with his chest high, like a man huffing, puffing, about to blow your house down with a lowered shoulder. His rookie year in 1963—726 yards on 35 receptions for a whopping 20.7 yards per reception—served as an exclamation point to everything Ditka originated in 1961. Curry notes that Mackey also returned kicks as a rookie, and when he pauses to let those words sink in, it feels more like a moment of silence for the brave souls willing to step onto those train tracks.

Grainy film does neither tight end justice because, physically, there was nothing remotely close to Ditka and Mackey before they arrived.

"They weren't," as Curry puts, "regular human beings."

During the course of a game, Curry would call for a huddle roughly ten yards behind the line of scrimmage and, then, everyone leaned in to hear what play quarterback Johnny Unitas was calling. Inevitably, many would look at No. 88 and thank the heavens Mackey was in their huddle. "We've got 'Superman' on our team," Curry said to himself. Often, he wondered why the Colts didn't simply throw the ball to Mackey every play.

"He didn't have a chip in his computer," Curry says, "that allowed him to do anything but dominate the guy across from him. If you were lined up across from him, you were going to have a nightmare all day long."

To fully grasp the impact of Ditka and Mackey in the 1960s, another old salt from the gridiron insists you need to travel back in time even further.

Ernie Accorsi first met Mackey as the Colts' public relations director before he became the team's assistant general manager and general manager. From there, he took over the Cleveland Browns and then the New York Giants. With a career that spans decades, Accorsi is unquestionably one of the game's finest historians. With the Giants, he also had access to a man whose NFL career went back to the '40s.

Long before Ken Kavanaugh spent nearly a half century as an assistant coach (1955–1970) and scout (1971–1999) with the Giants, he was an end for George Halas's Chicago Bears. Back then, in the '40s, everything was tight. Players did not stray from the scrum because NFL offenses universally deployed three running backs with no flankers, no split ends. The Bears won four NFL titles that decade and, while Halas ran his team with an iron fist, he was smart enough to let quarterback Sid Luckman draw up his own plays. One day, Luckman and Kavanaugh came up with the wild idea of Kavanaugh splitting ten yards off the line of scrimmage. Upon breaking the huddle, Kavanaugh took his spot out wide and Halas was incensed. "Kavanaugh!" he growled. "Who in the hell are you going to hit out there?"

Into the 1950s, that tightness suffocating offensive creativity started to loosen. Through the advent of the "pro set," a split end and flanker emerged. Baltimore had one of the best split ends ever, too, in Raymond Berry. The two ends attached to the offensive tackles were solid blockers with good hands but, as Accorsi notes, "no speed merchants." Accorsi watched his first pro game in 1949 and cites the Detroit Lions' Leon Hart as one of the best ends. A number one overall pick in 1950, Hart averaged 454.8 yards per season for his career at end. The Colts had a darn good end themselves in Jim Mutscheller, whose difficult six-yard catch in the 1958 NFL Championship, aka "the Greatest Game Ever Played," set up Alan Ameche's historic one-yard touchdown.

Then, Ditka and Mackey changed everything.

Their instant success forced everyone to use the word "tight" in front of "end," Accorsi adds, as a way to differentiate this pass catcher from the one split wide. At Syracuse, Mackey caught only 27 passes in three seasons. He also played running back on a team that ran all the time, but even then, he was mostly a blocker for Heisman Trophy winner Ernie Davis. Still, Colts head coach Don Shula saw something. He made Mackey the Colts' second-round pick in '63 and, to Accorsi,

Mackey is the player who best ushered the tight end into the mainstream because of his raw *"explosion."* Speed met power in a way the game had never seen. One bit of advice from his predecessor helped. Mutscheller taught Mackey how to fire off the line a half count before the ball was snapped.

Not that he needed any help.

"He was just different," Accorsi says.

The grandfather who watched John Mackey in real time could watch a montage of the tight end's punishing splendor today with his grandson, and both would enjoy the wreckage equally. Mackey's game was timeless. Be it tipping a pass to himself before ramming through New England Patriots defensive back Don Webb, or delivering a right hook of a stiff arm to the chin of a Washington Redskins' DB, or ducking underneath a Dick Butkus clothesline to race seventy-nine yards to pay dirt. Mackey became a main attraction for NFL Films, which was romanticizing the beautiful barbarity of the sport. "I decided the only thing you can do," Mackey once said, "is just try to hurt someone. There's the play I ran over the nine guys against Detroit. I caught that diagonal pass and, when I turned up, it was like the whole team came over there."

He wasn't exaggerating. Six of his nine touchdowns in 1966 came on plays of fifty yards or more and none were more dramatic than this sixty-four-yard conquest that remains one of the sport's most improbable escapes of all time. It's a scene straight out of *Kill Bill*. After sidestepping one defender, Mackey was suddenly fenced in by a horde of enemies. With no feasible daylight, he simply closed his eyes and slammed the accelerator. The linebackers and defensive linemen within range either took terrible angles or completely quit on the play. Wise decisions, in retrospect, considering Mackey thrashed all four Lions defensive backs on-site. He began by exploding through Bruce Maher and sticking a forearm in Bobby Thompson's face. The player he initially juked after catching the ball, Wayne Rasmussen, reappeared and tried leaping atop his back. That failed in comical fashion. Mackey then ran over one of his own teammates and—on his way to the end zone, opening his eyes—shooed away future NFL defensive coordinator Dick LeBeau.

"It's physically impossible to do what he did," Curry says. "You have to watch it over and over and over and just chuckle. Because he couldn't do it, but he did. There was no remorse, no let-up, no relenting, no 'Let's give this guy a break.'"

As he crossed the goal line, Mackey displayed the emotion of a mannequin.

That was part of the mystique, too. His switch. The same specimen terrorizing defenders hardly reacted after the whistle. Late in the 1970 season, the Colts appeared to be bottoming out. Super Bowl hopes were fading fast against a Chicago Bears team entering the doldrums. Unitas threw three interceptions in the first seven minutes to give Chicago a 17–0 lead. Yet, the expressions of both Unitas and Mackey never changed on the sideline, in the huddle, anywhere, and Baltimore climbed back to give itself a chance in the final minutes. Down 20–14, a hunched-over Unitas uncorked a fifty-four-yard touchdown to Mackey to win it.

When both players walked off the field, their demeanors still hadn't changed.

"Like they just finished a nice practice," Curry says. "Even though they were very different human beings, both of those guys had the most utter sense of calm. You better be damn sure you had them on your side because they were cold-blooded."

That was how Mackey conducted himself as a leader, too. He didn't say much, but his words always carried so much weight. Ahead of this Super Bowl season, he managed to speak up at the perfect time. The Colts swapped wide receivers with the Pittsburgh Steelers, welcoming in Roy Jefferson, who was fresh off back-to-back thousand-yard seasons. It was the age-old gamble that either gets a contender over the hump or spontaneously combusts. He had also clashed often with head coach Chuck Noll. And when Jefferson arrived at the Colts' training camp, the new partnership got off to a rocky start almost immediately. Coaches told Jefferson they wanted to time him, to test his speed, and he refused. After watching this all unfold on the field, Mackey later told the coaches to make Jefferson his roommate. "We win here," he said. "I'll take care of him."

The Colts obliged, and Accorsi declares Jefferson the team's best player that season. Easily.

"That's the kind of power that Mackey had," Accorsi says, "the influence he had."

The Super Bowl that 1970 season was an ugly affair. Baltimore could hardly move the ball offensively against the Dallas Cowboys, turning the ball over seven times and averaging 2.2 yards per carry. "They ate our lunch," Curry says. "It was embarrassing." But as he had many times before, Mackey delivered. A Unitas pass in the second quarter that was tipped by two players—Colts receiver Eddie Hinton and Cowboys cornerback Mel Renfro—landed in the tight end's hands and he rumbled seventy-five yards to the end zone. Jogging a good twenty paces behind his pal, Curry only thought, "There goes 88 again! Run, John, Run!" Baltimore won, 16–13. A fine payoff for a decade's worth of defenders hurling their bodies into his legs. Very quickly, defenders realized the only way to tackle Mackey was by chopping him down.

Nothing could knock him out for good—Mackey missed one game in ten seasons—but "Superman" did have his kryptonite.

He couldn't stand needles, refusing to get jabbed for flu shots and pain injections alike. The bubonic plague could've engulfed all of Baltimore. Curry is positive Mackey still wouldn't have allowed anyone holding a needle in the same room as him. He also got nervous around animals. Curry once found Mackey in nothing but his jockstrap, a strange sight in this training facility where families walked all over to watch the team practice. When Curry implored Mackey to get in the locker room, he said he couldn't. "There's something in my locker," Mackey told him, "and it's breathing."

Dennis Gaubatz, the team's middle linebacker, had placed a live possum in Mackey's locker.

This is another reason Mackey was so beloved by teammates. He didn't cold-cock Gaubatz for a stunt like this. He laughed. The same person with the impenetrable stare could also take a joke. There were many jokes, too. Running back Tom Matte, the team's preeminent prankster, took it to a new level when the seventeen-year cicadas swooped in one summer. Knowing that Mackey didn't wear thigh pads because his legs were already tree trunks, Matte sneakily stuffed the thigh slips in Mackey's pants with handfuls of the live insects. Halfway through a scrimmage, the cicadas started to get loud. Everyone was in on the joke...except for Mackey.

"Those things start going, '*Keh-keh-keh-keh-keh!*'" says Curry, rolling his tongue to imitate the sound. "We're in the huddle and everybody's cracking up."

It took a few moments but once Mackey realized where the sound was coming from—as Matte rolled on the ground in laughter—he freaked. "Huddle around me!" he said. With so many fans watching practice nearby, he wanted players to give him cover so he could once again strip down to his jockstrap.

"He got rid of those cicadas, out of his britches, in about thirty seconds," Curry says. "He always laughed at himself. I think that's the gift of a great person."

His impact on the position is obvious. The John Mackey Award has been given to the best tight end in college football since 2000. Older fans undoubtedly have flashbacks every time Rob Gronkowski or George Kittle squash a defensive back downfield. Accorsi describes the tight ends of today as "aircraft carriers" compared to those in the '60s. But John Mackey? To Accorsi, it all started with him. That's why it was so strange that it took twenty years for a true trailblazer to get into the Pro Football Hall of Fame. When Accorsi grew frustrated with the snub a few years before his 1992 induction, he asked one of the selectors what the problem was, and this selector said someone in the room was adamant Mackey had bad hands.

That set Accorsi off because Mackey rarely ever dropped anything. So what if he used his body, instead of his hands? "If you look at a million pictures of him in action, you'll see the ball is against his chest. But he *knew* that. He didn't drop the ball!"

One reason it possibly took so long for the Hall to call is the same reason Mackey resonates today—he was a needed thorn in the NFL's side. When the NFL and AFL merged, Mackey became the first NFL Players Association president and vigorously fought for the right to player movement. In a 1972 suit, Mackey was the lead plaintiff repelling the Rozelle Rule, which extremely limited a player's right to free agency. Named after the league's commissioner, this rule permitted Pete Rozelle to compensate one team that lost a player to another team by taking something of equal value from the club that signed the free agent. In fear of losing high picks, teams simply didn't sign talented veterans. The rule's existence alone prevented players from shifting team to team and/or selling their talents at the highest possible price.

Mackey looked around the country, saw that this was not the case in other lines of work, and challenged the status quo.

Over time, the player's union became strong enough to put Mackey's vision into full action. "The privilege," as Curry puts, "to say, 'I'd rather play over here than over there.'" Mackey passionately fought for the players on long-term issues such as better pensions and short-term issues like higher per diems in training camp. Curry, who succeeded Mackey as head of the NFLPA in 1973, still remembers when players received all of $6 per day. Mackey had a knack for commanding respect and gaining unanimity in a room full of people from different backgrounds. He did it with stoicism, too. Once, the location of a meeting had to change from a Westchester country club to a hotel in Manhattan because the country club wouldn't allow African Americans on the premises. When a representative for an owner asked Mackey—in an insulting way, as Curry recalls—why he was wearing a purple jumpsuit, the tight end hardly reacted. Instead, he looked the man up and down and asked why he had white socks with dress shoes.

When the rep replied that he liked white socks, Mackey said, "I like purple jumpsuits."

"Charisma," Curry says. "When he walked into a room, the room changed."

For all the lives he affected on a football field, Mackey changed far more off it. Today's players have unprecedented control of their destinies. And if serious health issues set in after this game ejects them back into mainstream society, their families have options. Thanks to Mackey. As his own health deteriorated to scary depths, the league passed the "88 Plan," named in his honor, to supply up to $88,000 per year in financial help for players diagnosed with dementia, ALS, or Parkinson's disease. The mass media coverage of Mackey's tragic battle with frontotemporal dementia also helped raise awareness for what the sport can do to a man later in life. Mackey died at the age of sixty-nine in 2011, after spending the final four years of his life in assisted living.

The tight end position can be a glorious endeavor, one that brings the very best out of the sport itself, but it's not always rainbows and touchdowns. This game, as one of Mackey's contemporaries learned, has a way of sticking with you.

One play is all it takes.

Chapter 3

A MINDSET

The good times are rolling for Jackie Smith. He's basically your lovable grandfather from the jump with eighty-two years of stories that twist and turn and always land on a profound point. His vivid memory is rivaled only by a vivacious personality. If Mike Ditka finds his peace at a golf course, cigar in hand, Smith relaxes at a spot like this, Syberg's restaurant in the St. Louis area, with a twenty-two-ounce beer in hand.

It's packed. It's loud. In a perfectly ironed, buttoned-down shirt, the former St. Louis Cardinals great has the sort of gentle eyes and cheeks that are frozen in a thin, permanent smile. What a joy it is for him to detail his rise. Smith was the first tight end to truly emerge out of nowhere—a dirt track in Kentwood, Louisiana—and dominate pro football. He was a bad, bad man who could both run like a gazelle and kick some ass. Yet when everyone hears his name, these aren't the memories that autoplay. Unless you're a football diehard who's at least seventy years old, these memories are forgotten. Chances are, *Jackie Smith* elicits a totally different moment. A nightmare. At a tabletop nearby, right underneath one of those neon beer signs and televisions that replay Tom Brady highlights on ESPN, sits the elephant in the room. One we cannot ignore. Close friends advise against bringing up the night of January 21, 1979, because they know the pain it brought Smith.

Like Ditka, he dismantled defenses from the tight end position.

Like Ditka, he took a circuitous path to Tom Landry's Dallas Cowboys in the twilight of his career and, like Ditka, a football was thrown to Jackie Smith in the end zone of a Super Bowl.

The ball arrived, ricocheted off his fingers, and everything changed.

Be it the stakes, the iconic radio call, or the image of his body levitating off the Orange Bowl surface, these scant 5.5 seconds defined the man. And it's not fair. When Smith retired, no tight end in pro football history had more receiving yards. He was the first of his kind. A star. Yet his legacy was distilled down to one mistake that, in truth, wasn't fully his mistake. Whereas Ditka overcame his depression to become one of the sport's most beloved ambassadors of all time, people mostly associate Smith's name with failure. Imagine if a moment so brief in your profession grew to define your very existence to millions. It wouldn't matter if you're volatile by nature or, like Smith, the epitome of southern hospitality. Psychological damage is a guarantee.

So, through a four-hour chat, we ever...so...gently...ease into this subject.

Once Smith is displaced to Super Bowl XIII, he doesn't hide. He basically orders that elephant an IPA, relives it all, and never breaks that smile.

"I guess they can kill you," Smith says, "but they can't eat you. People can look at it how they want to look at it. I did the best I could do. It's an emotional game for the fans, too. When things like that happen, it's something to be talked about. The thing that helped me a lot was the attitude I had—I was so lucky to be there. How can you cuss and get upset and be depressed about something that gave your children..."

His voice trails off. That tends to happen when his kids come to mind.

Smith reaches into the front pocket and pulls out two sheets of paper held together by a staple. Right here are a collection of typed quotes from one his favorite authors, Ralph Waldo Emerson. For several minutes, Smith is quiet. He reads the prose to himself with pursed lips and striking intensity.

Finally, Smith pauses and recites one quote aloud.

My life is a May game, I will live as I like. I defy your straight-laced, weary social ways and modes. Blue is the sky, green the fields and groves, fresh the springs, glad the rivers, and hospitable the splendor of sun and star. I will play my game out. And if any shall say me nay, shall come out with swords and staves against me to prick me to death for their foolish laws, come and welcome. I will not look grave for such a fool's matter. I cannot lose my cheer for such trumpery. Life is a May game still.

This is the one that helps most. Asked to interpret what the quote means to him, his voice rises.

"There's a lot more to life than a freakin' football game. It's a wonderful game. But it's a game. It's not the essence of life."

Few have a clue that it took years—no, *decades*—for Smith to reach this state of serenity. He doesn't want to sound completely rehabilitated, either. Smith drifted from family. From himself. Only recently, about two years before this chat, did Smith sincerely take his demons head-on. Precisely what drove Smith to such amazing heights in the NFL—his mind—became weaponized against him. More than any other sport, football can define a man. And who Jackie Smith was, to his core, was a man obsessed with outworking everyone.

What happens when you bleed and sweat and bleed a little more for 214 games, then your world comes crashing down in Game No. 215?

Somehow, you must find yourself again.

———

His rise begins with a tale American as apple pie: a high school crush. At Kentwood High, there were only thirty kids in his class, but one of his pals had a cousin in Baton Rouge who'd visit every so often and, by golly, the tenth grader was smitten. Aware that this girl's father was Al Moreau, a record-setting high hurdler in the 1930s, Jackie Smith reckoned he'd join the track team to impress her.

He didn't know the first thing about clearing a hurdle and the school didn't even have its own functioning track. They'd count one lap around the football field as a quarter mile. Even worse, a leaky water tank would form a huge mudhole near the fourth light pole on this makeshift track—there was no way around it. Training in such slop might sound miserable, but in truth it actually helped the Kentwood track team. Once they competed on an actual track for their meets against other schools, about thirty-four miles south in Hammond, Louisiana, they could fly. "It was like running uphill," Smith says, "and, all of a sudden, it leveled out." The crush didn't last, but his pure love for running sure did. He'd eventually fall for a girl with a white Corvette named Gerri from a town five miles north, too.

Smith won states in the hurdles with one flat-out refusal to lose.

"I was determined," he says. "It's a game of arms and legs played mostly from the neck up. Once you have the ability to do something, it's about how you think about it and how you position it in your mind."

He played football, too, as a way to stay in shape for track. Five total games, anyways. After riding the pine as a junior—only punting occasionally—Smith got his shot as a "spinner back" in Kentwood's single wing offense his senior year. Translation: He'd catch the direct snap and usually hand the ball off to somebody else. Then he broke his shoulder in the fifth game. After getting shoved out of bounds, Smith started to lift himself up, and another defender leapt on top of him. That following week, Mom drove him to New Orleans to see a specialist. Smith's shoulder was so damaged that for six weeks he needed to wear a body cast that wrapped around his entire body and rested on his hips. Sleeping was impossible many nights. His cracked shoulder never did fully heal, either.

No, Smith did not resemble a Ditka-like predator. The track was his home.

Little did Smith know that thinking on his feet at the state track meet would trigger an NFL career.

The meet was held in Natchitoches, Louisiana, at Northwestern

State University, the same school that had already offered Smith a partial scholarship. Which was nice. Unfortunately, his family didn't have the money to split the difference. Dad was a good man, a quiet man, who eventually worked hard enough as a welder to open up his own shop thirty miles from Kentwood, but Smith knew his only realistic shot at attending college was a full ride. After taking first in the hurdles, he was greeted by Northwestern State's track coach, Walter Ledet, near the finish line. The two went for a short walk, with Ledet reiterating how much he'd love for Smith to join his squad. Smith saw an opening. He informed Ledet that Southeastern Louisiana in Hammond had contacted him, too. It wasn't a lie. Southeastern *did* call him and Southeastern *was* much closer to home, too. The statement was simply marinated with a microscopic drip of embellishment and a pinch of urgency.

The maneuver worked. Soon after, Ledet called Smith to say the university could grant him a full scholarship under one condition. He also needed to play for the school's football team and could not quit.

He didn't think twice and, to this day, the counterfactual still confounds him. He's still not sure where his life would've floated without this offer.

Of course, the last time Smith had played football, he ended up in a hospital bed. For whatever reason, Smith wasn't afraid one bit. "I would just move it along." In college, he served as the team's punter and caught a pass once every blue moon. In 1960, Smith had 10 catches for 129 yards. In 1961, he had 9 for 95. The school doesn't even know how many passes he caught in '62, only that the team's leader had 13. The Demons, indeed, were a run-first operation. Playing in the NFL wasn't a speck of a dream in his mind. Little did Smith know that St. Louis Cardinals trainer Jack Rockwell stopped by campus one spring. Rockwell watched the spring game and, Smith thinks, saw him sprinting around the track, too. The 1963 NFL draft arrived and, as the seconds ticked down at number 129 overall in the tenth round, the Cardinals couldn't decide who to take. That's when one person in the room blurted out, "Ah, hell, just take that redheaded kid from Louisiana."

Smith got the call. Smith couldn't believe it. He thought St. Louis made a mistake. Once he realized this was real life, one thought crossed his mind: "If they're crazy enough to draft me, I'm crazy enough to make this damn team."

The only person Smith knew with any pro football ties just so happened to be one of the best flankers in the sport. Charlie Hennigan was tearing up the new American Football League and had a background similar to Smith. After originally attending Louisiana State University on a track scholarship, Hennigan transferred to Northwestern State and wasn't thinking of pro football as much of a career, either. He went undrafted in 1960 and became a high school biology teacher. The Houston Oilers got around to signing Hennigan and he was an instant sensation. In 1961, he caught 82 passes for 1,746 yards (21.3 yards average) with 12 touchdowns. Thus, Smith had a hunch Hennigan—"a running machine, a godsend"—could supply a few pointers. With his newlywed wife, he headed to tiny Arcadia, Louisiana, to work out with him. This was where forty or so kids attended Hennigan's football camp at an old schoolhouse and Smith convinced him to carve out some one-on-one time on the field.

There were no hotels out in the boondocks, so Smith knocked on the door of a woman who lived across the street and begged her to let him and Gerri sleep on a bed inside her screened-in back porch. For two weeks, Hennigan then supplied Smith the cheat codes needed to dominate pro football. Defensive schemes were elementary through the '60s. Almost all teams ran man to man, so Hennigan meticulously broke down the footwork it took to leave a defender in the dust.

No doubt about it. These two weeks are the number one reason Smith even made the Cardinals team as a rookie.

Here, at Syberg's, he jolts off his chair to demonstrate. Right away, Smith learned to never curve his routes. To, instead, explode—"Boom! Boom!" he says—out every single cut. The best way to do this was by throwing his legs and arms one direction at the same time. Inside this packed restaurant of patrons in their twenties, thirties, forties, this eighty-two-year-old pumps his arms like he's back at Busch Memorial Stadium. "You have to be able to stop," he explains, "and then give everything you can going the direction you want to go." So engrossed in reliving the origins of his football career, Smith still hasn't touched his beer. Part of me thinks he might even knock the glass over reliving this breakthrough.

Two middle-aged men who work at a bank in St. Louis spot Smith from across the room and visit for a few minutes. When they hear Smith is chatting for a book on the tight end position, they bust his balls.

"You'll get some good information," one jokes, "once you get through all the bullshit."

"Believe it or not," says Smith, "they're friends of mine."

He laughs and picks up where he left off. The Cardinals decided to plug Smith in at tight end, where his set of skills was foreign to a burgeoning position. Whereas Ditka and Mackey were more apt to catch a short pass and steamroll a defender, Smith used his speed. He burnt that same defender down the field. In Week 5 of that 1963 season, Smith put the Cardinals on his back in a 24–23 win over the Pittsburgh Steelers with 212 yards and 2 scores on 9 receptions. Year to year, his role steadily expanded from 445 yards as a rookie...to 657 in Year 2...to 648 in Year 3...to 810 in Year 4...to a record-setting Year 5. That season, Smith caught 56 passes for 1,205 yards (21.5 yards average) with 9 touchdowns. Only two players in the entire league had more receiving yards. With most defenses trained to expect the tight end to run five yards and turn around for the ball, Smith would often sprint directly at the safety twenty yards downfield and turn *in* to the post or *out* to the flag. The Cardinals threw deep. Often. "A bad habit, I guess," jokes Smith.

Central to his success was a work ethic. No X's and O's, rather an old-fashioned motor. As a 205-pound rookie, Smith told himself he'd either need to pack on muscle or carry a gun on the field. Each off-season, he traveled to Baton Rouge to train with Alvin Roy, a man ahead of his time who helped Smith put on fifteen pounds without sacrificing his torrid speed. Roy became pro football's first full-fledged strength and conditioning coach in 1963, helping the San Diego Chargers win an AFL Championship, before winning Super Bowl titles with the Kansas City Chiefs (1970) and Dallas Cowboys (1976). He's now in the Strength and Conditioning Hall of Fame for sculpting human beings like this. The chiseled, 225-pound Smith maintained 4.5 speed in making five straight Pro Bowls from '66 to '70. Remarkably, his career average of 16.5 yards per reception remains a tight end record and is more than a full five yards better than the position's all-time receiving leader, Tony Gonzalez.

One day, Smith was hanging out with two of his best pals on the team—offensive tackle Dan Dierdorf and linebacker Tim Kearney—when Dierdorf asked Smith if he ever got tired on a football field. Kearney immediately began to laugh. "Of course he did!" he said. Unfazed, Dierdorf told him to let Smith answer the frickin' question. Smith kept thinking, and thinking, and, no, he couldn't remember one instance. He was dead serious. After working out all off-season long before one season in the late '70s, Kearney wanted to test his endurance against Smith. He was ten years younger than the aging tight end and figured he could take him. Without warning, he asked Smith to go for a run. Smith grabbed his shoes. And mile to mile, as Kearney breathed heavily like a dying fish, unable to talk, he couldn't believe how Smith tried to carry normal conversations in a normal voice. After five miles, Smith asked if he wanted to kick this run "in the ass." Kearney declined.

"I said, 'I'm good,'" Kearney recalls. "I put my hands on my knees and go, 'Jesus, Mary, and Joseph. Look at this guy. Ten years older than me and he's running me into the ground.'"

That was Jackie Smith's secret. Late in games, when most everyone else got tired, his speed would not wane. Dallas Cowboys safety Cliff Harris, a six-time Pro Bowler, believes Smith was the first wide receiver type playing tight end.

"Oh my gosh, he was fast," he says. "He was big and tall and lean and muscular and *fast*."

In real time, Smith had zero clue he was defining a position. He never imagined what a tight end would resemble twenty years down the road. He was grateful, only grateful, repeating his favorite line here: "Can you imagine how lucky I was?" A day prior to this lunch, Smith filmed a TV commercial where the director asked if he'd refer to himself as a Hall of Famer. He couldn't do it. Felt too awkward, too conceited, too...not him. He always lived by an old saying: "When you're green you're growing and when you're ripe, you're dead." He never wanted to think he had arrived.

Most remarkable was that all factors seemed to be working against Smith in St. Louis.

The team mostly stunk. Even when they started winning with new head coach Don Coryell, in 1973, one of the game's greatest innovators ever wasn't yet experimenting with the tight end. Smith stayed in a three-point stance next to the tackle. The most he ever split out was three yards, and it wasn't even to run routes. If Smith strayed off the line it was because he needed to block a linebacker on a sweep play. Thinking back, damn, he wishes he was able to split five, ten, fifteen yards outside to test this speed against linebackers in open acreage. Unfortunately, nobody was doing that through the '70s. Back then, Kearney would clothesline opposing tight ends. He cannot imagine what Smith would've done if he didn't have to deal with a linebacker. "They would've had to outlaw him," he says.

In practice, linebacker Bill Koman hit Smith so many times that Smith started to think it was normal to look out of his earhole. He learned quickly that if he could avoid Koman's kill shot, he could toast any linebacker downfield. As a result, few even had a chance to clothesline him. God help them if they did. Dynamite pass-catching ability never came at the expense of renegade toughness. Judging by his name and take-no-prisoners game, running back Terry Metcalf jokes that he always thought Smith was African American before they became teammates. His best memories are Smith accidentally tackling him ("He was coming down to help and, 'Pow!'") and the time Smith ran through what felt like the entire Cowboys defense for a TD. This locker room was full of the most hostile players in the sport, mind you. In 1977 alone, right guard Conrad Dobler was named "Pro Football's Dirtiest Player" by *Sports Illustrated*, and left guard Bob Young competed in the World's Strongest Man Competition.

But the one player *everyone* knew to never mess with, Kearney says, was Jackie Smith.

Especially opponents.

Once, a defensive back for the Washington Redskins punched Metcalf and . . . Smith snapped. He didn't give a damn that he was in street clothes, on the bench, out with an injury. Smith immediately ran onto the field to attack the perpetrator. Officials ordered Smith to get the hell off the field, thinking this was some crazed fan. Once they realized it was perennial Pro Bowler *Jackie Smith*, they made Smith sit in a special seat up against the stands far, far away from the bench. Thinking back, Metcalf chuckles. Cheap shots always did "raise the hair on his neck." Smith was the team's protector. In the midst of this particular melee, Smith made a mental note of that Redskin player's number to one day get his sweet revenge. One year later, he thought the moment had arrived. He visited his mother in Jackson, Mississippi, and couldn't believe it when she said a Redskin player had just moved in one block away.

"Really?" said Smith, tensing up. "Did he tell you what number he is?"

He hadn't. But Mom did say the player wanted to see Smith.

His jaw nearly hit the floor. Right then, Smith told himself that Jesus Christ himself must've delivered him this opportunity at vengeance. "Divine providence!" he thought. "I can get my shot in." Smith walked right to the player's front door with a clenched fist behind his back. He knocked, the player opened, the player was extremely friendly.

"Hi, Jackie!"

Smith ignored him. His blood was boiling. "What's your number?" he asked.

The player told him. It was somebody else. Smith unclenched that fist.

"Nice to meet you!" he said warmly, extending a handshake. The two had themselves a fantastic visit, and Smith returned to his mom.

Then there was Harris, the Cowboys safety. One game, he tried tugging and pulling Smith's jersey to get inside his head. Nothing abnormal. Nothing he hadn't tried with any other player. But, no, Smith was not having this. Irate, he looked Harris squarely in the eyes and said to meet him in the parking lot after the game. He was not bluffing.

No wonder he loved challenging the most cannibalistic linebackers of his era. He'd get his bell rung by Green Bay's Ray Nitschke and Chicago's Dick Butkus and return for seconds. His primary foil was Butkus, a man who never referred to Smith by name—only "punk." One game, Smith had enough of his shit and got a good shot in, but unfortunately, Butkus had the last word. He kicked Smith, crushed his facemask in, sent him to the sideline. Like Ditka, this tight end bonded with his enemies off the field, too. When Smith visited the Packers Hall of Fame in Green Bay, Wisconsin, he remembers Nitschke grabbing one of his sons and plopping him right on his knee. It was a different time.

"Back then, they didn't care what happened," Smith says. "They just asked me, 'Do you know where we're playing?' And, 'How many fingers do I have up?' And that's it. 'Go back in. You're good to go!' It's not that I could block 'em or hit 'em or hurt him or anything. But going against people like that? What an honor."

The beatings added up. Against one team—he cannot remember who—Smith caught a pass and didn't wake up until he was on the bus heading to the airport. It was horrifying. He had no recollection of getting dressed or walking onto the bus. Only his momentum carrying him out of bounds and everything going black. He did the math and figured he was out cold for an hour and a half. "What the hell?" thought Smith when he came to. He reenacts the scene here with wide eyes darting to his left and right. "I didn't want to say anything. I sat there and said, 'How did we get here?'" From what he was told, an opposing player who was already on the sideline hit him.

The field they shared with the Cardinals baseball team at Busch Stadium was terrible, too. Once, a torrential downpour before kickoff against the New York Giants rendered the infield swath of the football field a total mudpit. Players all resembled mud zombies. Running a ten-yard pattern felt like running the mile because the weight of the mud on Smith's uniform was unbearable. Of course, this was paradise compared to the AstroTurf installed in 1970. The padding, if you could even call it that, laid underneath the turf was designed for a baseball team so the ball would bounce high off it. "That didn't mean our ass bounced off it!" Smith kids. He started wearing cleats with steel tips to keep his footing even if that meant gouging an opponent's flesh. Hey, it was survival of the fittest out there.

And after fifteen seasons, it was time. He retired.

The end of his Cardinals tenure was marred by a spinal injury that would make his arm go numb on contact. When he initially injured his neck, he couldn't walk. Teammates helped him off the field. "Like it paralyzed me," Smith says. "That was the first time anybody helped me off the field." The final blow, in 1977, was when the arch in his foot was flattened. He still gets on running back Jim Otis's ass for that one every time he sees him here in St. Louis. Otis—"the king of cutback," as Smith called him—changed direction (yet again) and stepped right on his foot. Smith was done...or so he thought. Right before the '78 season, Cardinals coach Bud Wilkinson asked the thirty-eight-year-old if he wanted to return. The tight end underwent a physical and—after a week of silence—called the team himself for the results. That's when he claims the Cardinals told him he had failed the physical and that one more hit could leave him paralyzed. Part of Smith later wondered if Cardinals owner Bill Bidwell simply didn't want him back. To this day, his relationship with the team is strained. He's still emotional about it, too, banging the table with his fist as he relives painful memories.

Smith is the team's only Pro Football Hall of Famer whose name isn't in its Ring of Honor.

The '78 season began. Then, exactly as he did nine years prior, Tom Landry picked up the phone to call an aging tight end great. Thinking this was a prank, Smith first hung up.

When Landry called back, the Dallas Cowboys coach asked if Smith was in shape and convinced him to head south to see the Cowboys' doctor. He coveted his leadership and knew that Smith—like Ditka—would bring something extra to his locker room. This was also a golden opportunity for Smith to pursue the one accolade that eluded him all those years in St. Louis: a Super Bowl ring. The Cowboys were the defending champs and had spent most of the decade serving as big brother to the Cardinals in the NFC East. Smith had played in all of two playoff games, catching one pass in each contest. Landry told Smith not to worry about his neck. So he didn't. He headed south, met with a team doctor, and estimates the physical took all of fifteen minutes. In fact, it hardly felt like a physical at all. When Smith informed this doctor that the Cardinals' doctor thought one hit could paralyze him, he waved it off.

Only later did Smith learn that this doctor was in a hurry because he was also a farmer and had to get a load of cattle off to an auction.

"So," says Smith, chuckling, "he rushed me right through the whole deal."

He's glad. This was the most fulfilling season of his career.

The same players who had been trying to take him out for years embraced Smith with open arms.

That Monday, walking to the training room, Harris peered into the locker room and couldn't believe his eyes. "Cliff!" yelled Smith, with a warm handshake. "I'm on your team now!"

"Oh, thank goodness," Harris replied. "I thought you were here to whoop my ass."

When Smith ran into Lee Roy Jordan, the longtime linebacker reached into his mouth and pulled out two partial dentures. "I always wanted to show these to you," he told Smith. "They're compliments of you." Jordan had since retired. But apparently in a long-ago Cowboys-Cardinals bloodbath, a different linebacker (Jerry Tubbs) gave Smith a cheap shot, and Smith sought revenge. On a sweep play shortly after, instead of blocking the safety as assigned, Smith waited back for Tubbs. He saw a silver helmet, threw a forearm and, whoops, wrong guy. The blow knocked Jordan's two front teeth out.

They laughed it off.

Smith fawns over the unflinching head coach in the fedora, just like Ditka. There were no pregame speeches sending players through the nearest wall. The motivation came in wanting to execute Landry's brilliant game plans. They were so specific, so detailed, that nobody wanted to let him down. What impressed Smith most was Landry's knack for identifying an individual player's weaknesses and attacking. He'd explain to everyone why exactly the Cowboys were going to run ten specific plays, detailing how one set up the other. His demeanor was stoic, but his schemes? Cold-blooded.

"That's what made him so extraordinary," Smith says. "The players didn't mess around. They *wanted* to make sure they didn't miss anything or they didn't upset him about anything. They didn't actually say that, but you could tell by their actions."

This was the same year the Cowboys earned their "America's Team" nickname from the legendary narrator John Facenda. Even though he caught exactly zero passes in twelve regular-season games, Smith's value to this 12-4 team was undeniable. Harris could tell this was a player willing to do anything for a championship. He could still run a 4.6 but his role, now, was to block. And lead. And stand up for his guys. One night in the middle of the season, Charlie Waters had a party at his house, and Harris couldn't believe that one person at the party was flirting with his girlfriend. It wasn't a player. Smith had no clue who this was, either, and it did not matter. He beelined in that direction, grabbed ahold of this joker by the collar, and held him straight into the sky. "Hey! Don't you mess with Cliff Harris's girl!"

In the playoffs, against the Atlanta Falcons, Smith had arguably the best catch of the day. His two-yard touchdown reception tied the game up, 20–20, in the fourth quarter and was anything but easy. In for a concussed Roger Staubach, back-up Danny White rolled right and flicked it to Smith, who deftly boxed out a defender along the goal line and tapped his toes down before absorbing a hard hit to the midsection. The Cowboys won, 27–20.

Sensing that this conversation is inching closer to his nightmare when I bring this touchdown up, Smith redirects to other topics. He praises Landry. He goes off on chicken wings, of all things. After we order another round of beers, Smith asks the waitress if any of the Sybergs are around because they once tried to swipe his world-famous chicken wing recipe. Smith originally plucked the recipe from a teammate, Irv Goode, and used it at his own restaurant, Jackie's Place. Now, Smith can always tell when any restaurant is half-assing wings. There's a top-secret ingredient, he notes, that most cooks neglect.

"I still have the recipe," he says. "Something was written where I was given credit for bringing the buffalo chicken wings to the Midwest. My name was in there! I said, 'I've got it made now!' "

If only this was how everyone remembered him.

In the NFC Championship, the Cowboys pummeled the Los Angeles Rams, 28–0, to tee up a Super Bowl showdown with their dreaded rival, the Steelers.

Smith is ready. He'll discuss the drop now.

"I've never said this to anybody," he begins. "I've never talked about it."

———

So many of Jackie Smith's closest friends—Kearney and Harris, included—have never dared to bring this play up to their pal. They know how much it has haunted him. In truth, the devastation at the Orange Bowl in real time spoke for itself. The reactions of all parties involved may be the reason why a play that occurred with two minutes and forty-six seconds remaining in the third quarter, not even the fourth, still resonates today.

On the Cowboys' radio broadcast, play-by-play man Verne Lundquist famously stated, "Bless his heart! He's got to be the sickest man in America!" On the NBC national broadcast, Curt Gowdy shouted, "He dropped it! Drop! Jackie Smith! He's a great human-interest story: Fifteen years with the Cardinals, it's the first time he ever had a chance to go to the Super Bowl. And he let a sure touchdown pass get away." On the field, it was worse. The ever-emotionless Landry threw his hands up in dismay. Quarterback Roger Staubach threw his head back in disbelief. And, of course, there was Smith. He clenched his fists and kicked his legs into the air.

This was how everyone at home consumed the play. In reality, the details that went into this moment and game have been mostly ignored over time.

Start with the play call. On third-and-three from the Steelers' 10-yard line—with the Cowboys trailing 21–14—Landry sent "47 QB Pass Y Corner" into Staubach. The quarterback called timeout because this didn't make sense. This was a goal-line play, one Dallas had implemented all but one week before. Why would Dallas call it at all, in the *Super Bowl*, let alone from the 10? Not once did the Cowboys practice "47 QB Pass Y Corner" this far from the goal line. Landry instructed his quarterback to run the play anyway. The design sent two receivers to the pylons. Running back Tony Dorsett motioned left to right before the snap and dripped into the flat. And Smith? He was the fourth option, instructed to go to the back of the end zone and wait. Staubach later told *Sports Illustrated* that the Cowboys should've never called the play. "We can blame what happened," he said, "on Coach Landry."

Nonetheless, the play did scheme a player wide open.

After Staubach faked a handoff to running back Scott Laidlaw, linebacker Jack Lambert stormed in on a blitz and Laidlaw stoned him. That gave Staubach ample time to locate Smith in the end zone.

With those tenders polished off, Smith begins by explaining that he needed to block his man off the line a second longer to sell the run fake. This was a goal-line play call, after all. Smith released, stripped through the line, and never saw Staubach release the ball. For fifteen years, that was something he always looked for on plays like this. If he could've seen how the football was leaving the quarterback's hand, Smith knows he would've made the same adjustment as Staubach. The quarterback later told Smith that he was shocked to see him so wide open, so he tried softly floating it to him. He took a few RPMs off this pass.

Once Smith realized this? It was too late. He hit the brakes, slipped, and dropped the ball.

"He told me later, 'You were so damn wide open, I wanted to make sure I got the ball to you,'" Smith says. "So, it wasn't like a regular pass he'd throw to me. He didn't throw the ball as hard. In other words, if there was somebody (covering) me, he would've zipped it in there to get through. But I was so wide open. That being the case, I had to stop, and it was behind me because it was a little bit lofty. When I had to put the foot down to get back to get it, I didn't get back far enough.

"It's as simple as that."

Everlasting, too. It didn't matter that Staubach threw an interception at the end of the first half, with Dallas driving, and the Steelers quickly drove to score a touchdown of their own. Nor did it matter that Randy White fumbled a kickoff return in the fourth quarter or that the NFL's No. 2–ranked defense allowed Pittsburgh's Terry Bradshaw to throw for 318 yards and 4 touchdowns on only 17 completions. Nor did it matter that both Harris and White lament their own gaffes to each other still to this day and that Harris tried telling Smith the entire team lost that night in Miami. In the locker room afterward, Smith answered questions from reporters for forty-five minutes. "I hope it won't haunt me," he said then, "but it probably will." He was proven correct.

Here, his words slow to a crawl. Asked how he coped with the drop over the following days, weeks, months, a man who could literally talk all day clams up. He forces a slight chuckle.

"They were different. For a while. It was, it was..."

Another long pause.

"...different."

That night at the Orange Bowl should've been the crowning achievement he deserved. Instead, here is what "different" entailed. Strangers called the family's house to inform Smith he blew the game. One angry caller who phoned the Häagen-Dazs store Smith opened in St. Louis was especially malicious. This person, *Sports Illustrated* explained, told Smith the drop cost him $20,000. All four of his kids were ridiculed at their high school and college sporting events. His daughter, Angie, was walking back to her car after one race in track when someone mocked her about the dropped pass. She proceeded to beat the hell out of the kid.

Catch that pass and he's a conquering hero. Instead, this became everyday life. A game he grew to love suddenly was bringing him nothing but an avalanche of negativity. The best way to cope—the only way—was to remember the good football provided his entire family. When he fielded all those questions in the losing locker room, fourteen-year-old son Darrell was at his side. Dad clung dearly to the fact that playing in the NFL for sixteen seasons afforded his kids so many opportunities.

An optimistic man to his core, he is beyond proud of them all.

He chokes up thinking about the lives that Sheri has saved as the principal at Danforth Elementary, a school full of kids from impoverished backgrounds that desperately need guidance. She possesses the innate ability to either "kick them in the ass or love 'em," he says. "The kids love her. They go from one classroom to the other. They'll get out of line, run in, give her a hug, then run back out. She's touched them all because of the way she is." Both his sons, Greg and Darrell, are in sales. Darrell went to Arkansas and Greg to Dartmouth, and he cannot stop thinking about the trip he has planned with Darrell this month to head back to Louisiana. They're going for Jackie's birthday, and you better believe they're ready to hit up all the Cajun music and food joints possible.

His other daughter, Angie, was a phenomenal athlete just like him. Tall, strong, with a stride to leave all in the dust. Now retired, she's excited about a property she purchased way out in the country.

Altogether, Smith now has fourteen beautiful grandkids, too.

"Playing a football game, for God's sake," he says, voice raised. "Look at what it's given us!"

All the blowback was worth it. He can live with how people treated him because, hey, he could've been hauling pulpwood for a living.

"I have nothing—*nothing*—to complain about," he says. "No regrets at all . . . I knew how important it was for our family. It's paid off. And they're doing well because we did this. I don't give a shit about anything else, when it comes to how it affected me. That's the biggest blessing. That being the case, it was worth that. If I had to go through that deal to have the family life we do and for those kids to be as successful as they are, and people like to see me and talk about football? I feel so lucky."

Physically, he's no doubt in the top percentile of players from his era. That shoulder he injured back in high school finally quit on him about twelve years ago, and Smith needed it replaced. Soon after, he jokes, the other shoulder got jealous. He needed to replace that one, too. Otherwise, he's felt phenomenal. Getting into the Pro Football Hall of Fame sixteen years after retiring was validating. The first phone call he received when the news broke was from Mackey, a gesture he still treasures. He's wearing his enormous Hall ring today. Nobody can ever take this away from him even if no player's legacy in this hallowed ground has been so drastically warped.

Yet, the scars from that night never healed.

A passion that filled Smith up with so much joy was now hammering him with despair and he became distant. He refused to address the man in the mirror directly and never wrote a book or spilled his guts on national TV as a form of a catharsis. There's still no relationship with the Cardinals, either. He believes it all stems from an interview he did with the Dallas media upon signing, when he simply explained what transpired. Worst of all? He never opened up to family like he should have. He allowed the drop to hijack the relationships with the same people he loves so dearly. An Emerson quote may keep him on track today, but for too long Smith admits he was "wandering around" mentally. He felt sorry for himself and flat-out ignored what's most meaningful in life. It wasn't until 2020, into his *eighties*, that Smith looked deep within and told himself, "You're one stupid son of a bitch."

"I was making excuses because of the Super Bowl and all that bullshit. Maybe I was trying to find something to help me forget about stuff that was going on in my mind. Because what happens is you condition yourself for that, to do what you need to get done. And when you do that, you take away from a lot of other things. And a lot of those other things are your family. Quite frankly, they're not going to be able to understand. They just can't imagine that a mind can be so...almost... a *different* mind. They can't imagine how that can change. You have to pay the price for things you didn't do. The ways you didn't think. The affection you didn't show.

"You're trying to look at other things and trying to say other things are important. 'This is the way I should think about it.' And while you were doing that, you're ignoring your family."

A tear rolls down his cheek. With one deep breath, it's as if Jackie Smith is releasing a burden.

"I know what I did and what I didn't do."

Seconds later, his phone rings. Check that. His ringtone is actually a hilarious duck quacking at full blast.

It's Angie calling for the third time today. Something as simple as seeing her name appear on his phone is what Smith lives for now. The phone quacks again and he's stunned to see the name on the screen. It's a friend Smith actually thought was dead. He answers. "It can't be. It could be. It is!" he says to the caller, overwhelmed with joy. "What are you doing, nutcase?" Smith jokes that he's sitting down with someone for a book, telling lies about how good a guy he is and that he could use some help. "Get your ass on over here!" He laughs and the two agree to meet up at two o'clock the next day. "Love you," says Smith, before hanging up.

Phone calls like these mean the world now. Especially with so many loved ones passing away.

Koman, the linebacker who hardened him, died in 2019. Former Cardinals quarterback Tim Van Galder died of cancer just a few weeks before this chat. Through Mackey's "88 Plan," Smith has been helping Van Galder's family transition. As so many teammates and opponents die, here's one of that generation's best tight ends just now experiencing an awakening. Whereas a phone call from Tom Landry boomeranged Mike Ditka into football immortality, Smith spiraled into a darkness that took decades to escape.

Finally, he's genuinely happy. Relationships with loved ones are closer than ever.

Kearney knows he can call Smith any day, anytime, to grab some beers. ("As good of a football player as he is, he's an even better friend. He'll do anything for you.") Metcalf lives in Seattle now, but it meant so much to see his old protector at his induction into the St. Louis Sports Hall of Fame. ("He was a humble man. When he put the uniform on, that humbleness became very, very aggressive in trying to accomplish what he needed to. He had a big heart. Jackie loved people.") Harris lives in Dallas but has made a point to visit his old friend in St. Louis. In Smith's office, he spotted the image that everyone should think of when they hear *Jackie Smith*. Blown up as a poster, it's a completely horizontal Harris, getting spun around, trying to tackle Smith downfield. That's who Smith really was, he says. The two still talk regularly.

Nothing will ever again detract from family. The older Jackie Smith gets, the more this reality dawns on him. He stays busy, but never too busy. For years, Smith ran his restaurant, sold fishing shows, sang the national anthem at sporting events. Now his labor of love is building a Vietnam War memorial eighty miles south of St. Louis in Perryville. Now, whenever his plate gets too full, he pulls something off it. He reprioritizes. As for his legacy? How he wants everyone to perceive him as a player? He hopes folks remember him as a nice guy. That's about it. He's not concerned about what others think because he reclaimed his identity on his terms. Smith doesn't even like the suggestion that he "persevered" because that insinuates that he was doing something he didn't enjoy. And he sure enjoyed being an NFL tight end. At the heart of the position, he loved the idea of answering to one person: himself. That was how this whole wild journey began in Kentwood and why he worked so hard to make the team with Hennigan and trained harder than anyone else every off-season.

"To keep fooling their ass," he kids. "Nobody liked to work out with me because I liked to *work*."

It was never the drop that made him emotional. The drop, given all those variables, he can live with. What makes him emotional is how he allowed that play to steer him away from the people he loved. He needed to rediscover the person he's been all along. That's a man who'll reach out to one of his children just because and a man who's still working out like he's trying to make an NFL team. Perhaps the best proof that Smith is a man at peace can be found in a gym where he still throws dumbbells around and climbs a StairMaster with a purpose because he never wants to just "look pretty" on a machine. What good is that? If he's going to sweat, he must *sweat*. He's still leaving friends in the dust on runs, all at the ripe age of eighty-two.

It's psychological more than physical. Working out forces Smith to once again answer to himself. He views each run, each lift, as a way to pay a price for all the blessings that have come his way.

"I have to feel like I deserve what I'm getting," Smith says. "I've got to be content with myself."

OK, so he's not knocking teeth out. He is finding that edge within all over again.

"I would've hated if I would've had the opportunity to play and do something for the family, like that, and then I didn't make it. If I would've gone through the process of trying to make the team and slacked off a little bit or took shortcuts or done things I shouldn't be doing. I didn't want to be released from the opportunity and say, '*If* I would've had a different way of looking at it' and '*If* I would've tried a little bit harder.' To me, that's why people kill themselves."

His legacy can be found within the very soul of the sport and has nothing to do with those 5.5 seconds. So many tight ends who followed Smith have emerged from the strangest locales. Cornfields in Iowa. Group homes in North Carolina. The roofs of houses in sweltering summer heat and, why not, a bar fight or two. Smith was the first to truly prove that relentless tenacity can overcome all circumstances. That's the lifeblood of this position. So, heck yeah, he wakes up with a smile every single morning. He asks to see pictures of my two kids and lights up at the shot of a two-year-old Ella posing. "She's sassy!" he says cheerfully. With that, Smith starts tapping away on his phone to show off pictures of his family. Initially, he's seeking one specific shot until, for a good ten minutes straight, he cannot stop scrolling and scrolling and sheds a tear for all the right reasons.

Moments later, he doesn't want to hear about any visitor of his traveling via Lyft or Uber. He invites me into his trusty black Pilot—the "sled," he calls it—and takes off. There's more than 246,000 miles on this vehicle and he fully intends to run it into the ground. As we drive around St. Louis, Smith explains how difficult it was for this city to lose its football team a few years back. Fans were quite emotional.

He pauses. He appears to be thinking about everything that happened in his life after January 21, 1979, once more, but this time he lets the words hang in the air.

Big plans are set for Wednesday. He'll see that long-lost buddy, stop by his daughter's school to say hello, and, of course, make sure he's cherishing every second.

The Ghost

Dave Casper wanted nothing to do with this book.

He didn't recognize my phone number, so he answered, and I

might as well have been a nagging telemarketer. Told that *The Blood and Guts* was examining the best players at the tight end position—*his* position—Casper was not amused. He said he speaks publicly only when one of his former teammates passes away. Otherwise, he'd prefer to be left alone.

Fair enough, and not necessarily surprising. Casper was known as a recluse through a career that spanned from 1974 to 1984. The five-time Pro Bowler also was central to two of the most iconic plays in league history—the "Ghost to the Post" and the "Holy Roller." Two former Raiders who faced Casper daily in practice were willing to speak and claim Casper was a tight end ahead of his time. To cornerback Lester Hayes, the best way to understand Casper's game is to watch Kansas City Chiefs tight end Travis Kelce.

Both have "4.4 feet" that waste defenders with each cut.

"And that is not normal," Hayes says. "That's a gift from God. I've watched sixty years, plus change. Dave Casper's feet are not typical feet of a man, who is six foot four, 250 pounds. That was his blessing. How he moved a safety. How he'd stop, step, and would burst. Chasing Kelce, you can't catch him. Chasing Casper, you can't catch *him*! And he's a 4.6 guy. What the hell!"

That's basically what the Baltimore Colts were asking themselves in the 1977 AFC divisional playoff round when the "Ghost" went to the "Post." Trailing 31–28, with just over two minutes to go, the Raiders needed a big play to get into field goal range. Casper took off on a deep post route and quarterback Ken Stabler appeared to overthrow him. Somehow, Casper changed direction and chased it down. Neck craned back, he cradled the ball over his shoulders for a forty-two-yard gain. An Errol Mann field goal sent the game to overtime, and the Raiders were victorious.

Casper later remarked that he could not recall catching a pass on this play all season.

"Willie Mays," says former Raiders safety George Atkinson, referencing the former San Francisco Giants outfielder's legendary catch.

"Over the shoulder. Running it down. He made it look easy. I couldn't believe it. But he'd do that in practice, so it wasn't anything new. Every day."

If this play required immense skill, the "Holy Roller" the following season certainly did not.

Against the San Diego Chargers in September, only ten seconds remained when the Raiders had the ball at San Diego's 14-yard line, trailing 20–14. While getting sacked, Stabler fumbled the ball forward toward the Chargers' goal line. Running back Pete Banaszak tried to recover it at the 12, couldn't stay upright, and shoveled the ball closer to the goal line. Casper was next. He swatted and kicked the ball into the end zone before then falling on top of it for a game-winning touchdown shrouded in controversy. Per NFL rules, if a runner intentionally fumbles forward, it is a forward pass. After stating publicly that it was a fumble, Stabler was asked by NFL Films in 2008 if he could convince them he did not flip the ball forward. "No, I can't convince you of that, because I did," he said. "I mean, what else was I going to do with it? Throw it out there, shake the dice."

Nonetheless, Casper did need to be in the right place at the right time. That was no accident to Hayes, who notes that Casper played for Ara Parseghian at Notre Dame and John Madden in Oakland. A "seed," he believes, was planted in the tight end's brain to never quit on a play.

"Dave is mentally a footballholic," Hayes says. "A player who loafs on certain plays, they are not a part of those plays. His focus was 100 percent. Go, go, go. On that day, Dave found the presents on Christmas."

Atkinson? He cannot make this same leap. He calls this a "zany" play that required "no skill whatsoever." Maybe it's no shock that strange player would score the touchdown on one of the strangest plays ever. Atkinson would try to agitate Casper in practice to no avail. Casper stared back at him without saying a word in return—he was utterly "nonresponsive." Quite damaging to a defender's ego, Atkinson notes. Through the ruthless '70s, nobody could get under Casper's skin. And when Hayes watches football today, he takes tablets upon tablets of notes. The way Casper used to spin safeties around in practice "as if they're a top," is best reflected in Kelce.

Those feet are making Hayes awfully suspicious.

"You know what I believe?" Hayes says. "Travis Kelce is Dave's son! He made that boy! Check to see if Travis Kelce's mama dated Dave."

Chapter 4

CALM IN CHAOS

In the forty-seventh game of his career, on December 14, 1980, Ozzie Newsome dropped a pass.

This made no sense to teammates, to coaches, to anyone associated with the Cleveland Browns who'd been around the tight end his first three pro seasons.

The odds of a UFO landing in the middle of Metropolitan Stadium were higher than quarterback Brian Sipe feathering a perfect ball over the tight end's shoulder and Newsome, a six-foot-two, 232-pound human spiderweb, letting the ball graze off his fingertips. The Vikings went on to win that day with a Hail Mary heave. It didn't matter that this sort of play happens all the time in football. Teammates told Newsome they had never seen this from him, and he took it to heart.

"I wanted to make sure," Newsome says, "they never said that again."

From Game 48 to Game 208, Newsome cannot recall ever dropping another pass. Seriously.

Know this about Newsome, too. He's the antithesis of hyperbole, downplaying all monumental moments of his life through this conversation. If he were telling a fishing story, his big catch might actually get smaller over the years. Yet thinking back, not one drop comes to mind because if Newsome got his hands on the football, he caught it. Period. "No drops," he adds. "I didn't like dropping the ball. If you drop the ball, they won't throw it to you." The Browns kept throwing the ball to

54

Newsome and he kept catching it more than any tight end before him. Amazingly, he did this through one of the league's most ruthless eras, too. Headhunters still lurked through the late '70s and early '80s. Any brave soul wandering over the middle of the field risked impalement. Like the time Newsome dared to venture into the teeth of the Pittsburgh Steelers' secondary as a rookie, and safety Mike Wagner delivered an elbow to his head. Newsome totally blacked out with what'd instantly be diagnosed as a concussion today.

Back then?

"You get whacked. You lay there for a while. And then, all of a sudden, you come to your senses and you line up to play again."

Newsome never missed a game due to injury—not in college, not in the pros—and shattered the tight end records for receptions (662), yards (7,980), and touchdowns (47) before retiring after the 1990 season. His 662 catches ranked fourth among all NFL players. Somehow, Newsome found a way to evolve the position into more of an art. Whereas Ditka and Mackey mashed, he pranced. And leapt. And contorted his body at circus angles to make highlight-reel catches that'd pop off the screen in any era. So...how? How does a tight end released downfield dominate in such an era?

The answer is Newsome's steadfast calm amid chaos. Nothing ever derailed him from changing the game. Not growing up in the segregated south and not any blow to the head. Not a string of heartbreaking playoff losses and not being handed the keys to an NFL franchise that left that city behind. His hands were historic. But when it comes to Ozzie Newsome, it's always been about his eyes. It's how he perceives that chaos around him, processes it, keeps moving in one direction only.

Because, honestly, the world around Newsome started shaking immediately.

In Muscle Shoals, Alabama, Newsome grew up in the throes of segregation. The same year Newsome was born, 1956, the Montgomery Bus Boycotts rocked the nation. Sparked by the arrest of Rosa Parks the previous December, this thirteen-month boycott led to the Supreme Court ruling that segregation on public buses was unconstitutional. When Newsome was six years old, George Wallace became governor of his state and vowed "segregation now, segregation tomorrow, segregation forever." Eight months later, 112 miles south, four young girls were murdered by the Ku Klux Klan in the Sixteenth Street Baptist Church bombing, one of about fifty explosions in Birmingham that earned the city the nickname "Bombingham." Nine days before Newsome turned nine years old, another eighty-five miles south, hundreds of peaceful marchers headed southeast on the Edmund Pettus Bridge in Selma and were brutally attacked by state troopers on "Bloody Sunday."

When Newsome was twelve, Martin Luther King Jr. was assassinated.

He attended a predominantly African American school his first five years of education but—even as racial strife gripped the south—Newsome asked his parents if he could attend a white school in sixth grade. He had read that this could lead to more opportunities in life so, suddenly, there was Newsome taking a bus across town as the only African American in his class. The first few days were difficult but, soon, Newsome saw the inherent good in humanity. "People learn to respect you," he says, "if you give them the respect." Newsome believes he proved he could compete with white kids academically and in athletics, and that was that. By ninth grade, schools were consolidated, and he'd go on to lead the football and basketball teams to state titles in 1972. He played baseball, too, as the team's catcher.

The last thing Newsome wants is sympathy. He's intensely private. Decades later, some of the closest people in his life still knew very little about his childhood. However, even Newsome knows the reality of his youth is not as neat and tidy and painless as he first makes it sound.

There were separate water fountains, of course, and whenever he went to the movie theater Newsome needed to enter through a back door where someone then led him to the balcony. When Newsome and his brother were the only two children of color on their Little League

All-Star team, they traveled to Georgia for a tournament and stayed at a camp near a lake. One day, he was walking among other white kids and white families and thinking nothing of it. The next? His entire team was staying in a new hotel. It'd be another twenty-plus years before the coach of that team told Newsome they moved because management said he and his brother were not welcomed to stay.

"There were the white cafes and the 'white this' and the 'colored this,'" Newsome says. "There was major segregation that was going on. When you're going through it and all you can do is be with your color, that's just the way that things were. And then eventually when things started to change, I was allowed to be a part of that change. I started to see some different things in my life. Having lived through it made me a better person and made me the person that I am today."

He's a product of his parents. Their message was always the same: "Work hard, be respectful of people, stay humble, believe in Christ." They experienced such racism—and then some—a generation prior. Before Ozzie was born, the political powers that be in Muscle Shoals demanded an extra $25 per week from Ozzie Sr. just to operate his restaurant, "Fats Café," and the politicians were found not guilty of extortion by a jury that was nearly all white. Blatant racism was woven into the fabric of everyday life. But, Newsome cuts in, "that was the *world*.

"You were able to do what you were allowed to do. You make the best of the times you're dealing with."

Newsome had a gift, of course. His athleticism was coveted by colleges throughout the south. After whittling his decision down to Alabama, Auburn, and Vanderbilt, he chose 'Bama. He'd be part of Bear Bryant's 1974 recruiting class only three years after Alabama finally integrated its football team. The two were a match made in football heaven. This was the same kid who once picked cotton after school on weekends for three cents a pound—one hundred pounds made him all of $3. If Newsome wasn't playing sports or working in the field, he was probably helping his dad at Fats Café, too. All he knew was work. And contrary to what many believe, Bryant actually helped nudge Alabama's football team toward its long-overdue integration. As Newsome points out, Bryant made a point to play schools that had African American players on their team for that reason. He wanted the alumni, fans, and powers that be to understand they needed a diverse roster if they wanted to win.

Day to day, he says Bryant treated everyone exactly the same, that he didn't see color. "You were an *Alabama football player*." Offensively, the Crimson Tide ran the wishbone, which meant attempting a meager 11.4, 12.5, 11.8, and 11.3 passes per game in Newsome's four seasons. But when they did throw it? Newsome drew one-on-one coverage, it was often a deep ball, and he caught it. Of Alabama's 71 total pass completions in 1977, Newsome caught 36 of them for 804 yards. He finished as the school's all-time leading receiver, and Bryant—not exactly one to douse any individual with praise—once called Newsome the school's greatest split end ever, adding, "That includes Don Hutson."

Newsome looked up to Bryant as a fatherly figure. The consistency of the coach's message struck him most. How to be unselfish. How to create value for yourself. How to become 1 percent better every day because that's the mindset that can destroy complacency. Newsome was essentially a living embodiment of the coach's all-time quotes.

"The price of victory is high but so are the rewards."
"In life, you'll have your back up against the wall many times. You might as well get used to it."
"There's no substitute for guts."

So just imagine the pit in Ozzie Newsome's stomach when he let Bear Bryant down.

Like Ditka, he can pinpoint a very specific turning point in his life. Thankfully, his struck much sooner. Newsome admits that going into his senior season, he had not been disciplined with his workouts. He passed his fall conditioning test without a problem, but the Bear wasn't pleased and the Bear wasn't shy. At Media Day, off to the side, the two had a conversation Newsome will never forget. He can still hear

Bryant's voice in that moment—"a growl, very distinct." Chances are, Newsome would've still been drafted the next year and had a fine pro career.

But Newsome knows there's zero chance he would've ascended to the heights he did without this talk.

No wonder he still owns a photo of this exact conversation that someone took. It's a daily reminder.

"He is reading me the Riot Act about what he thought my attitude was and I hadn't prepared myself for my senior year and I had let my parents down. It was an unbelievable conversation that he and I had—and it wasn't much of a conversation on my part. I was listening. But that ended up helping me turn that corner to be the type of person that I am today. I had to listen to him paint the picture of a person that I did not want to be. It taught me about work ethic and being the type of person that shows class all of the time. It was a lesson to be learned. The reason I'm sitting in the position I'm in right now is because of that conversation. Everything that's happened between now and back to then is because of that conversation."

The sport's ultimate prize eluded Newsome in college. The Crimson Tide banged on the door. They finished in the top five each year, accumulating a record of 42-6, but were never national champions. If Newsome thought he knew heartbreak in football, he didn't have a clue.

What a year 1978 was to go wide receiver hunting in the NFL. *John Jefferson. Wes Chandler. James Lofton.* Armed with a pair of first-round picks, the Browns planned on landing one of these future All-Pros. Unfortunately for Cleveland, two of those receivers flew off the board—fast. Chandler to New Orleans at third overall. Lofton to Green Bay at sixth. And with Jefferson still available at twelfth, the Browns decided to roll the dice that he'd fall to their twentieth overall pick and, instead, chose linebacker Clay Matthews.

Jefferson went fourteenth to San Diego, and Browns head coach Sam Rutigliano scrambled to one hell of a Plan B in trading back to the twenty-third pick, where he took Newsome. Locally, the pick was heavily criticized and, honestly, Newsome gets it. He was the classic "tweener," not quite a wide receiver or a tight end. He had played in that prehistoric wishbone, too. "But good scouts," Newsome points out, "do their job." Indeed. Those Browns most certainly did. Before the draft, Rutigliano had dispatched his wide receivers coach, Rich Kotite, to Alabama to work out Newsome primarily for one reason. He wanted to see if his, uh, butt was large. That's all. Rutigliano couldn't tell on film if Newsome had the body type to beef up to 230–240 pounds. Kotite returned with a full derriere report—the kid checked out—and Cleveland felt comfortable taking Newsome in the first round.

Of course, Rutigliano loved everything else. He said on draft day that Newsome could "catch a BB in the dark."

Newsome wasn't at rookie minicamp—for good reason. He didn't want to miss his college graduation. As the first person in his family to get a diploma, he wanted Mom and Dad to see him on that stage. When he headed north to Cleveland for regular minicamp, Newsome initially practiced at wide receiver as expected. Kotite told him afterward that Rutigliano wanted to see him one-on-one. "You didn't do anything wrong," Kotite said. "He just wants to talk." And that was when the head coach took the sport in a daring new direction. Rutigliano told Newsome he could be a *good* wide receiver but they believed he'd make a *great* tight end.

One more thing: They planned to throw him the ball. A lot.

Say no more.

"The magic words," Newsome recalls. "And once I got involved and I saw the matchups I was getting, yeah, it became fun. When you're having fun, you can enjoy yourself."

For the late '70s, this was a radical position switch. Typically, teams worked from the inside out. They turned *offensive tackles* into tight ends. Five years prior, the Buffalo Bills drafted Michigan tackle Paul Seymour seventh overall and converted him to tight end, where he caught all of sixty-two passes in five years as a road-grader for O. J. Simpson. The Browns knew they'd need to teach Newsome how to block, but so what? That was a minor detail. He'd present a totally new threat. Lumbering linebackers wouldn't be able to stick stride for stride with him. Whereas Mike Ditka and John Mackey did their damage on shorter routes—bruising defenders after the catch—*this* tight end would be released on deeper patterns into the third level of the defense. Rutigliano envisioned Newsome exploiting the soft spot in the middle of a Cover 2 defense.

Newsome would force defenses to trash this coverage.

"Because you didn't want a linebacker trying to run down the field with me."

Slashing downfield with elegance and acrobatics, "the Oz" flipped the script. He was proof that an offense didn't necessarily need to combat your ass-kicker with an ass-kicker. The football field remained a cruel place. Out were linebackers like Ray Nitschke and Dick Butkus sneering over your motionless body. In were safeties like Donnie Shell and Jack Tatum and Bruce Laird. "You have to put your head on a swivel," former Bills and Browns guard Joe DeLamielleure says. "Those guys were hitters." Newsome brought a maneuverability to a malevolent realm. He didn't throw fists between whistles or take mental notes of a player's number to get revenge later. Forget trash talk. He barely spoke to his own teammates and rarely ever showed any emotion on the field. In his first pro game, at San Francisco, Newsome emphatically spiked the ball in the end zone after a touchdown and, moments later, heard Bear Bryant's voice replay in his head. He thought back to Bryant telling his players to act like they've been there before in the end zone. So, as soon as he could, Newsome called Bryant to apologize and promised to never spike the football again.

"Humble as a mouse and smart as an elephant," DeLamielleure says. "He was a great team leader without saying a lot. His actions spoke louder than words. He practiced hard all the time. I never saw him take a day off in the five years I was with him. He was a superstar in everybody's eyes but his own. I tried to emulate him. Work hard every day. He showed up and wasn't a showman. He was a silent killer."

The team's longtime left tackle, Doug Dieken, never remembers Newsome calling for the ball in the huddle. He "didn't say boo." Nor was Newsome out to assert his physical dominance on Day 1. Instead, Dieken had fun at his expense in the trenches. Against the six-foot-six Fred Dryer, Dieken instructed Newsome to chop low and said he'd go high. He knew Dryer would probably be irate and go after Newsome, but that was the kind of guy the Oz was, he says. "You ask him to do something, and he did it." Dryer was pissed and Dieken, to be sure, had his tight end's back.

Meanwhile, when it was time to throw, Newsome digitalized what had been an analog world. He ran routes like a wide receiver. "Very fluid. Very smooth," says former Browns receiver Reggie Langhorne. "Very decisive in what he was doing. It was quite effortless for him to get open."

Maybe the Steelers' Wagner did concuss Newsome, but he doesn't remember crunching him. The only memory that replays in his mind is having Newsome blanketed, getting in front of the tight end and jumping as high as he could... for nothing. His efforts were futile with Newsome virtually propelling off a springboard. One play, Newsome plucked the ball above his head, the two tumbled to the ground, and Wagner only said one word to himself: "Wow."

"He could go up and take the ball out of the sky," Wagner says. "Tight ends don't have leaping ability."

Up into the sky, Newsome was a master contortionist. He bent his body at bizarre angles to tip balls to himself while completely horizontal or cradle a deep shot over his shoulder or—as he did in 1982 against the Philadelphia Eagles—bat an underthrow pass out of safety Roynell Young's hands to himself for a score. Such athleticism, to Newsome, is the direct result of playing three sports through high school.

Then, there were those hands. Those glorious hands. DeLamielleure can't recall Newsome dropping a pass in any practice, any game. Yet, obsessing over any aspect of a visually exquisite game fails to see the forest for the trees. Everything started with his *eyes*, with his laser-beam focus on the football traveling his direction. Newsome possessed the ability to block out everything else. The basketball background helped with his hand-eye coordination. Especially pushing the ball upcourt on a fast break, when the sport becomes a game of hot potato toward the rim. Baseball, too. As a catcher, he'd need to react quickly to tipped balls and this fed muscle memory. He learned to trust the natural synergy between his hands and eyes, a tunnel vision rooted in the segregated south and sharpened by Bear Bryant.

No madness flusters him. Just keep those eyes on the ball.

"I was told by Coach Bryant at a very early age, you always look the ball all the way in," Newsome says. "You have to use your eyes as much as your hands to catch a football. You're going to get hit, so you might as well catch it. It's like shooting free throws. You can be a great free-throw shooter if you shoot it, if you practice it all the time. A good hitter in baseball. Watching the ball and making sure you get contact. All of that comes into play."

Not only did he never drop another football, but Newsome also did not fumble on his final 557 touches. Meanwhile, he played through the pain. Which, of course, explains why he needed hip and ankle replacements later in life. The worst of them all was a high ankle sprain in 1986. Newsome played all eighteen games because he knew his presence alone would demand attention from a defense and open up opportunities for others. "Steady as a rock," Langhorne says. "Week in, week out and day in, day out. That was the Wiz."

The Drive. The Fumble. Red Right 88. No injury hurt more than the ceaseless playoff heartbreak in Cleveland, too. Newsome was part of iconic losses that still send a shiver up the spines of Browns faithful. In thirteen pro seasons, he made the playoffs seven times, and one loss topped them all.

"Red Right 88. That one was a tough one. That team could've gone to the Super Bowl."

That team in 1980 was affectionately known as the "Kardiac Kids." After the Browns beat the New York Jets in overtime of the 1979 season opener, as morbid legend has it, a doctor at the Cleveland Clinic visited the team's training center in Berea and showed the quarterback (Sipe) a paper readout from a cardiac machine. Someone had died right when Don Cockroft kicked the game-winning field goal. The following year, thirteen of the Browns' seventeen games were decided by a touchdown or less. Sipe was named the league's MVP. Rutigliano was the coach of the year. Newsome was entering his prime.

Then, came an unforgiving wind off of Lake Erie. The 11-5 Browns hosted the Oakland Raiders in what was then the coldest NFL game since the Ice Bowl. The wind chill dropped to thirty-six degrees below zero, calcifying the field into a sheet of ice and turning the basic exercise of kicking the football into a Charlie Brown–like odyssey. Cockroft missed two field goals, from forty-seven and thirty yards out, had one extra point blocked and another field goal attempt aborted due to a botched hold. So even as the Browns drove all the way to the Raiders' 13-yard line with less than a minute left, down 14–12, they weren't thinking field goal. On second down, Rutigliano wanted Cleveland to take a shot at the end zone, called "Red Slot Right, Halfback Stay, 88," and if it wasn't open? He told Sipe to "throw it into Lake Erie."

Sipe's pass to Newsome suspended in the wind and was intercepted by Mike Davis. The Raiders went on to thump the Eagles, 27–10, in Super Bowl XV. DeLamielleure is also convinced the Browns would've won it all that season and actually blames the holder for the Browns' kicking woes.

Backup quarterback Paul McDonald wore "scuba gloves," he says, which made it difficult for him to corral and place the snap.

"All the players were saying, 'Take the fucking gloves off! What are you doing?'" DeLamielleure says. "This was new to everybody. He thought, 'Hey, they're rubber. They'll stick well.' Well, it was worse. The ball went right through them. They were frozen. He couldn't get it on the ground. I guarantee you if he kept his hands warm until the last second, Cockroft would've kicked it in. Everyone in the huddle was shocked that we didn't just take one play to get the ball in the center of the field and take a knee to get in position to kick the field goal. Win the game. Run off. We win by one."

It would only get worse. The Browns lost AFC Championships in 1986 and 1987 and 1989. For someone so team oriented, it was an agonizing decade.

"You gain a hunger and a thirst," Newsome says, "to be able to take it to the next step."

Through the turmoil, Newsome's steadiness never wavered. The wave of receivers drafted through the mid-'80s all followed his lead. Langhorne tried to watch exactly how Newsome conducted himself daily. There were no spikes, no first-down signals, yet when Langhorne chatted with Newsome, he could tell the tight end had an eye for talent. Owner Art Modell clearly liked him, too. When Modell visited practice on Fridays, he always made a point to shake Newsome's hand first. "I got envious," Langhorne says.

To no one's surprise, Newsome stayed in the organization after retiring. First, he was a grunt of a scout under head coach Bill Belichick. No ask was too small with Belichick delegating the lousiest of the lousy jobs to him, from scouting players that weren't any good to drawing up the cards for the Browns' scout team. As he did his whole life, Newsome put his head down and worked. One of his jobs was escorting Kirk Ferentz around the building when he interviewed for the Browns' offensive line coaching job ahead of the '93 season. After Ferentz got the job, and couldn't help but live and die with every play, Newsome told him that was no way to operate. "You're not going to last," he warned. "It's a long season. You learn how to deal with it." Ferentz never forgot.

If Newsome was the glorified grad assistant on offense, Phil Savage was the GA on defense. And Savage had to pinch himself. As a ten- and eleven-year-old growing up in Mobile, Alabama, he idolized Newsome and even scored his autograph at the Senior Bowl. Local TV carried all of Newsome's Browns games. Now here they were running the Browns' scout teams. Those five years under Belichick, he's sure, helped lay a true foundation for Newsome as a scout because he was a total sponge. He learned how to study tape and write advance scouting reports.

Not that Belichick could find a tight end to replace him. The joke in the building was that the Browns were constantly using *Ozzie* as the bar. Ferentz also noticed that whenever the Browns faced a team with two dynamic tight ends, Belichick's antennae went up. It was odd. Nothing seemed to faze Belichick in putting a game plan together— this did. The Browns spent extra time preparing for the Packers' Mark Chmura and Keith Jackson in '95. That early, Newsome identified a larger trend developing. He believed football was losing the six-three, six-four, six-five high school athletes to basketball because AAU organizations were selling kids on the NBA dream. And that meant a drier well of tight ends and linebackers.

Next came an entirely new level of chaos.

On November 6, 1995, Modell announced the Browns were moving to Baltimore. The team's owner could've personally reached inside the chests of fans to extract their hearts and it would've hurt less.

At the NFL Combine, after walking out of the bathroom, Savage asked Newsome if they'd even have jobs. "I think we're going to be OK," he said. On February 14, 1996, Modell fired Belichick, Newsome became the de facto GM, and Newsome made Savage his college scouting director.

Calling the state of franchise "bare bones," as Newsome does, is kind. This new team didn't have a name or team colors or a functional team headquarters. It took a good three months to refurbish the football facility the Baltimore Colts had left behind thirteen years prior. Over that time, it had since been transformed into police barracks. There were still old bullet casings on the field where the police academy had apparently done some pistol training.

The roster itself was decimated. Newsome recalls only forty-some players being under contract. On March 29, the team finally had a name. Modell put it up for a city vote and revealed that the "Ravens" prevailed. And two and a half weeks before the draft, a small group that included Newsome, Savage, and Ferentz settled into that ragtag facility. The rectangular-shaped building wasn't much to look at. There was a racquetball court, a weight room, a tiny snack room on the first floor. Nobody could believe this was actually the NFL. It was embarrassing, humbling. They'd tell each other that "it's not the walls, it's the people within them." Which was fine and all, until they then looked at those walls.

The Ravens needed to line up roughly 3,500 VHS tapes around the entire perimeter because there was no shelving available.

And if anyone wandered into Modell's office, they would've found shag carpeting on the floor.

"We had a mountain to climb trying to get this franchise moved," Newsome says. "It was a monumental task, but when you have a good team of people working with you—and everybody working toward the same goals—you can accomplish things, and that's what we did. We started from scratch and we built it. And we built the way we wanted it to be built.

"Guys just rolled up their sleeves and we just went to work."

In other words, the Baltimore Ravens took on Newsome's personality. He led the way he lived.

The day before the 1996 draft, the powers that be were split. With the fourth overall pick, the Ravens had a feeling they'd be picking between Nebraska running back Lawrence Phillips and UCLA offensive tackle Jonathan Ogden. The two elders, Modell and head coach Ted Marchibroda, wanted Phillips. The Ravens needed to make a big splash in Modell's mind, so he was able to look past the fact that the running back was arrested for assaulting his girlfriend in college. Newsome and Savage wanted Ogden, the highest-rated player on their board. Both players trickled on down to number four and Modell gave Newsome one more chance to change his mind. Baltimore had a perfectly adequate left tackle in Tony Jones, but Ferentz assured Newsome that the six-foot-nine, 345-pound Ogden could play guard for a season.

Newsome didn't hesitate. He trusted the entire process that went into a draft. The way he viewed it, all the work the Ravens had done for five months would've gone out the window if they didn't select their highest-rated player. He would've lost the confidence of his scouts, of everyone associated with this first draft.

"It's not a one-person board," Newsome says. "You're entrusting a lot of people but you're entrusting the work that's been done. A draft is the Super Bowl for all of the staff and personnel people."

The mood was not celebratory. Savage needed to assure Modell they'd never regret taking Ogden. Then, with the twenty-sixth overall pick, the Ravens selected linebacker Ray Lewis.

This team looked like the Mean Machine in *The Longest Yard* during rookie camp. Their generic black-and-white uniforms were laughable. But when Ogden picked off a blitzing corner from his left guard position, Ferentz turned to Savage. "This guy," he said, "is an absolute phenom." Newsome's first two draft picks combined for twenty-two Pro Bowls, hoisted two Super Bowl trophies, and jump-started a GM career that's worthy of Canton itself.

He's the antithesis of a micromanager. Scouts can freely do their jobs and offer their opinions without feeling like those opinions will be used against them. Newsome has "the patience of Job," Savage says, in carefully collecting everyone's thoughts. He's freakishly consistent. You knew when Newsome was working out, getting his haircut, and talking to Modell. He's forever selfless. When Modell tried to replace Marchibroda with Mike Holmgren in 1999, the understanding was that Holmgren would take over personnel and Newsome was OK with it. Instead, Holmgren headed to Seattle and Newsome maintained personnel control when Brian Billick was hired.

He never forgot Marchibroda's one request as the coach, too: "Find good players who love to play the game." Forty times and vertical leaps in spandex could not cloud this judgment.

"Ozzie's greatest strength," Savage says, "is that he's gifted with common sense."

The Ravens' football department became the gold standard in league circles, and it all starts with Newsome.

Oh, his former team is well aware. The Browns returned to the NFL in 1999 and spent most of two decades losing to one of their best players ever.

Homecomings to Cleveland early on were not warm receptions. Newsome declines to get into specifics, only saying he experienced "a couple of incidents that were, you know, not very 'warm.'" Yet in evolving into one of the NFL's best GMs of all-time, Newsome never forgot how the Browns found him. It took a vision to put *his* skill set to use, not the other way around. Not a team forcing him to do something he's not good at. This was his exact thought process in selecting Louisville quarterback Lamar Jackson in 2018. Where some extremely bright football minds, like fellow Hall of Famer Bill Polian, believed Jackson needed to play wide receiver in the pros, Newsome saw a quarterback… on Jackson's terms. Baltimore didn't force Jackson to be a pocket passer immediately. Instead, they built an offense that accentuated his gifts and, by Year 2, Jackson was the league's MVP.

The Oz Effect is felt in the very soul of a roster, too. He takes pride in the fact that in 2021, the Ravens kept fighting despite twenty-five players landing on injured reserve. Where most all other teams fold, that squad lost five games by a combined eight points down the stretch. Down to third- and fourth-stringers, they refused to quit.

"That's your charge," he says. "There's a lot of things that are out of your control."

Langhorne thinks those Browns fans who gave Newsome grief have come around, too.

"People of Cleveland may have hated Art Modell but they didn't hate Ozzie Newsome," he says. "They still revere and love Ozzie Newsome. They still wanted him to come back and run this organization."

The tight end position was never the same. Newsome believed he proved this player can do more than catch a six-yard pass and run over a few defenders. That's also why DeLamielleure and Dieken wish the

Browns flexed Newsome out wide more often, like the San Diego Chargers did with Kellen Winslow. Rewatch that Browns-Vikings game in 1980 and you'll see this a bit, but even then, Newsome's hand is comically in a three-point stance. As the NFL's first African American general manager, his reach extends beyond offensive schemes, though. Newsome created a new dream for kids in Alabama and beyond. One conversation still sticks with him. After he was officially given the GM title by Modell in Baltimore, longtime Georgetown University basketball coach John Thompson told Newsome that he'd now inspire African Americans everywhere to be GMs one day.

He hopes so. And he points to Bear Bryant giving him a chance to play college football. That was all it took to get his remarkable football life rolling. Today, the Ozzie Newsome General Managers Forum helps people learn how to be GMs. More doors are bound to bust open. Newsome isn't the general manager anymore, but as the executive VP of player personnel, the man who built this football team from scratch is still visiting practice. Shortly before this conversation, in fact, Newsome stopped by.

A few players dropped passes and, naturally, they turned their heads toward Newsome. They wanted advice and he provided it.

"You didn't look it in," he told them.

"You have to use your eyes."

Chapter 5

THE MATCHUP NIGHTMARE

Football was killing a man in plain sight. By overtime, Kellen Winslow wilted into a staggering corpse of a tight end.

It was overtime. Third-and-twenty. A victory over the Miami Dolphins the night of January 2, 1982, would send the San Diego Chargers to the AFC Championship. So, despite his body temperature reaching 105 degrees and despite losing thirteen pounds, Winslow caught his thirteenth of thirteen receptions and turned upfield with a surge of adrenaline conjured somewhere from the depths of his soul. He slid behind a block by wide receiver Wes Chandler, took safety Mike Kozlowski for a ride past the first-down marker and lifted himself up off the shoddy grass surface to supply Chandler the deadest of dead-fish handshakes.

His head bobbed loosely. His arms dangled. He began wobbling back toward the Chargers huddle before turning toward his sideline and grabbing ahold of the nearest body he could to stop himself from fainting, that of Dolphins defensive back Fulton Walker. The two shared an awkward five-second dance before Walker realized he shouldn't be helping this player in the midst of an all-time game. A trainer rushed over to keep Winslow upright and, as the tight end nursed an apparent shoulder injury, color man John Brodie said on the broadcast that Winslow would probably like "a brand-new right arm."

Multiple trainers were needed to help Winslow lay down on the bench—it appeared he could not move his limbs on his own. The simple exercise of transporting oxygen to his lungs was a chore with the humidity (80 percent) eclipsing the temperature (seventy-six degrees). The Chargers drove deep into Miami territory and Winslow's gutsy play was for naught. Kicker Rolf Benirschke hooked a twenty-seven-yard field goal.

He pressed on. All teammates could do was watch in awe.

"When you see him in the zone," Chandler says, "you let him stay in the zone. You don't interrupt him. You don't go to him and say, 'Hey, man, you need some water.' You let him stay in that zone and be in the condition he's in. It's a mental thing. He's beyond the fact that he knows if he's hydrating. But not to the point where he can't perform. I just marveled at it and was so glad he was on our team. You could see his focus was 100 percent on leaving everything on the field, and that's what he did that night."

Of course, Benirschke's second attempt in overtime was successful and the Chargers were victorious, 41–38. Lined up as the left flanker on the protection team, Winslow hurled his flesh and bones into the middle of the pile and the silence was eerie. The Dolphins fans were dejected, of course, but even the Chargers' celebration was muted. Everyone had just expended every drip of energy at their disposal, and nobody was running on empty quite like Winslow, who laid sprawled and motionless. Tight end Eric Sievers remembers trainer Ric McDonald first running onto the field and getting into an "F you" shouting match with a photographer or reporter. McDonald and another trainer first tried to pick up Winslow and, obviously, were unsuccessful. The man was six foot six, 250 pounds, after all, so Sievers and tackle Billy Shields stepped in.

"All we've got is 100 percent and most of us might get up to 90," Sievers says. "He gave 100 percent that day. At the end of it all, he had nothing else to give."

Head down, towel around his neck, Winslow was carried off the field like a wounded soldier heading to the infirmary. This 166-yard performance supplied the nation a master class in resilience. People in all walks of life could relate to this moment on NBC more than any in the sport's history because right here was a beaten, bloodied competitor refusing to succumb to cowardice. Mike Ditka made us fall in love with the sport's brutality. Ozzie Newsome was proof that the tight end could be unleashed down the field with a flair of finesse. This night, Winslow reintroduced the NFL tight end to the country as a superhero.

On the national stage, in a game chock-full of drama, right to its pulsating conclusion, this position entered an entirely new galaxy. The reason? The Chargers were warping offensive football like no team before.

OK, this is what real swagger in the NFL looks and sounds like.

Even for the early '80s, the scene inside a San Diego Chargers huddle was unmatched badassery.

Quarterback Dan Fouts knew for a fact that his Chargers would score a touchdown every time they took the field and what a glorious feeling this was. Turning the scoreboard into an oversized Lite-Brite for 34 first downs, 564 yards, and 41 points as they did at the Orange Bowl that night in '82 was nothing new. At the peak of his powers, Fouts would see where the ball was spotted, step into his huddle, and peer into the eyes of the other ten players with cold-blooded conviction. "Eight plays, eighty-five yards." Everyone slapped their hands, broke the huddle, and by the time they stepped up to the line? "Bang! We'd do it. It was laughable," former Chargers running back Hank Bauer says.

There were only two possible outcomes. "We'd be ahead of schedule," says Chandler, chuckling, "or right on time."

If Fouts didn't like a play call at any point along this joyride to the end zone, he'd glare back at his coaches and give them a double-bird salute. "The hell with that," Sievers remembers the QB saying before calling a new play and threading a strike downfield. Passing records were shattered constantly. All involved were fully aware that they were doing things no team had tried before.

And yet, before injecting everyone with this sense of inevitability, Fouts was a nobody for five excruciating seasons.

"Personally," Fouts says, "my career was in the shitter."

To put it mildly. The sixty-fourth overall pick in 1973 stumbled through a 12-30-1 run as the starter those five years with 34 touchdowns and 57 interceptions. One potential savior, Bill Walsh, slipped away after one season as his offensive coordinator. Into 1978, the misery continued. The Chargers started 1-4, and the same day of the fateful PSA Flight 182 crash that killed 144 people in San Diego, Don Coryell was hired as the team's head coach. The hire generated a speck of attention locally and nationally but proved to change football forever. The new boss spoke with a pronounced lisp that was awfully easy to imitate, and while he looked like someone whose belt was pulled three buckles too tight, Coryell was simply a fitness nut. He loved the outdoors so much that his dream was once to be a forest ranger.

"All I remember," Bauer says, "was watching this crazy maniac run around the practice field. Yelling at guys. Patting them on the back: *'Oh, hell! Jesus Christ!'*"

Bauer also remembers standing next to Coryell during his first game. The new guy wanted to go deep right out of the chute with "989 F Rub Sneak." The team's offensive line coach, Jim Hanifan, sent the play into Fouts and quickly called him back.

"Dan, Dan, Dan, if we get a Cover 6, the tight end's going to sit down and adjust the 8 route."

"I know, I know."

Fouts trotted back out, and Hanifan called him back to remind him that if they get "man free" coverage—man to man across the board with a free safety deep—to hit the go route up the right sideline.

"I know this," said Fouts, growing irritated.

Fouts started to run onto the field. Hanifan started to call him back *again*, and Coryell finally lost it.

"Hey, Dan! Fuck all of that and throw that son of a bitch to JJ!"

The architect himself knew the Chargers should never overthink this sport.

Fouts hit John Jefferson deep and this "Air Coryell" offense led the league in passing for six consecutive seasons. The coach had been around—twelve seasons at San Diego State, five with the St. Louis Cardinals—but the cosmos truly aligned for a Big Bang in 1978 when Coryell took over these Chargers. That same year, the NFL instituted what became known as the "Mel Blount Rule." No longer did the field resemble international waters with cornerbacks like the Steelers' Blount permitted to maim receivers until the quarterback released the ball. Now, a defender could make contact with a receiver only within the first five yards of the line of scrimmage. Furthermore, the NFL allowed offensive linemen to extend their arms and open their hands when they pass blocked.

Coryell smelled blood.

By releasing four or five options at a time—often deep—Coryell forced individual defensive players to cover large areas of the field. One of his play calls may sound intimidating to the layman when, honestly, anyone capable of counting to nine could learn it. Take "635 F Cross H Swing." Each play read *left* to *right* so, on this call, the wide receiver farthest left ran a "six" (a curl in), the next man inside ran a "three" (a short out) the next a "five" (a curl out) and whoever was lined up as the "F" receiver ran the cross with the running back looping out for a swing pass. Until Coryell, play calls in the NFL included the literal names of the routes themselves. A post. A flag. A dig. His route tree, numbered one through nine, allowed the Chargers to streamline complicated designs. The higher the number, the longer the route. Even numbers turned inside, odd numbers turned outside.

Timing was essential. With cornerbacks no longer stuffing receivers into body bags, the Chargers could drill routes with eerie harmony. Once, 20/20 came to practice to film a story on San Diego's passing game, and Fouts completed balls to his receivers at full speed while blindfolded. Cornerbacks could still get their licks in within those five yards. Bump-and-run coverage became the rage. But Coryell had answers for this, too. Presnap, the Chargers would send receivers in motion so it was tougher to lay a finger on them. This also tipped off Fouts. He could see whether the defense was playing man-to-man or zone coverage. And by deploying one running back and two tight ends more than any other team—"12" personnel—the Chargers balanced the field out. Defenses couldn't automatically tilt a strong-side linebacker and strong safety toward an obvious heavy side of a formation. Drop that strong safety down on Sievers's side and Winslow drew a linebacker in man coverage.

The cherry on top? Routes could change midplay, depending on how a defender played a receiver. "Conversion routes," Chandler calls them. Intelligence was still a must.

Keep up and the offense was guaranteed to score at will. A Coryell game plan was downright lethal. He'd obsess over an opponent's most recent two games, target a specific weakness, and attack.

"We'd see, 'OK, when we go to a slot formation, they flip their corners over to go man to man,'" Fouts says. "Then, we'll split out Winslow to the other side and they can't stop it. There's no way to stop it. The only way is to double him. The big thing was always being a step ahead of our opponent. We would put the game plan in on a Wednesday and we would practice our first fifteen plays on Wednesday, Thursday, and Friday. On Saturday, we would walk through them. So, on Sunday, when we'd run our first couple of plays, we had it down so cold it was scary. We knew on Wednesday, 'OK, on this play, they can't stop that. And if we have time to throw it and the quarterback is on his target, they can't stop *that one*. And they can't stop *that one*. And they can't stop *that one*.'"

San Diego quickly accumulated the artillery needed to execute Coryell's vision. The veteran Charlie Joiner was a future Hall of Famer. Jefferson was the team's fourteenth overall pick in 1978. Winslow was taken thirteenth in 1979. Running back Chunk Muncie was a severely underrated running back who, Bauer insists, was more physically gifted than both O. J. Simpson and Bo Jackson. Fouts was the "mad scientist" behind it all. A "Superman of game plans," Bauer says. No wonder he hated the shotgun. The split second it took to corral the ball was precious time he wasn't using to read the field.

The true genius of Coryell was that he listened to these players, too. This wasn't Vince Lombardi teaching a power sweep on the chalkboard. Coryell would constantly ask Joiner or Jefferson or Winslow if they liked a certain play, and if they hesitated? "Screw it," he'd say. And that play was trashed. On the flip side, if there was a route they loved to run, Coryell worked it into the game plan.

"That gives the player ownership," Fouts says. "And when a player has ownership, what is he going to do? He's going to try really, really hard to make his suggestion work. So, he's going to play better. He's going to be engaged."

They just needed to get used to his idiosyncrasies. The same coach who sincerely loved his players, who'd get genuinely upset if another player on another team said anything bad, could walk right by his own guys in the hallway without saying a word. It was nothing personal. Coryell simply had something else on his mind. He was too consumed with investigating and obsessing over every advantage imaginable to make petty small talk.

When Coryell realized running back Lionel James was an option quarterback in high school, he infused that into the playbook. Chandler was left-footed? He used the receiver as a punter. When Seattle Seahawks quarterback Jim Zorn was driving him batty with his legs, Coryell told his defense they needed to play like wild dogs and proceeded to bark throughout practice. He was a paranoid fellow, too. He felt the need to protect his X's and O's like nuclear codes. The fencing around the Chargers' practice field was completely covered by vinyl shielding to prevent anyone from peering through, but there was also a ridge on the other side of the freeway—about one mile away—that sat elevated two hundred feet. Fearful that someone could watch their practice with a telescope or high-powered binoculars, Coryell would send team employees to clear the area for spies.

During Raiders week, they took no chances with habitual line-stepper Al Davis and practiced right inside the stadium. Not only that, the team's head of security was instructed to patrol the premises. This dude meant business, too.

"It always seemed like that guy showed up with a silver Colt, pearl-handled revolver," Sievers says, "and would walk around the stadium like he was going to gun down some spy."

One training camp, Coryell had all players eating Popsicles during breaks. Bauer still has no clue why.

"That was Don World."

The system was equal parts brilliant and bizarre, with only one blind spot. It was just that: a *system*. The Chargers were not consciously force-feeding one particular player all game long. There was no lead vocalist around here because, for starters, Winslow couldn't sing a lick in real life. Sievers remembers Winslow and linebacker Linden King playing at local nightclubs and events as the duo "Kellen and King" and…yeah. Not great. This offense was more of a grand symphony with Fouts serving as its conductor. Nobody griped for the ball more than Winslow, and Fouts wouldn't put up with it. Nor would he put up with any imperfection whatsoever.

He cussed Winslow out for "tippy-toeing" out of his breaks. Winslow told him to find another tight end. Fouts said he would.

"Fouts was the boss," Sievers says. "It didn't matter who was the field, who the player was, how big or strong. There were arguments on the field. But moments later when the ball's snapped, we're focused on what we have to do."

In Cleveland, Ozzie Newsome hardly squeaked. In San Diego, Winslow berated officials and opponents and stuck a finger in the faces of defenders. Winslow was also four inches taller than Newsome. The first time he walked into the locker room, Bauer thought, "Holy shit? Where did we get this guy? The Lakers?" He was enormous. And athletic, and strong, and unbelievably smart. Very quickly, Fouts embraced Winslow's ego because this attitude gave the offense a bite and Winslow was the centaur who brought Coryell's master plan to life on the field.

There was no football comparison. The best way to understand Winslow's talent, Sievers explains, is to watch Bruce Lee in slow-motion. In real time, it's impossible to decipher the martial artist's flurry of kicks and punches and blocks. But slow that footage to a crawl and how in sync all those moves are will blow your mind. That was Winslow. He could maneuver his hands and upper body just like that off the line of scrimmage. He dipped his shoulder "as well as a guy who was five foot three."

"There weren't many guys in the league," Sievers says, "who had the power he did to control a game."

So, back in the lab, Coryell took that novel concept by Luke Johnsos in Chicago—the two-way release—and shoved it into a microwave. Attached to the line, Fouts recalls Winslow as a devastating blocker, but Coryell knew that quarantining Winslow to the trenches would waste his limitless potential. Instead, Winslow was flexed out wide as much as possible because this was what put the defense in a foreign bind. Drift a linebacker out with him, and good luck. He'd run past him. Try a defensive back, and he'd bully him. San Diego dared a defense to double-team Winslow. Both Joiner and Jefferson were ready to feast on the other side of the ball.

This exact predicament was what triggered one of the greatest schematic evolutions in the sport. Through the '70s, the Oakland Raiders were the toast of the AFC West and played the Chargers man to man with a free safety over the top. Then, Winslow sifted on out wide. A linebacker couldn't cover him. A safety couldn't. The Raiders had zero choice but to replace a linebacker with a cornerback. "And that's when people started playing what's called a nickel defense," Bauer says. "Because of Kellen Winslow." The Chargers always had a dangerous third option at wide receiver, too, so defenses were soon forced to replace *two* linebackers with *two* defensive backs. And the dime defense was born. All because of this chess piece of a tight end who fittingly played on his high school's chess team because his mother wouldn't let him play football until his senior year.

"Kellen was a monster," former Steelers safety Mike Wagner says. "Kellen would just make space. If he caught the ball, he was more dangerous because he just loved running over you. He wouldn't elude you. He'd drop a shoulder to run over you. If you were tackling him, he wanted to punish you."

Not that this monster was exactly pumping iron in his spare time. Sievers came from a college program (Maryland) that demanded tight ends bench 450 pounds—and Winslow was no gym rat. Rather, he threw other humans around on sheer natural strength. Attitude. He absolutely loathed being tackled, especially by smaller defensive backs. If a cornerback managed to wrestle Winslow down, Fouts adds, he took it as a shot to his pride. The quarterback loved such wickedness but soon found himself begging and pleading for Winslow to live for the next down.

"He would literally try to run guys over and it would drive me nuts," Fouts says. "I'd say, 'Kellen, give me five yards instead of five stitches in that kid's head.'"

In 1980, Joiner, Jefferson, and Winslow each eclipsed one thousand yards as the Chargers advanced to the AFC Championship and fell to Oakland, 34–27.

In 1981, it was time.

When Jefferson wanted a new contract, San Diego refused to budge, traded him to the Green Bay Packers, acquired Chandler from the New Orleans Saints for first- and third-round picks, and didn't miss a beat. A 44–23 loss to the wretched Seattle Seahawks on *Monday Night Football* served as the wake-up call. After a team meeting, the Chargers swiftly turned their season around with a simple plan: Get the ball to Winslow. The following week, the tight end scored *five* touchdowns in a 55–21 blowout win over the Raiders. The first was hysterical. At the 7-yard line, cornerback Odis McKinney got both of his arms around the tight end's waist, and Winslow shucked him away with his right arm. "Slung him off like a rag doll!" Chandler says. He frolicked in the end zone all day, too. Unlike Newsome, this was a tight end who relished a good spike. After each score, he tried spiking the football in a new way. Running out of ideas, after Touchdown Number 5, Winslow did more of a slow-motion toggle under his legs before dunking the ball with two hands over his head.

All while leaving a pile of bodies in his wake.

"He reminded me of Derrick Henry when he comes around the corner," Chandler says. "These cornerbacks know they're going to get the stiff-arm, and no corner wants to come up on Derrick Henry in that situation. That's how Kellen was with these safeties. He'd just fling 'em off. You're talking about a guy who's six foot six and had agility and strength, size. It was going to be a load for them to handle. He would just beat 'em up. Just a bully! That's what Kellen was. Kellen was just playing bully ball. Sometimes, I would just laugh.

"We'd hug and, hell, my facemask would be in his chest. I'm like, 'Damn. My face is in his chest!' I'm a six-foot guy. It's like, 'Oh my Lord.' It reminds me how big he was. He had great flexibility, outstanding hands, strong hands, could catch the ball in any position. Behind him. He'd reach back like it was nothing. Catch it over his shoulder."

Adds Sievers: "He had the best hands I've ever seen. His ability to snap his hands in position to grab a pass was remarkable."

Nobody had an answer. For the second straight season, Winslow led the league in receptions. The Chargers won the AFC West and took their "eight-play, eighty-five-yard" swag to Miami for a divisional playoff showdown with the Dolphins. On the flight 2,200 miles east, Coryell took the microphone to speak to the entire team. This was never his forte. The coach always seemed uncomfortable speaking to the team as a whole but, as always in "Don World," this was of vital importance. Coryell told everyone to drink a ton of water because you lose ten ounces an hour in your body on a plane. Each player was also told that there were bananas waiting for them in their hotel rooms. Coryell had researched that the *"phosphorus"* from bananas—he meant "potassium"—helps players ward off cramps and, well, the forecast called for quite a bit of heat and humidity.

In Miami, the team's business manager, Pat Curran, went to five different locations to buy as many bananas as he could find. Not everyone ate them. Fouts drank a couple of beers instead. Winslow actually did eat his bananas. But in retrospect, both Curran and Coryell should've spent all of New Year's Day scavenging the state.

Humidity to this extreme sucks the life out of visitors. The Orange Bowl transforms into a scorching sauna, the air becomes unbearably sticky and opponents wither away.

The Miami Dolphins saw it all the time. Hard-hitting safety Glenn Blackwood remembers the telltale signs. First, a player appears dizzy. Next, they put their hands on the knees. Finally, they cave. Once, against the Chicago Bears, Blackwood saw 315-pound guard Noah Jackson puke all over the field and linebacker A. J. Duhe turned around to yell back, "We got 'em!"

This night, he had a feeling it was only a matter of time. Through the first quarter, the visiting Chargers acted as if this was a climate-controlled dome in racing to a 24–0 lead. Back in his home state, Chandler took a punt back for a touchdown and San Diego added two more scores off Dolphins turnovers. Winslow was living his best life, too. After Chandler's electric runback, he wrapped his teammate in a hug and smiled like a kid in Disney World. Dolphins head coach Don Shula pulled quarterback David Woodley for Don Strock, and the career backup caught fire. Miami's hook-and-ladder touchdown as the final seconds of the first half melted off the clock cut the deficit to 24–17. On the broadcast, play-by-play man Don Criqui set the scene best in saying the crowd went from "stunned silence" to "absolute mayhem." The ear-splitting boom could be heard inside the locker room where, as Blackwood says, the Dolphins felt like they were ahead. They could hardly hear Shula speak.

"Then," he says, "it was like two heavyweights laying on the ropes slugging each other."

Into the third quarter, Winslow's twenty-five-yard touchdown catch up the left seam from Fouts gave the Chargers a 31–24 lead. Blackwood blitzed off the right edge and was blasted onto his can by running back John Cappelletti. From the grass, Blackwood couldn't help but marvel at Fouts's pump fake and release. A release he calls one of the best ever. After Winslow crossed the end zone, he dunked it over the crossbar and was swiftly reprimanded by the color man, Brodie, for showboating. "Don't do that once you get in there," he scolded.

Then, the humidity started to take its debilitating toll.

As cramps grabbed ahold of Winslow's muscles, the game turned. Again. Miami answered with a pair of touchdowns to go up, 38–31, and were driving yet again with only 4:39 remaining.

From their own 20-yard line to the San Diego 21, the Dolphins ate up precious clock to set up a game-clinching field goal. And that was when defensive lineman Louie Kelcher ripped the ball out of running back Andra Franklin's hands. With new life, the Chargers turned it on. On the first play, Winslow trotted in motion wide left. Fouts stumbled to his knees while dropping back, popped up, slung a short completion to Joiner over the middle and Winslow had a perfect, beeline angle to obliterate the 187-pound Blackwood. He stormed in and hurled a vicious right shoulder into the safety who, miraculously, stayed on his feet. The safety knows it should've been much worse. A collision like this sends players to the ER. Only "by the grace of God" did Blackwood catch Winslow in the corner of his eye in time to dip his shoulder. The fact that Joiner was continuing to run helped, too. Something was giving Joiner hope.

"So I glanced right at the last minute and saw where his hope was coming from," he explains. "Kellen wasn't afraid to sacrifice his body to help his team win and that's a good example of it right there. I've heard people say lots of stuff about that game and people getting carried off. There is no way on God's green earth I'm going to criticize him. As much as I hated having to play against the guy, it was a work of art to watch him play. . . . I hated his guts every time he caught the ball. But you look at it and say, 'Daggome.' Kellen Winslow, to me, was a wide receiver in a tight end's body. He was so fluid and so...he was just a tremendous football player. I'd like to say it was a pleasure battling him, but it wasn't. I usually ended up on the wrong side of things."

Thankfully, for his brain cells, this was not one of those times.

Instead of drilling Blackwood into tomorrow, Winslow was the player heading to the sideline with a pinched nerve in his shoulder. The cramps were really getting bad now. His thigh. His calves. His lower back. Everything hurt. Winslow later told *Sports Illustrated* that the back pain felt something like "paralysis." All those 8s and 9s thirty-plus yards downfield in the Air Coryell offense were adding up. Fast. Fouts threw the ball fifty-three times in all this night and, as Sievers notes, the Chargers were no dink-and-dunk operation. The team's gargantuan tight end was sent on vertical routes all game.

The Dolphins beat him up, too. A linebacker would shuck Winslow with a forearm. A safety would ding him over the top. This was when men were men. One Dolphins cornerback, Don McNeal, played this night with a broken right arm in a cast.

"Back then, you could spear, you could chop a guy at the line," Sievers says. "There was a lot of punching. A lot of head shots. All of us were taught at that stage to lead with your head. That's how you developed the toughness of a football player. A lot of guys didn't like to do that so they became receivers. Kellen was tough. He could go across the middle and take a shot in the ribs. Guys would chop his legs. Everybody wanted to get a shot in. The Miami guys would say, 'Oh, that guy's a pussy. He can't get himself off the field.' There might've been some dramatic moments, but it definitely was earned. He was exhausted. It was a unique set of circumstances that night—the heat, the humidity, the volume of plays we did vertically downfield."

Adds Bauer: "I hate it when people say, 'He wasn't a tough guy. He got hurt.' Bullshit. Kellen was tough, man."

There's a reason Sievers was the player lifting Winslow to his feet during the game, too. The rookie was scared to death he'd need to take his spot in the offense. His nerves spiked each time Winslow staggered off. *Oh my God*, he told himself. *Get up. Get up.* The parts are interchangeable in this offense, after all, and he knew it'd be impossible to mimic someone redefining the position. At 50 percent, Sievers adds, Winslow was the better option. And, actually...

"If he was breathing, he was the better person to put out there."

Every time Winslow tapped out, he tapped back in.

On this game-tying drive, his eleventh catch of the night advanced the ball to Miami's 29-yard line and set an NFL playoff record. Winslow shoved Kozlowski at the top of his route to create separation and, luckily, ducked in time to avoid a kill shot from Blackwood. Fouts hit Chandler for nineteen yards on a post with 1:07 to go and, inside the huddle, the plan was to get the ball to Winslow. Fouts asked him to run a "three," and out, and didn't give a damn if Miami doubled him. Fouts figured he could buy some extra time and loft it up to Winslow for a jump ball. Unfortunately, Winslow was gassed. When Fouts let it fly, the tight end didn't have enough energy to leap. "The next thing I know," Fouts recalls, "there's this flash in the back of the end zone and it's 'JB' with a touchdown." Out of nowhere, running back James Brooks flew in to catch what should've been an overthrown incompletion. On this play, Brooks was supposed to stay in and block but decided to scramble into the end zone when there was nobody rushing.

Tie game, 38-all. Winslow wasn't done.

When Miami drove into position for a straightaway, forty-three-yard attempt, the weary tight end sauntered on out with San Diego's "desperation" block team and—with every code-red siren blaring for mercy inside his body—Winslow launched into the sky, extended his right arm, and nicked the football with his pinkie finger. In that exact moment, his entire body cramped up. He was a battered man before this game even began, unable to put on his own shoulder pads due to a bruised left shoulder and strained rotator cuff. Now? He had a gash in his lip that'd require three stitches, a bad shoulder, and cramps that Winslow said afterward made him feel like Muhammad Ali boxing Joe

Frazier in The Thrilla in Manila. "I'd never come that close to death before," Winslow told *SI*. Again, he was helped off the field.

After his thirteenth reception, he laid on the bench. Defeated.

San Diego missed a kick. Miami had a kick blocked. Once more, Winslow reentered the game and the huddle was an unforgettable sight. Indeed, this was a punch-drunk heavyweight holding on for dear life. Sievers remembers seeing Winslow's eyes closed and his mouth agape with drool pouring out. He wasn't the only one, either. Sievers had flashbacks to his college days at Maryland, when players would sit around in disbelief that they survived another day of practice under coach Jerry Claiborne, a disciple of Bear Bryant, who ran "Junction Boys"–style camps. As Sievers's roommate, Lloyd Burruss, told him later in life: "What they did to us was criminal."

That was how all eleven players felt in this huddle. He's sure of it. There wasn't a dry spot on anyone's jerseys or pants.

"Go run an 880 as fast as you can," Sievers says. "Try to set your record time. Then, go directly to sit in the sauna for forty minutes at 120 and, while you're in there, do push-ups and sit-ups if you want to feel what it felt like. You're just down to the guts. When you're completely exhausted, you're not rigid in any sense. It's fortunate he was even able to hold on to the ball. Your body's just rubber."

Fouts hit Chandler over the middle…and Chandler was knocked out of the game. Fouts chucked it deep to Joiner for thirty-nine yards… and Joiner was knocked out. This time, Benirschke's kick was true from twenty-nine yards out. Winslow collapsed one final time, and the image of the tight end being carried off was immortalized. Once Winslow got to the locker room, he was able to walk under his own power but, years later, one comparison struck Sievers. Why Winslow collapsed made a little more sense. When Sievers battled cancer himself, his wife would fall into a heap the second a CT scan result was in. "Everybody's body reacts differently," he says, "when you have put every ounce of what you are into something."

Elsewhere on the field, longtime guard Ed White looked over to Bauer. "Have you noticed they never carry the fat guys off?" he said.

Inside that visitor's locker room, nobody was in a celebratory mood. In full pads, cleats, everything, White sat in the showers as the cold water blasted. Blackwood was devastated but admits he wouldn't have been in a cheery mood if Miami won.

It's no shock the Chargers had nothing left to give. Especially with what awaited them next.

On to the AFC Championship, they swapped the sauna for an igloo. In minus-*fifty-nine* wind chill, the Chargers fell to the Cincinnati Bengals, 27–7. Winslow wore two pairs of gloves and still got frostbite in his right thumb. Even worse, it took their departing plane three hours to deice and players couldn't even drink their sorrows away. No alcohol was sold in Boone County, Kentucky, on a Sunday. In the strike-shortened 1982 season, the Chargers torched defenses (again) and Winslow played hero (again) in a 31–28 wild card win in Pittsburgh. With one minute to go, Fouts faked a run to Brooks with an exaggerated rollout right. Pittsburgh took the bait, and he threw it back to Winslow on a screen to the left side. A thirty-four-year-old Mel Blount was waiting for Winslow at the goal line. He stood no chance.

"Kellen just put his head down like a running back and bowled through him," Chandler says. "For years, it was the final resting place for people to go into Pittsburgh and lose to the Steelers in the playoffs. We took care of business."

One week later, Miami got its revenge with a 34–13 win in the same divisional playoff round. A turf toe and twisted ankle rendered Winslow 50 percent by his own admission, and nobody could fill that void. Blackwood is still proud of his "de-cleating" hit on Sievers that day and that was it. The Coryell-led Chargers never made the playoffs again. All those stitches Winslow gave opponents caught up with him, too. He logged a third thousand-yard season in 1983 but was never the same player after a ghastly knee injury in 1984. Witnessing this first-hand remains one of the worst days of Sievers's life. Against the Raiders, Winslow was hit by linebacker Jeff Barnes, and the ligaments in his knee were so mangled that the man who performed the surgery,

Dr. Gary Losse, told the Associated Press his knee resembled "spaghetti." The posterior cruciate and medial collateral ligaments were both severed, so Dr. Losse needed to extract a spare tendon from the front of the knee to graft a new ligament.

The sight was so nauseating that, to this day, Sievers turns away from the TV whenever a player suffers a severe injury.

"It makes me cringe and curl up right now just thinking about it. For him to come back, it's a miracle."

Winslow's hands never left him, but his speed was shot. He played two and a half more seasons and retired at age thirty.

The legacy of Coryell lived on. The Dallas Cowboys won Super Bowls in 1992, 1993, and 1995 with quarterback Troy Aikman calling the same plays Fouts did a decade prior. Four years later, "Air Coryell" evolved into the "Greatest Show on Turf" with the St. Louis Rams going on a surreal Super Bowl run. A quarterback who was stocking shelves five years prior, Kurt Warner, won NFL MVP as the Rams scored an NFL-high 32.9 points per game.

"Air Coryell and Kellen really changed the way teams played defense," says Bauer. "Everybody else was pretty basic up to that point. And Kellen and Coryell and Dan Fouts and our group, we caused that change. Our offense, to this day, is being run! All of the offenses you see, they're using our packages and running our routes, our route tree."

Coryell isn't in the Pro Football Hall of Fame. A "shame," says Fouts, despondent. Winslow did get the nod, in 1995, and his legacy has also lasted decades. He forced NFL teams to consider an entirely new body type at the position. Up to that night in Miami, teams mostly pursued the six-foot-three, 240-pound, Sievers-like grunts at tight end. Winslow cannon-blasted the position into a new realm. Whenever a team thinks about drafting a tight end now, and they're staring at a draft board, Fouts believes they're saying one thing: "We need to find a Winslow."

That was impossible in the early '80s, of course. Kellen Winslow was an anomaly. Nobody looked remotely similar in that one-on-one matchup at the top of your screen. But year to year, decade to decade, more *Winslows* did emerge. From strange places, too. On one coast was a terrified kid in Cali who hated football. On the other was a kid brawling with his brothers during mini-stick hockey games in Buffalo.

Many had Winslow-sized egos, too.

"Which is fine!" Fouts repeats. "That's part of your makeup. As long as you keep it under control and you keep it in the proper perspective, it's important to have one."

One tight end in particular rerouted the position this colorful direction. Instead of spiking a football, this tight end was much more creative. He'd mock you in pregame and, in the midst of a blowout win, pick up a phone and pretend to call the president of the United States to send the National Guard in.

This tight end is still talking, too.

Chapter 6

CLUB SHAY SHAY

When the Denver Broncos reconvened for their first practice ahead of the 2000 season, players lined up to stretch like they had done an infinite number of times in their football lives. It doesn't matter if it's a group of mighty mites at the neighborhood park or millionaires. Every football practice at every level essentially starts with the same calisthenics. At its core, football is a bunch of friends playing a game that's supposed to be fun.

This is where the personality of an NFL team can take shape, too. Before players disperse into positional factions for drills, they're here. They're together. And for the first time in a decade, Shannon Sharpe was gone.

Nobody had a clue what to say.

"It was dead," former Broncos running back Anthony Lynn recalls. "It was like we were at a funeral—for Shannon. There was no 'Club Shay Shay.' It was just *dead.*"

That was what they called it, too: Club Shay Shay. Warmups never lasted too long for the Broncos. About seven or eight minutes. But Sharpe's baritone voice—part gospel preacher, part drill sergeant—had a way of grabbing everyone's attention. Players shut up in unison because they absolutely could not miss Sharpe's latest comedy set. His jokes killed. His impersonations were flawless. There was always a lingering fear that you would be his next victim. And if anyone didn't have a nickname, it was only a matter of time. Whatever moniker Sharpe chose stuck forever.

For a decade, one man siphoned the monotony of the pro football out of the Mile High air.

"It was the Shannon Sharpe Comedy Show," Lynn says. "You just never stopped laughing."

What Sharpe accomplished as a player was unparalleled in his era. At his first press conference with the Baltimore Ravens, that same off-season, Sharpe said he couldn't have imagined a better destination since he always admired general manager Ozzie Newsome as a player. "I can see the guy every single day," said Sharpe, his cheeks molding into a smirk. "And he can see me every single day as I break his records." Then, he did exactly that. Won a third Super Bowl, too. The numbers sparkled but Sharpe's imprint on the position—and the sport—was most evident out of the public eye.

On that Denver practice field. In 2000. When an entire team felt fossilized.

Players always knew their locker room was tight but, now, it was painfully obvious why.

"We all play the game because we love the game," says Lynn. "But there are some days you just don't like football. Football is brutal, hard, physical. It's mentally and emotionally exhausting. To have somebody like that in your locker room and on the field that can lighten things up and bring that humor where you actually laugh? And enjoy it? It creates energy and momentum. The intangibles were something that we didn't think about when we let him go."

The thoroughbred powering those Broncos teams to back-to-back Super Bowl championships, running back Terrell Davis, believes we all lob the word "great" around far too liberally. It has become watered down. "Great," to him, is what everyone felt that day.

"The soul of the locker room was gone," Davis says. "Stripped away. It was an example of how important locker rooms are. Chemistry. It's hard to manufacture it. A lot of times it's organic."

Memories of the man rouse laughter, and not just any sort of laughter. Rather, the sort of deep-bellied seizure that makes players'

stomachs burst and eyes well with tears. This feels more like reminisc-
ing of Clark Griswold–level family vacations. For three decades, nobody
said much of anything at the tight end position. Mike Ditka spoke with
violence. Kellen Winslow was more cranky than colorful. Newsome
and Ben Coates were mutes. And in came a wide receiver from Savannah State incapable of shutting up.

To Sharpe, talking trash was a lifestyle. He brought an electricity to
what had been a stodgy profession.

The tight end position, he proved, should be fun as hell.

―――――――

"Where's Shannon Sharpe!? Where's Shannon Sharpe!?"

A slight pause.

"He ain't getting nothing today!"

That was the voice of a defensive back for Clark College ahead of
a game against Savannah State right in Savannah, Georgia. Before
Sharpe turned stretching into a daily roasting as a pro, *he* was the target during warmups in college. The game wasn't even close to starting,
so nobody on Savannah State's team was even in pads yet. They were
on their butts doing leg stretches when this poor fool stood up on his
side of the field and sashayed around enemy soil. Sharpe was a Division
II All-American—the DB surely watched him on film. But this was
also 1989. Media coverage was nonexistent. "Shannon Sharpe" was an
urban legend to this DB, more Loch Ness monster than reality.

Quickly, Savannah State teammates started to chime in. This was
common. They knew it was smart to escalate any situation involv-
ing Sharpe. "You're going to be shut down tonight!" one yelled. "Oh
baby!" And the team's quarterback, Richard Basil, can still picture it
now. Seated at the 50-yard line, right where the Tigers' field crowned,
Sharpe had enough. When he stood up on this elevated hump—with
all teammates still seated—it looked like Sharpe was seven feet tall.

"Who out there," Sharpe shouted, "is looking for *me*!?"

The DB cowered. No way did this DB expect Sharpe to be so big, so mean. An *Oh Shit* paleness overcame his face. The air so visibly left his body that Basil felt bad for him.

"Shannon is not the kind of guy you want to call out," Basil says. "I'm looking at the DB like, 'Dude, do you know what you're doing? I'm sitting right here beside him and I do have the ball in my hands first. I'm going to feed him. You're saying he ain't gonna get nothing and I haven't seen it yet. So, let's see.'"

That defensive back—"No. 32," as Basil recalls—retreated to his Clark College teammates. There was nothing left to say. Savannah State finished up with some jumping jacks, the ball was kicked off and, again, Sharpe was unstoppable. This was the theme in college: Sharpe routinely crushed spirits. Anyone who talked junk to Sharpe lost their football manhood on-site.

It's also true that everyone who encountered Sharpe in college for the first time experienced iterations of the same shock. When Basil first met his new wide receiver at the mall, Sharpe extended a hand and said, "Pleased to meet you." It felt more like Sharpe's five fingers were eating his right hand. "Wow," Basil told himself, "this is a *specimen*." They hit the field for practice and Sharpe was thrilled when Basil overthrew him by fifteen yards on a bomb deep. "Yeahhhh, baby!" he shouted on his way back to the huddle. "I've got somebody who can let it go!" Basil was thrilled, too. He realized all he needed to do was lob the ball in Sharpe's zip code. Especially in one-on-one coverage. Their two seasons together, Savannah State went 15-4, and it didn't take long for Basil and Sharpe to burn secondaries with "sight adjustments." They'd eye the same vulnerability in a coverage and shoot each other a subtle look. No words or hand signals were needed. The two shared a telepathic chemistry that'd also flummox friends during card games at the student center. Nobody could understand how Sharpe and Basil kept winning.

In intramural basketball, Basil would hear a thunderous "I'm coming!" and knew to lob it off the backboard for Sharpe to slam.

This wasn't the SEC, but he was clearly a different breed. At night, friends got used to the sight of Sharpe walking through the front door as a fountain of perspiration. He'd train to the point of literal immobility, obsessed with testing the limits of his body. More suckers would challenge him, too. At Savannah State, Sharpe racked up the W's like a young heavyweight dominating inferior chumps at rundown gyms. Basil remembers a DB on their team calling Sharpe out during a one-on-one blocking drill. This junior college transfer was brought in to help at free safety. "I want Sharpe," he declared. Again, teammates incited chaos. "Shannon! He's calling you out!" The two players lined up and, after piledriving him ten yards, Sharpe deposited this free safety on his ass.

This was the player's final practice, too. He quit.

"If you go up against a big man like that and he slams you on your back in the game of football," Basil says, "you don't want to play anymore. He wanted a piece of Shannon. I don't know why. All the other guys out there, and you call on him? OK! Cool! We'll sure watch the show."

The production was too bonkers for the NFL to ignore. Sharpe finished with 3,744 receiving yards on 192 receptions with 40 touchdowns at Savannah State, all while mastering the routes that win in the pros: the 10-yard out, the flag, the curl. After his NFL Combine workout in 1990, one coach for the New England Patriots told Basil that no receiver caught the ball better in Indianapolis than Sharpe. Still, he measured in at six foot one and 220 pounds. He ran a slow 4.67 in the 40. His older brother, Sterling, was asserting himself as the best wide receiver this side of Jerry Rice, but teams weren't sure where Shannon even fit into the pro game. Was he a wide receiver? A tight end? Mike Shanahan, the Broncos' quarterbacks coach then, remembers viewing Sharpe as a "brick shithouse." The offensive staff wanted him badly in the sixth and, luckily, he was still available at 192nd overall in the seventh round.

This was no Ditka or Winslow tearing the league up in Year 1 or Year 2. On the *All the Smoke* podcast, Sharpe said he once asked a

Broncos teammate which route to run and was intentionally told the wrong one—the two were competing for a roster spot. He vowed, on the spot, to never do the same thing as a veteran. Halfway through the season, with injuries crippling the tight end position, head coach Dan Reeves decided to move Sharpe to tight end. He was still light then, and had no clue what he was doing as a blocker, but torched Denver's number one defense on the scout team. After big plays, Sharpe would chuck the ball right into the woods. Finally, defensive coordinator Wade Phillips spoke up to Reeves: "Put his ass in the game. Let's see if they can cover him. Because we can't."

He was still clueless. He only caught twenty-nine passes in two seasons.

When Sharpe glided behind John Elway in motion before the snap, the quarterback would need to turn around and tell him what route to run. Elway had approximately a thousand more important things to worry about play to play—he easily could've told Sharpe he wasn't a babysitter and that Sharpe should read a playbook—but, instead, Elway knew this patience would pay off. "We knew," Shanahan says, "we had a diamond in the rough."

In 1992, Sharpe caught fifty-three passes and made the Pro Bowl. Reeves was fired, but he still made a point to call Denver's incoming tight ends coach, Les Steckel, to make sure he knew he was inheriting a budding star. These two bonded quickly. When the coach grew tired of Sharpe dismissively referring to him by his last name—"Hey, Steckel!"— he gave it back to him. He started calling Sharpe "Sweetheart." From '93 to Sharpe giving Steckel a second-row seat at his Hall of Fame Induction in 2011 to today, that's still what they call each other. Steckel tapped into Sharpe's inner desire to smother all challengers. After practice, when players caught 50 "bad balls" at the JUGS machine, Sharpe waited for everyone to leave and caught 100. The pigskin was fired off the wheels at all angles—high, low, to the side—and had such an effect on Sharpe that Elway thanked Steckel after the first training camp.

Elway only had one request. He wanted Steckel to talk to Sharpe about his propensity to order double cheeseburgers, fries, and chocolate malts from Wendy's. He knew Sharpe had another gear in him if he cut the fat from his diet. Steckel told Sharpe that his "number one asset" was his body, and Sharpe listened. In due time, he was cutting little pieces of chicken breast up for dinner and posing shirtless for muscle magazines.

There was always something deeper motivating Sharpe beyond a random adversary yelling his name back at Savannah. Steckel could tell. Whenever he chided Sharpe, the tight end's go-to line was "I've eaten enough cold oatmeal." Another time, "Sweetheart" said to "Steckel" that he should've seen his suitcase when he headed to college. When Steckel asked if it was all beat up, Sharpe's response shocked him. "No," he said, "it was a grocery bag." The entire world eventually learned of Sharpe's singular motivation at his Hall induction speech. It brought a tear to Basil's eye, and he wasn't alone.

That night, Sharpe said he was raised by his grandmother and, as a kid, he asked her once what she'd want one day. It wasn't a car. It wasn't jewelry. Mary Porter said it was a decent home. She wanted to be able to go to bed at night—have God let it rain as hard as He possibly could—and to wake up dry. For sixty-six years, if it rained, those inside got wet. The tin roof was full of leaks. Shannon and Sterling would set up pots and pans to catch the rain, then use those same pots and pans to cook the next day. They lived in a one-thousand-square-foot cinder block home with cement flooring and no indoor plumbing.

"That's what drove Shannon," Sharpe said in Canton. "That's what got me here."

So, it was no surprise Sharpe put in the work. He mastered what Steckel labeled the "stair step." All receivers who ran drag routes tended to run in a straight line. He taught Sharpe how to start in that same straight line but—after crossing the center—take a "step" vertical, like you're going to streak up the hashes. Even two or three steps. Then, slam that outside foot and turn horizontal again along a new straight line toward the sideline. "When you go vertical, guess what that guy does?" Steckel says. "He backs off because he's afraid you're going vertical. Now, he has to change his body to go vertical with you. All of sudden, you go flat again."

Steckel is shocked players don't run this route today. He hasn't seen it himself.

Elway loved what he saw, and now Sharpe was sitting next to him in meetings asking him exactly how he wanted every route. He was targeted 110 times in '93 and a career-high 140 times in '94.

Once in a while, Sharpe would phone Steckel up in the booth to snipe, "Steckel! Tell Elway to take some mustard off the ball? He's throwing it a hundred miles an hour. My hands are ripping apart!" and Steckel would remind Sharpe that this was Elway's first-quarter adrenaline. Also, Sharpe was more than capable of asking Elway himself. Then, they went back to connecting for touchdowns. Each one seemed to inflate Sharpe's ego, open yet another floodgate of trash talk and, while Steckel admittedly hates "hot dogs" on a football field, there was an authenticity to Sharpe. He loved it when Sharpe flexed his biceps in the end zone. It was funny. It was *fun*. The two grew so close that Shannon had Sterling call Steckel for advice when he was deciding whether or not to continue playing after injuring his neck in 1994. After a half hour, Steckel told the twenty-nine-year-old that if Sterling was his son, he'd say to never play again.

It was around this time that "Club Shay Shay" opened up, too. After wide receiver Anthony Miller signed a big contract in free agency to play for the Broncos, he initially struggled with the playbook. Right on cue, Sharpe grabbed his virtual mic during stretches and shouted that Miller should use half of his money to hire a tutor and learn the plays. They soon competed in everything from shooting hoops in the locker room to getting phone numbers from girls. Everyone hung out together, but at times it seemed like this specific feud got a smidge too intense.

Fridays were a riot. Elway and company raced out of the shower as fast as they could to listen to Sharpe.

"He was the most coachable, enjoyable, fun—capital 'F-U-N'— player I ever coached," Steckel says. "He had me laughing all the time. He had everybody laughing."

OK, maybe not everybody.

Before busting out in '93 and '94, Sharpe was still slated to play on special teams. Coordinator Richard Smith tried rallying the group with one of classic "fire-and-brimstone" speeches, Lynn says. That was his MO. All energy. All juice. And this particular speech was one of the best Lynn had ever heard. Smith showed the entire team in the room specific plays and dissected all the different ways they'd bust a wedge on kickoffs. Damn right, they'd torpedo bodies right through those 1,200-pound walls. Then, he offered a fair warning: *If you don't agree with what I just said, you can get the fuck out of here.*

Retelling this story, Lynn laughs so hard he can hardly speak.

"And Shannon," Lynn says, "politely put his one finger up like he's in church, got up, and walked out of the room. And the whole team was in there! He's like, 'I'm not hitting no fucking wedge. You're out of your damn mind!' Everybody wanted to bust out and laugh because we all knew Shannon. But Richard was a serious dude. So, we couldn't laugh. We're like, 'Oh my God. I can't believe he's doing this.' But Richard said it two or three times, 'If you're not down with this, get your ass up and walk out now!' He gets up and walks out."

This was a ballsy maneuver for someone who had started all of one season at tight end. Smith watched Sharpe exit the room and turned to Lynn. "Fuck him!" he said. "You replace Shannon!" And just like that, Lynn started for all three special teams units. He became a team captain, too. Twenty years later, Sharpe tells Lynn there's no chance he would've become an NFL head coach if he didn't walk out that day.

One taste of greatness went right to Sharpe's head and, Lynn jokes, there was no turning back.

"He knew he wouldn't get cut so he had Richard by the balls," Lynn says. "We told jokes about that for a month. You can imagine how that stretch period went...He's going to speak his mind. Some people appreciate it. Some don't. But his sense of humor? He could've been a comedian."

He is also an acquired taste. Nobody in the locker room had ever experienced a character remotely close to this before so, initially, Shannon Sharpe had everyone scratching their heads. Especially the team's sixth-round pick in the '95 draft, a running back out of Georgia named Terrell Davis. When he first came in, buried on the depth chart, Davis tried to observe the full dynamics of this Broncos locker room and barely said a word. To him, the leader of the tribe was obvious. The second Sharpe walked into a room, everyone responded to him. Only later did Davis learn Sharpe didn't drink. "I assumed the dude acts this way because he's always liquored up," Davis says. "Like, 'This cat is hitting it hard.'"

Nope. Clowning everyone just happened to be the man's daily nutrition. He needed to poke and prod and insult to survive the day. Long before the two teammates shared busts in Canton, Davis endured a miserable rookie year. There's still an exhalation of shell shock in his voice.

"Shannon," Davis says, "embarrassed me so much."

He tended to sink his teeth into teammates most on flights to away games and the team bus ride to stadiums because that was when players were required to dress up, and Sharpe was a fashion fiend. He poured his earnings into the finest fitted suits money could buy. Conversely, Davis was not in his same tax bracket back in '95. He visited a local Men's Wearhouse, bought what he could afford off the rack, walked onto the Broncos' bus and, no, no, no, absolutely not. Sharpe would not stand for this. A blazer? With tan khakis? In those Bobo shoes? Sharpe roasted the rookie. He was always surrounded by a posse, too, that featured special-teamer Keith Burns as his sidekick.

It did not matter that Davis made the team with a crushing hit on special teams in the preseason and would go on to rush for more than one thousand yards as a rookie.

Sharpe was relentless.

"If you show any emotions toward it bothering you?" Davis says. "Oh, he's going to be on you from the time you're on the bus to the time you're at the hotel to after the game. You just hope that somebody gets on the bus with a worse suit than you. I mean, shit, I was trying to put together the best outfit I could put together. You'd laugh it off outside. But inside you're like, 'This mother…' And then you not only have Shannon, but his whole crew. My rookie year was not fun."

Lynn was a man making league minimum himself and knew nothing about fashion. He recalls getting on the plane in a navy jacket with khakis. The gall. The horror. No, Sharpe would not stand for this, either.

By then, the tradition for players was to bring Popeye's onto flights. As Sharpe polished off his chicken, he asked Lynn if he could wipe his mouth on his collar.

"Can you do *what*?" Lynn asked.

"Well," Sharpe said, "my hanky costs a lot more than your shirt, so I'd like to wipe my mouth on your collar."

Lynn wasn't pleased but Sharpe actually lent a hand. He gave his teammate two of his suits that he didn't wear anymore, two suits that were easily the most expensive pieces of clothing Lynn has ever worn in his life. Even the players who absorbed the most ribbing knew Sharpe wasn't malicious about anything. He just had no off switch. Sharpe enjoyed crafting his material 24/7. He wouldn't go in for the kill unless he liked you. Of course, you better like that nickname Sharpe bestowed upon you. It stuck for life. Lynn was "Bullwinkle," or "Wink" for sure. Defensive end Alfred Williams thought he was a receiver with a towel hanging from his pants, so Sharpe called him "Prime Plate" and "Hot Plate." Davis was "Ju Ju," and has no clue why. Wide receiver Rod Smith was "Foots." Burns, "Tic."

To this day, teammates refer to Anthony Lynn as "Bullwinkle," too. His best friend from high school, Rocky Jones, used to hang out with everyone, so Sharpe seized the moment. "Bullwinkle" it was. Nothing changed when Lynn became an NFL head coach, either. When Lynn bumps into old teammates on the coaching trail, like former Broncos quarterback Gary Kubiak, they ask, "How's it going, Bullwinkle?" He turned on the TV once and ex-Broncos guard Mark Schlereth, now an NFL analyst, called him Bullwinkle. "Mark!" Lynn told him. "You can't do that! I'm a head coach!"

Those comedy routines during warmups only sharpened over time. Mike Shanahan returned to Denver as the head coach in 1995, and even he needed to listen in.

"Shannon would talk the whole stretch," Shanahan says. "He was giving everybody all kinds of shit. He'd give people a hard time, but people would endure it because usually he was hilarious. He'd always say, 'Mike, remember, nobody's going to beat me talking. They may try but they're not going to beat me.' You could see that was true."

Of course, we're talking about practice. Not a game. When the game arrived? Good Lord, did Shannon Sharpe bring the goods. In the midst of a 34–8 blowout win at New England in November of the 1996 season, Sharpe grabbed the red phone on the sideline and alerted the Patriots fans that he had the president on the phone. "Mr. President," he said, "we need the National Guard. We need as many men as you can spare because we are killing the Patriots. So, call the dogs off. Send the National Guard, please! They need emergency help, please! Help these folks!"

After hanging up, he looked back toward the fans and assured, "Help is on the way!" When Shanahan saw the clip days later, he could not stop laughing. "Only Shannon," he says, "could get away with that."

The cameras only captured a fraction of Sharpe's act, too. His best work was in between plays on the field where he wasn't so nice. He could be unapologetically sinister. After signing with the Seattle Seahawks, linebacker Chad Brown decided to open up a retail reptile store in Denver. Somehow, Sharpe acquired this information ahead of their matchup at Mile High Stadium against the Seahawks and filed it away for the right moment. On a running play, Brown destroyed Sharpe with a violent blow. As he laid on top of the tight end, he let him have it, too.

Sharpe? He didn't miss a beat.

"That's all right," he told Brown. "I'm going to burn your store down tonight."

Brown had no comeback. He was silent. He knew he'd be on a flight back to Seattle that night so, if Sharpe wanted to burn Pro Exotics Reptiles to the ground, he certainly could. Honestly, he was impressed, too. *Brown* was the one who embarrassed Sharpe. *Brown* was the one with every right to talk shit. Yet even after getting flattened, Sharpe went for the kill.

"I've heard all different types of shit-talking over the years, but that one shocked me," Brown says. "I have clearly won the play. That is my play to brag about. But his shit-talking was so perfect and directly to something that was important to me that he was able to shock me with it."

Before a game at Lambeau Field, in '96, Sharpe walked over toward the Green Bay Packers' side of the field to jaw in the direction of All-Pro safety LeRoy Butler. He knew Butler covered the league's best tight ends every week and figured he'd let Butler know what his stat line would look like. "Roy-Le!" Sharpe yelled. "I got your number Roy-Le! Nine for 150!"

The Packers cruised, 41–6. Sharpe went 4 for 34.

Without question, the man's magnum opus came against the Broncos' perennial rival, the Kansas City Chiefs, on *Monday Night Football* in 1998.

The game was all but over. Denver led, 23–7, with seven minutes remaining. Yet five unsportsmanlike penalties by the Chiefs led to seventy-five yards and a short TD run. Linebacker Derrick Thomas had a full-fledged meltdown with three of those penalties. Two of them were the result of grabbing Sharpe by the facemask and apparently trying to remove his head from his torso. It was beyond strange. Thomas was one of the most terrifying pass rushers in the NFL, the Chiefs' all-time sacks leader, but also renowned as a pillar in the community. The 1993 Walter Payton Man of the Year Award winner never lost his cool like this. Further, these two had even trained together in the off-season. They knew each other well. On the broadcast, color commentator Dan Dierdorf called this one of the most embarrassing moments in recent Chiefs history.

After the madness, Sharpe pled the Fifth. He assured all he had "perfected the talent to make people upset." He then hid from the press during the forty-five minutes of open locker room that following Wednesday and said little on his morning radio show the same day. Thomas, meanwhile, was suspended a game and issued a formal apology. Even Chiefs owner Lamar Hunt felt the need to address Thomas's antics, saying this "disgraced" the organization and the community.

So, what happened? What possibly pushed him over the edge?

In earshot, Sharpe recited the phone number of Thomas's girlfriend to him one...digit...at...a...time. Years later, he later referred to this as his "finest moment." Did he know her? Please. One Bronco teammate assures Sharpe more than just *knew* who this girl was. Sharpe had been saving this for the perfect moment. And while Thomas tragically passed away two years later in a car accident, players are sure he'd still want a piece of Sharpe if he were alive today. Sharpe had made it that personal.

Adds Davis: "The way that he talks, he is able to get in your skin to where he got him completely out of his game."

This could backfire. Sometimes, opponents were able to harness their fury for good. Davis also remembers guard Brian Habib telling Sharpe to shut the hell up when he was pissing off Minnesota's John Randle, another trash-talking savant. Randle was ravaging their line.

Granted, no words coming out of Sharpe's mouth would've meant a thing if he couldn't back it up. And he did. Sharpe was the first muscle-bound wide receiver to masquerade as a tight end. Yet this alone wasn't enough for Shanahan when he returned as the head man. The Broncos went 8-8 in '95 and, into '96, rumors swirled that Shanahan was shopping Sharpe. When he heard this, Sharpe naturally approached Shanahan to ask why the head coach was trying to trade him. First, Shanahan tried to set the record straight. He told the tight end he hadn't initiated the call—a team reached out to him—which obviously did not satisfy Sharpe.

"Why are you listening?" he sniped.

"We listen to everyone," Shanahan said. "If somebody makes an offer for anybody, we always listen."

"Mike, what would make you even *think* about trading me?"

That's when Shanahan was ruthlessly blunt. He told Sharpe that the tight end apparently only cares about one thing: catching passes. He loved the fact that Sharpe could line up outside and inside and making the Pro Bowl may be a neat individual goal, but the goal now was Super Bowls. To accomplish this, Shanahan told Sharpe he needed to practice more and he needed to be a more willing blocker. As fun as "Club Shay Shay" was those seven minutes to start a practice—Shanahan was all for it—the coach wanted his star tight end setting a new tone behind the scenes.

"If you would do that," Shanahan told him, "there's no possible way I would let you go."

Sharpe was in. Sharpe gave Shanahan his word. He vowed to set that tone. Very rarely did players ever ask such a point-blank question, so Shanahan believed Sharpe needed brutal honesty in return. Fifteen years later, on his hit TV show *Skip and Shannon: Undisputed*, Sharpe claimed that Shanahan tried to trade him to the Arizona Cardinals in a package for defensive end Eric Swann. Bring this up and Shanahan repeats he never actively shopped him.

Either way, the therapy session was needed and this was a marriage built on compromise.

Initially, Shanahan hated that Sharpe was the only player who didn't train with the team in their off-season program. Through the '90s, Sharpe preferred to work with his own trainer in Atlanta. After he thought about it, however, Shanahan decided to tell Sharpe to stay in Atlanta when the rest of the Broncos gathered in late March. Shanahan's only request was for neither of them to say a word about it. Not to players. Not to coaches. If anyone asked either party what was up, they simply said they were on the same page.

"That's all he did: work out," Shanahan says. "I thought if he saw how our guys worked compared to how he worked out, he'd be so pissed. He'd say, 'My off-season routine is so much better than your off-season program.' But he didn't understand that sometimes you've got to do the best thing for the team. I thought the best thing for the team was for Shannon to do his deal like he did in the off-season. Most people don't have bodies like that to start with. You take a look at his and would say, 'Oh, my God. This guy could be Mr. America.' Because he works at it."

Everyone who watched Sharpe lift weights in person was in awe. Lynn makes clear that Sharpe was never the genetic freak he's portrayed—he earned everything. He was in the weight room, on a treadmill, watching film, "constantly doing something." Eventually, Sharpe stopped ragging Davis and invited him to his house in Atlanta for two weeks to train in the off-season. Davis was more floored by this scene than any trash talking he witnessed on the field, too. He half-expected the two of them to hit the gym around 10 a.m. It wasn't like they had to sneak a lift in before meetings during the off-season—they had all the time in the world. But when Davis woke up, Sharpe was already done with a two-hour workout. Sharpe woke up each morning at 4 a.m. to get his first two-hour workout in.

"I realized that's what you have to do," Davis says, "to get your game to the next level. Plenty of players work out during the season. Plenty of players say they work out and do whatever. But this dude was committed. What he did on the field wasn't an accident."

He was never a great blocker. But he cared, and that was all Shanahan needed for his zone-blocking scheme to gain steam. As Davis enjoyed one of the best three-year stretches for any running back in NFL history from '96 to '98, Sharpe didn't gripe for more targets. Instead, the starting tight end unquestionably had something to do with this all because, Davis notes, not many tight ends in the entire NFL could've handled this scheme. Playoffs included, Davis totaled

1,310 carries over those three seasons, and it wasn't like Denver ran in the opposite direction of Sharpe 1,310 times. Shanahan needed a semblance of unpredictability, which meant sending Davis toward the Savannah State wide receiver.

Sharpe had zero choice but to sign up for the janitorial duties of his position.

The Broncos asked Sharpe to do something, Davis adds, that his body wasn't exactly designed to do.

The trick was striking a balance, a major problem for future play-callers in possession of an athletic tight end. Only once can Davis recall the volcano erupting during a game. On "16 Power," Sharpe was the front-side tight end asked to wrestle a defensive end by himself and, one game, Denver was having so much success with the play that Shanahan kept calling it. Hanging on for dear life, Sharpe finally screamed toward the sideline. "Stop running this fucking play!" Shanahan was able to tap into his entire playbook and is adamant that Sharpe's blocking ability was a major reason why. He might not always like it, but Sharpe was capable of walling off defenders all by his lonesome.

"He had the strength," Shanahan says, "and the mindset to know how important the running game was to be successful. That's why our running game was one of the tops every year. Because of that."

Shanahan did this without sacrificing Sharpe as a receiver, too. He knew he couldn't wear him down to maximize what Sharpe did best. And when the head coach's prophecy was fulfilled, when the Denver Broncos reached the Super Bowl, he had an idea.

The second Shanahan verbalized this idea to Sharpe, it really should've spilled lava all over the floor, too.

Terrible Towels lit Three Rivers Stadium up like the sun once more. Bill Cowher paced the sideline with his lower jaw fully locked. A touchdown had drawn the Pittsburgh Steelers within three points in the AFC Championship, and now the Steelers were a third-down stop from getting the ball back. Doubt started to creep into Broncos players' minds when the offense faced a third-and-six with two minutes to go.

Backed up at their own 15-yard line, the Broncos' season was on the line.

But Shannon Sharpe then lined up in the left slot with a dream matchup. The linebacker shadowing him, Jason Gildon, walled off the in-breaking route so Elway lasered a ball to Sharpe's outside shoulder. He caught it and sped upfield for an eighteen-yard gain. The kid who once picked tobacco by day and lived under a leaky roof at night, the adult who hurled around all those weights and bought into Shanahan's vision was now heading to San Diego, California, for Super Bowl XXXII. What a golden opportunity this was to talk smack for two weeks and truly introduce *Shannon Sharpe*, in all his glory, to the world.

Not only that. The Green Bay Packers were eleven-point favorites. This moment was built for Sharpe.

Then, the tight end sat down for another meeting with Shanahan ahead of Media Day.

"I know you're going to get sick and tired of listening to how good the Packers are," Shanahan told him. "But you've got to do me a favor. You can't say anything to the media the whole week. You have to promise me that you'll take it all in. We cannot respond."

"Mike," he replied, "it's going to be hard. I'm getting tired of hearing it already."

Shanahan explained that this could be an advantage for Denver. Refuse to give the Packers any reason to be pissed—any sliver of motivation—and the Broncos would enter this game infinitely hungrier. He wanted the Packers thinking that this would be a cakewalk. Sharpe agreed to bite his tongue.

Next came the game plan. Sharpe, who had just made his sixth of eight Pro Bowls, would be a decoy. Shanahan identified the safety Butler as the chess piece who keyed Green Bay's entire defense. Not defensive end Reggie White. If Shanahan split Sharpe out wide, Butler would follow him. And that would undoubtedly open up lanes for Davis. He wanted to physically wear the Packers down with the run and to neutralize a safety who had 10 interceptions and 9.5 sacks the previous two seasons.

Fine by Sharpe. He wanted to win.

And the Packers were wholly unprepared. Eventually, Butler says they realized Denver was using Sharpe as a decoy, so they shifted a cornerback out wide to cover him. But, for the most part, a safety who remembers "murdering people" all season long was rendered a nonfactor. Never before had an offense toyed with Butler like this. White was too powerful, too strong. Teams felt no choice but to attach a tight end next to their offensive tackle to somehow slow White down. One Super Bowl prior, against New England, he feasted for three sacks.

That's why Butler calls Shanahan a genius. Denver stunned Green Bay, 31–24, on the strength of Davis's 30 carries for 157 yards. Denver's offensive line forced Green Bay's heavy front to move laterally all night and, by dusk, they were gassed.

The key to it all was the loudest player on either team swallowing his ego.

That's why Butler liked him. At his core, this tight end was unselfish.

"Most guys would say, 'I don't want to be a decoy. I want to catch a bunch of balls. Let me see if I can catch it over him—just throw it to me!'" Butler says. "But the game plan works. Sometimes, you're in a duel and you shake his hand and say, 'Hey, man, you got me.' I have a lot of respect for those guys because they said, 'We're going to do everything different.' Shanahan said, 'If you believe in me, I know how to neutralize LeRoy Butler in the Super Bowl. For one game, it's not Reggie White. It's "36." If we do that, we can run away from Reggie.'"

Despite playing in opposite conferences, Butler faced Sharpe *six times* in all, and he labels him the greatest tight end ever. "Not even close," he adds. To him, there were no weaknesses to Sharpe's game. He had a gift for identifying what coverage the Packers were in as soon as he took off on his route. On the flip side, it was extremely difficult for Butler to diagnose which route Sharpe was running because, whereas most tight ends accelerated slowly into their routes, Sharpe operated at one speed. Thus, Butler couldn't win with his brain. Or his physicality. Or even his speed because Sharpe was sneaky fast.

He braced for Elway to test him. Instead, Davis—migraine and all—had one of the best Super Bowl performances in NFL history.

This is where Davis makes an important distinction when it comes to the fast-talking tight end. Sharpe might've been born for the camera lens, but Davis insists he did not possess an enormous ego. Nobody offensively did. As Davis became the center of this solar system and won league MVP the following season, receivers didn't bang Shanahan's table demanding the ball. More than any zinger he spent hours researching, perhaps Sharpe's legacy was truly made the night he caught 5 balls for just 38 yards because this night was a direct reflection of the camaraderie he had spent a decade building.

Talent alone doesn't win forty-six games over a three-year span. These Broncos had something extra.

"There was nothing we wouldn't do for one another," Lynn says. "We were like family."

It wasn't hard for Sharpe to live anonymously under those lights, but the week leading up to the game? Brutal. "Mike," he told his coach afterward, "I can't tell you how hard it was."

There were more *Sharpisms* into 1998. After the Broncos knocked out the Miami Dolphins in the playoffs, 38–3, he called Dan Marino "a loser" and said that coach Jimmy Johnson needed to evacuate his office because the Broncos would need it to watch film in Miami for the Super Bowl. And when the Broncos returned to the Super Bowl for a date with the Atlanta Falcons, this time Sharpe was not quiet. He bragged about that wild night in Kansas City, boasting that his mouth alone got Derrick Thomas suspended, Wayne Simmons released, and forced Marty Schottenheimer to resign. "I ought to go into politics," he said. He also staged an epic war of words with cornerback Ray Buchanan.

After Buchanan said Sharpe looked like "Mr. Ed," Sharpe brought out the big guns.

"Tell Ray to put the eyeliner, the lipstick, and the high heels away. I'm not saying he's a crossdresser. That's just what I heard."

Denver waxed the Falcons, 34–19.

The following season, Sharpe broke his collarbone and his Broncos career was over. Practice in Denver might've felt like a funeral but not so much in Baltimore. It didn't take long for Sharpe to find a new rookie running back to harass on the team bus. Oh, Jamal Lewis had himself a damn nice suit. There was no way Sharpe could critique his fashion sense. But as the rook inched toward the back of the bus, Sharpe looked closer and identified one clear violation.

Lewis was carrying the garment bag issued by the team. Unacceptable.

"Jahh-Mahl!" his voice boomed. "You're going to get on here with that nice suit on and you've got that bag!? You know you could've got a better bag than that! I know you're making more money than that!"

No, it did not take long for Sharpe to re-create what he built in Denver with the Baltimore Ravens. Once again, he ripped anyone who dared waltz onto the bus or the plane lacking the necessary swagger. He had a new posse, too. To his left and right sat linebackers Ray Lewis and Adalius Thomas.

"If you didn't have thick skin, you didn't want to get on that bus," Lewis says. "Trust me. They would let you have it. It was brutal. It was torture."

Everyone would end up laughing nonstop to their destination, too.

The 2000 Ravens went 12-4, won the Super Bowl, and no chance do they even get to that 34–7 stomping of the New York Giants without Sharpe. In the wild card round, against his old mates, one pass bounced off Lewis's hands, then Denver cornerback Terrell Buckley's chest, and Sharpe corralled it. He turned the corner and out-ran the entire Broncos defense to the end zone. In the AFC Championship, Sharpe caught a slant pass from Trent Dilfer and split the safeties ninety-six yards to the house. He was arrogant, obnoxious, celebratory. Everything Ozzie Newsome was not. Yet, Sharpe was also perfect for what Newsome was building as the GM.

As different as Sharpe appeared to be from both Newsome and the snuff-chewing country boy lining up at the other tight end spot, Ben Coates, all three had strikingly similar roots.

"I loved Shannon," Newsome says. "He's a very confident person, and he had to be, coming from where he came from."

Lewis actually had known Sharpe for a few years himself. He trained with him in Atlanta. From 1998 on, he forced himself to do everything Sharpe was and—after the Ravens took Lewis fifth overall—Sharpe made sure head coach Brian Billick knew he was a hard worker. Like Sharpe, Lewis learned to train at a heavy weight in the off-season and chisel down twenty pounds or so from there. He calls Sharpe a "machine," a "monster" who was still a student of the game. Sharpe talked trash because he knew he could back it. Not only because he treated himself like a bodybuilder. The same agitator who knew the opponent lined up across the line of scrimmage owned a reptile store was uncovering that same opponent's specific weaknesses. The same young pro walking out of a special-teams meeting now sat in the front row of his Ravens meetings, notepad in hand.

"He was always one step ahead of his opponent," Lewis says.

If Lewis ran toward Ben Coates's side of the Ravens' line that 2000 season, he knew he could put a hand on his back and ram through the hole with him. This was not the case on the other side, but Sharpe gave it to Lewis straight. "Three seconds," he'd say. He vowed to hook and hold and shove the defensive end for three seconds. It was up to Lewis from there.

As for his roasting, he never lost his fastball. If anything, it gained speed with age. The last time Sharpe bumped into Lewis, as retirees, the first thing he did was scan his body head to toe and lambast him. Like old times. Reenacting the encounter, Lewis puckers his lips and sticks his chest out. "Man!" Sharpe barked. "You need to lose some weight!" It should be noted that former teammates all have excellent Sharpe impersonations, and they all love that Sharpe now has a national platform to share his endless opinions. They only wish it wasn't on FCC-controlled cable. That way, the Shannon Sharpe they knew could really let loose.

Glorifying Sharpe's mouth alone, however, fails to see the forest from the trees. All these one-liners served a purpose. After two seasons in Baltimore, Sharpe returned to Denver for two more seasons and retired as the position's all-time leader in yards (10,060) and receptions (815). Numbers do not adequately capture the significance of his career, either.

When Sharpe was on a roster, that roster forged unbreakable bonds. Every day was a joy.

As soon as he finished his own playing career, Anthony Lynn became a special teams assistant for the Broncos and has coached for nine different teams over two decades. Sharpe's name tends to come up often. Lynn loves pointing out to his staff how Sharpe's career began. If Dan Reeves didn't have the vision to move a seventh-round wide receiver to tight end, he knows Sharpe would've slummed around on the practice squad for a couple of seasons, possibly made the roster for one season, and then he'd be out. Finished. A never-was. The tight end position as we know it only exists because a handful of coaches thought outside the box. Luke Johnsos, Sam Rutigliano, Don Coryell, and Bill Parcells all helped make an ordinary position extraordinary.

In this case, a slow receiver turned out to be a strong, fast tight end. As a coach, Lynn remembers to always "put a player in a position of advantage."

With players, the lessons run deeper. Whenever coaches give players breaks today, most immediately bury their faces in their iPhones. A sickening panoramic view. Lynn mocks them on the spot to point out the absurdity of fiddling around on Instagram when teammates are seated directly next to you. When his Broncos had these breaks, they played cards and dominoes and Sharpe emceed it all. When they went home, they actually hung out at each other's homes to build memories that last to this day.

They weren't trying to broadcast a fake life for millions of strangers. Or go brain-dead playing video games. Real friendships were built over time, and that is how a team can pull off a Super Bowl upset.

"The fact that Terrell Davis was going to be the star in that game?" Lynn says. "That didn't matter to Shannon. That was like his brother, and we wanted to win a Super Bowl. I keep telling these young men that doesn't just happen. It's got to be intentional. The only way you do that is you've got to be with each other and around each other. You learn to love and trust one another. Because if you're not, you can talk all you want, you're not going to trust people that you're not spending any time with. You can't! Because you don't know them, really."

The way Sharpe is wired, Lynn isn't sure how he would've survived as a player in today's game. It would've driven him nuts. Either those phones would've been smashed or, his best guess, Sharpe would've shut down and been the quietest guy on the team.

"He would've been in his little shell," he says, "and never said anything because he didn't fit in."

There is, however, good news. This element of the sport can be saved.

Era to era, future tight ends find ways to preserve fun.

Chapter 7

COUNTRY STRONG

Ben Coates is pissed. He still can't believe this. From a couch inside the living room of his North Carolina home, Coates stuffs a wad of tobacco into his lower lip and shakes his head.

For a decade, Coates went toe-to-toe with some of the most physically imposing humans on the planet. One known as the "Minister of Defense." Another who did "bad, bad things." Another who snapped a man's leg in half. He refused to back down from Reggie White, Bruce Smith, and Lawrence Taylor and missed all of two games in ten seasons. Nobody could break him. Then, as the birds chirped and his wind chimes sang out on his front lawn recently—all alone—Coates felt his knee give out.

He tore the medial collateral ligament.

"Walking out here in the fucking grass."

Disgusted, he spits into his bottle.

Of course, it takes approximately 3.7 seconds for Coates to connect the dots. That torn MCL was no accident. The reason he's in such agonizing pain today is everything he put his six-foot-five, 250-pound body through. He never once thought how the sport could affect him one day.

"I did it for so long that now," Coates says, "it's coming back to say, 'Remember this? When you got away with this? And you got away with that? Nah, I'm going to come back and get you.' You think you're in the clear, but no, no, no, you're not in the clear."

For ten seasons, Coates was determined to never come off the field. A proud man whose NFL rise defied the odds, he refused to let anybody take his spot. Whenever any body part hurt, he didn't think twice. Here, treating his body like a science exhibit, Coates explains why he is in a world of hurt.

Start with the elbows. He has bursitis in both and they do not look normal. ("See how pointed they are?")

His fingers were mangled through the '90s because, he says, "when you have a quarterback throw that son of a bitch a hundred miles an hour, each finger goes wherever it wants to go." He dislocated a thumb once, wrapped it in a cast, and didn't miss a game.

AstroTurf was a nightmare. Something like playing on a slab of concrete. Whenever Coates crashed to the ground, his skin would tear open. Those red sheaths covering his arms and legs would then crack open and bleed all game. The fraternity brand on his arm once ripped open at the Meadowlands and Coates needed to stitch it back up.

His earlobe was nearly ripped clean off. One collision spun his helmet sideways and a little metal piece inside caught his ear. Coates was so immune to pain by then that he didn't even know anything was wrong until a teammate informed him his ear was bleeding profusely.

The worst injury of all was the high right ankle sprain. He shredded this in the 1998 season opener. Coates had it taped up, returned, then injured his other ankle. This was the reason he missed one game. The other wasn't even related to injury—his mother died. Otherwise, Coates refused to miss time and, hell no, he wasn't going to line up for the weekly cortisone injection. He saw the team doctor wiggle, then re-wiggle, then re-re-wiggle that needle around in teammates—blood squirting everywhere—and decided, right then, *Thanks but no thanks.* So what if this bad of a high ankle sprain typically takes four to six months to heal? He'd fight through the pain.

His entire career, Coates was in survival mode.

"Tap it and it fucking started hurting! When you're playing at that level, you know the guy behind you is trying to get your job because in the NFL it's always 'next man up.' Always 'next man up.' My motto was—when I got the starting position—'I don't care who you draft, they're not going to beat me out.' And they drafted guys over and over and over. But that never would happen. It just never would happen."

Mentally, Coates is forever the son of a World War II veteran who started his own roofing company and put his four sons to work. Coates spent his entire childhood installing roofs, became the highest player ever drafted out of tiny Livingstone (NC) College and helped transform the New England Patriots from joke to juggernaut. Thinking back, Coates knows he could've saved his body by half-assing his blocking assignments or griping to coaches that he was purely a receiver. He could've made a few more business decisions by stepping out of bounds.

Any thoughts concerning his health, however, never entered his brain because that'd be akin to whining to dad for a day off.

There was always a new tight end in Foxborough, so Coates pressed on and made sure this position was fueled by grit. So much grit. We *see* everybody else. Shannon Sharpe screams on television with Skip Bayless. Tony Gonzalez is a broadcaster and an actor, and doesn't appear to possess one scar or scab anywhere. Greg Olsen is a rising star in broadcasting. Then, there's Coates. By comparison, he's a hermit. He's not in the public eye. The only sign that this is the home of an NFL player is a Patriots mini helmet near the front door. That's it. His wife wants to decorate the place with paraphernalia from Coates's Patriots and Ravens days but, eh, Coates sees no need to live in the past. He's fine leaving everything in a room upstairs, which might as well be Massachusetts since his body hurts too much to even get up there.

Don't let these tree-trunk-sized hamstrings and veins snaking all over his calves fool you.

"I may look good on the outside," Coates says, "but you don't know what the hell's going on inside."

He's gotten his knees and ankles scoped, in addition to a hip replacement two years ago. OK, he doesn't even drive anymore. Fine, he can't be in a car for too long, period, because his knees and hips ache. Coates stuffs two pillows behind his lower back and makes one other thing very clear: He would not change a thing.

"If I had to do it all over again, I would do the same, same thing. I wouldn't change it. Competitive. Teammate. The drive. The camaraderie. I'd do it all over again."

And in case anyone didn't hear him the first two times.

"I'd do it all over again."

As a kid, his reward for a hard day's work was a crinkly $10 bill. Everything that went into that $10 payout would blow the minds of kids today, too.

True, Coates grew up in Greenville, South Carolina. More specifically, he grew up atop the roofs of other families' homes. Initially, he was a gopher. Dad didn't want any of his boys tumbling to the ground halfway up the ladder so, as early as seven years old, Ben started carrying shingles over to his older two brothers and then they nailed the roof in with Dad. He'd pick up trash. He'd sift his hand through the blades of grass below for any nails that fell. He hated it, but he never complained.

Once his two older brothers headed to the military, up the roof he went. They didn't own a fancy electric nail gun, either. Coates would physically swing a hammer again, and again, and again, all day long. They'd try to get to work early in the a.m. to beat the heat, but there was no avoiding those ninety-degree workdays. For "fun," Coates would jump off the roof if he deemed it low enough. Then he'd hurl more shingles over his shoulder, climb on up, hammer away, leap and repeat. At summer's end, the work didn't end. During the school year, Coates was still required to chip in every chance he could. And when he headed to college? Even if he had a minimum wage job somewhere else back home that started at 4 p.m. to help pay for his tuition, you bet Coates was still required to do everything he could on a roof before 4 p.m.

House to house. In numbing succession. Age seven to twenty.

"It's just up and down the ladder. Up and down the ladder," Coates says. "It's that work ethic. That's what does it. Nobody else is going to do it. You've got to do it."

Hammering in a new roof wasn't even the hardest part, no, that'd be ripping out an *old* roof. Considering the Coates crew mostly tackled older homes, they were tearing off roofs all the time. Many homes already had one or two and—since a third roof would cave the house in, Coates explains—they'd need to physically rip off the old felt paper.

"Then, you've got to run around and put the paper back on. Then, you have to line it. Then once you line it, you have to cork it. So it was something. The only thing I didn't like to do up there, was doing the valleys. You know how houses come down and they have a little valley where the water runs down? You have to tie the valley. I'm like, 'Nope. I want straight up and straight down. If it ain't straight up and straight down? I don't want to do no valley.'"

A "valley" is formed where two different slopes meet. Screw up this tedious task and a house could develop a leaking problem.

Next, Coates holds his hand at an angle of about twenty or so degrees. Many roofs weren't too difficult to walk on. Others, however, were "like *this*." Coates tips his hand vertically. To nail in these—so everyone didn't slip and slide and become paralyzed—Dad would find two-by-four boards and temporarily nail those into the roof, so the boys had somewhere to put their feet. ("If there's a will," Coates says, "there's a way.") He doesn't remember any WWII stories coming up those hot summer days with Dad. They worked. Only worked.

Nobody's installing roofs in this manner today. Coates scoffs at electric guns because all anyone needs to do now is gently squeeze a trigger to install a roof. "Boom, boom, boom. All the way down." Even worse, there are now trucks that mechanically lift shingles up to the roof for workers. Talk about soft. Nowadays, a family could install a roof barely breaking a sweat. The strenuous labor could be miserable as a young teen but, also, this was everyday life. You don't know what you don't know in life so, looking back, Coates realizes he wouldn't have developed into an NFL tight end without roofing.

For one, this served as a daily training session. Jumping off roofs and carrying two loads of shingles over his shoulders built up his endurance, his upper-body strength. This all installed a mental edge, too. Like Shannon Sharpe working in those Georgia tobacco fields, such labor served as the foundation for everything the Coates boys did in life.

For his older brothers, the next step was the military. Kuwait. Afghanistan. Qatar. They've been everywhere. The oldest, the one who guided and pushed him most (Gary) became a reverend and died in 2018. Gerald still works in the Middle East as a civilian. All share the same temperament as their father, too. A few days before this conversation, Afghanistan was handed back to the Taliban. Yet no amount of unrest overseas stopped his brothers from wanting to help.

"We're not afraid. If something's going to happen, it's going to happen. You can't live your life in fear."

Ben played football through junior high, didn't like it, quit, and figured he'd also enlist. Yet when his senior year arrived, Coates had a change of heart. It helped that he couldn't stop growing. He was suddenly six foot two and busting out of his brothers' hand-me-downs. Nobody in his family could understand it. Everyone else was six feet—tops. Coates was just naïve enough to think he could pick football back up and that the sport could get him into a college somewhere. He didn't want to go to the military, nor stick around Greenville. Nothing against his hometown. Ben needed to explore.

Granted, 1986 was a turbulent year in his life. His father suffered from sleep apnea but, since this was before CPAP machines were popularized, he wasn't able to properly treat it and passed away. Coates's reaction was typical. He responded exactly as Dad would want—by only becoming more dogged. "We all have to go somewhere at some point," Coates says. "We can't all stay." That summer, Coates ran routes every day with an older brother. His confidence soared.

"After that, I had that drive that nothing was going to stop me."

It was too late for any power schools to discover and appreciate

Coates, but a few HBCUs were interested, and he whittled his choice down to Savannah State, Livingstone College, and Johnson C. Smith. On his recruiting trip to Savannah State, Sharpe was actually his host. ("Shannon was a receiver at that time. He *still* is a wide receiver. He's not really a tight end.") Coates had a very simple reason for not following Sharpe's footsteps to Savannah, too. When he stepped onto campus, the stench was unbearable. "Ew! What is that!?" he asked. Current players told him it was the paper mill nearby and that he'd get used to it. Coates assured them he most certainly would not and crossed Savannah State off his list. He planned to attend Johnson C. Smith on a full scholarship but, upon arriving, discovered it was only a partial scholarship. Livingstone it was. His mother and sister dropped him off at the Division II school, set his belongings on the sidewalk, and were gone.

Honestly, Coates could've been playing for a rec team on Mars. He sincerely did not care where anybody else on the football field came from.

"What's a five star? What's a one star? That's what I ask everybody now. Somebody has to classify what those mean. There's no difference once you step on the football field. A football player's a football player. Either you're going to play to your ability or you're going to play down to your competition. That's my total belief. I was looking for a shot."

Remarkably, Coates continued to grow. All the way to six foot five. Offensive coordinator Joseph "Jo Jo" White taught him a few releases off the line of scrimmage and Coates realized nobody could cover him. All defenses played man to man with most sticking their best cornerback on him. They were no match. Coates could obviously outmuscle the puny defenders, but he was also leaving them in the dust. Nobody had his stamina. Into the fourth quarter, he didn't tire. Larger schools started showing interest and Coates knew that heading to North Carolina State or South Carolina could swing an NFL door wide open, but transferring then still cost students money out of pocket. Money his family didn't have. He stayed at Livingstone, had 103 receptions for

1,268 yards and 18 touchdowns in three years, and declared for the NFL with a year of eligibility remaining.

Only four players from his school had ever been drafted, and none since 1978, but several HBCU players had gone on to star in the NFL. Coates could be ignored no more. He earned a trip to the 1991 NFL Combine and again didn't give a damn where anybody else came from.

One star. Five stars. Livingstone. Alabama.

"I was better than all of them tight ends," Coates says. "I didn't care what school you went to. I was better than every last one of them at the Combine. In my mind and spirit, I said, 'Ben, you're the best one here.' Somebody's going to take a chance on you. When they take that chance, they'll say, 'Wow. Tiny Livingstone College. Where's that?'"

That was precisely what was running through the mind of one, Dante Scarnecchia, that spring. He was the tight ends coach for the New England Patriots then, and the team's director of personnel, Joe Mendes, had him watch VHS tapes of this prospect from the CIAA. Scarnecchia loved what he saw. Coates was an "aggressive" and "tough" tight end, of course, but he also remembers seeing Coates dabble at safety and punter. Coates's 40 time at the Combine wasn't great—in the 4.9s—but the Patriots wanted to see this mystery man up close themselves. Granted, it was bad timing. Scarnecchia was in the middle of moving back to the northeast after two seasons with the Indianapolis Colts. The same day Mendes wanted him down south to work out Coates was the day his wife was flying in to house-hunt. Bracing for impact, he "pleaded insanity" with his wife and promised he'd be gone all of one day.

Scarnecchia flew down to Salisbury, went right to the football office to talk to the coaches and...nobody was home. Odd, he thought. He found Coates, headed outside to the football field and was greeted by an even stranger sight: There were no lines marked. Nothing. There was no way to tell how long forty yards was on the team's own football field. Scarnecchia headed back inside and found an equipment manager to help him rummage through storage for a yardstick. Then the coach measured out forty yards himself on the dirt track.

"I just kept flipping it and flipping it and flipping it to forty yards," Scarnecchia says. "I've gotta get a 40 time on this guy."

Coates ran three 40s, and each one clocked in the 4.7s. Scarnecchia then cycled him through blocking and receiving drills for an hour. All along, this hulking tight end refused to get tired. At all. Anything Scarnecchia asked him to do was met with a "yes sir" sense of duty. On the chalkboard, Coates understood everything, too. When Scarnecchia returned north, he told Mendes that the Patriots should draft Coates. Not too early—New England did have a perfectly fine tight end in Marv Cook—but certainly not too late. Scarnecchia envisioned Coates as someone who could do damage at all three levels of the passing game.

The Patriots drafted Coates in the nick of time with the 124th overall selection in the fifth round. A coach for the Dallas Cowboys later informed Scarnecchia that they would've pounced in the sixth.

His talent was obvious. Instantly. After the first seven-on-seven drill, Cook went right up to Scarnecchia and sarcastically said, "Thanks a lot." Where Coates had an edge over most all starting tight ends in the league, though, was in the run game. Scarnecchia was the right coach at the right time. Nobody had truly taught him how to block before and, now, he was getting the 101 training from a man who'd eventually go down as arguably the greatest offensive line coach ever. He loved Scarnecchia's abrasive style, too, how the coach would bark, "You've got to be shitting me! Go back and do it again, Coates!" Such is the order and discipline he craved.

Coates even liked Cook, too. He seemed like a nice enough guy who made the Pro Bowl in 1991 and 1992. Coates might've been one of the quietest players on the entire team, but in his mind? Cook was no different from anyone else in his path.

"It didn't matter," he says. "Once I got into my position, I don't give a fuck who you draft. He wasn't going to beat me out."

Losing was miserable enough. These wretched Patriots went 1-15 in 1990 and then 2-14 in 1992. Cheap ownership, however, had a way of exasperating the misery. Long before the monstrosity that is "Patriot Place" became its own village in Foxborough, the Patriots were not run like a normal professional sports team. There was no practice facility when Coates arrived in 1991. He'd park his car, see clouds forming overhead and... sigh.

"When it rained outside," Coates says, "it rained inside. Right inside of the locker room."

When the team finally built a bubble, it was only built large enough for a sixty-yard field. Coates remembers coaches, for some reason, cranking the air conditioner unit in the bubble before one cold-weather game, too, when it was already frigid outside. "We said, 'Fuck it, let's go play outside!'" The team was so cheap that players needed to sign for a new pair of socks. The organization was counting how many socks were being distributed to players. All that was missing above the building was an "Everything Must Go" sign. This felt like a busted-out Sears with a very real fear that the Patriots were St. Louis bound.

For most rookies, the culture shock was unfathomably disrespectful. Most were treated more professionally in college than the pros.

Coates was unfazed.

"I'm like, 'Damn, we get more than one pair of shoes? Let me get some more!'"

The conditions around Coates were irrelevant because he doesn't make excuses. A Pro Bowler in his tight end room, a leaky locker room, three bodies hanging on his limbs downfield, Bruce Smith staring into his soul. All were minor details. Through the '90s, Coates played the tight end position just as a country boy who spent his entire childhood building roofs would.

Soon, the right dominoes started to tip for both Coates and the

Patriots. On January 21, 1993, Bill Parcells took over as head coach. On April 25, he gambled on a gunslinger (Washington State quarterback Drew Bledsoe) over a game manager (Notre Dame's Rick Mirer) with the first overall draft pick. And on January 21, 1994, businessman Robert Kraft purchased the team for $175 million and ensured the team stayed in New England. There would be no more signing out for socks. And, immediately, Parcells took a stun gun to the team's sagging culture. His first training camp, for ten straight days, Parcells put his team through grueling *three*-a-day practices. The Hall of Fame coach later joked that a coach would get arrested for this today. When thirty-four-year-old Andre Tippett asked Parcells for a customary vet's practice off, not only did Parcells refuse. He continued to fine the star defensive end $250 for each pound he was overweight.

Surprise, surprise: Coates and Parcells were a match made in heaven.

A duo essentially drawn together by the tight end gods. Parcells first learned the importance of this position when he was the Patriots' linebackers coach in 1980. Both Mike Holovak (the director of college scouting) and Bucko Kilroy (the GM) detailed to him what constituted an effective tight end. Facing the six-foot-five, 245-pound Russ Francis and six-foot-seven Don Hasselbeck in practice helped. So did being friends with Raiders owner Al Davis, a man who valued the position. After winning two Super Bowls with Mark Bavaro as the New York Giants head coach, Parcells admits his standards were high.

And that's what helped him recognize the talent discrepancy between Cook and Coates. He wasn't going to settle.

"Ben hadn't had a lot of football experience," Parcells says. "I think some people were a little afraid of that. But once we saw him, he was big, he had really good hands, he was a willing blocker, and he learned how to block really well. He was our biggest weapon there for quite a while. The tight end position was very valuable for us at New England. Ben was a high producer."

The monster who burnt cornerbacks in college was now facing *linebackers* in the pros, a decision by coordinators that shocked Coates.

"I'm like, 'Y'all OK?' Holy shit. I'm licking my chops."

In practice, Coates started referring to himself as "7/11" to Bledsoe. He told the young quarterback to simply chuck it up to him because he had the ability to embarrass those linebackers, like the one he loved facing more than anyone: New York Jets' Mo Lewis. By 1994, it was no secret where Bledsoe was throwing the ball in every clutch situation. That season, the Patriots' rifle-armed quarterback targeted his tight end 148 times—more than Rob Gronkowski has ever seen—with Coates catching 96 of those balls for 1,174 yards and 7 touchdowns. The 96 receptions would stand as a tight end record for ten years and New England (10-6) reached the playoffs for the first time in eight years.

"Shit," Coates says, "everybody in the stands knows. Hell, the defense knows where the ball's going! And they can't stop it. After so many clutch catches from a guy, you get that security blanket where he knows he can count on you. And the coaches know: 'Get Coates the ball.'"

That was exactly what the offense became. Bledsoe threw his first touchdown ever to Coates on fourth-and-one, with Coates catching a quick out off play-action and shucking Buffalo Bills cornerback Nate Odomes away with ease fifty-four yards to the end zone. Bledsoe says he's not ashamed to tell anyone. Heck yes, Coates was his "security blanket" that point forward. After this play, he felt a magnetic pull to No. 87.

The only time Coates spoke up was when nothing else was working one game and he felt he had no choice: "Time to throw me the damn ball," he told his quarterback. Then, eureka, the Patriots started moving the ball with ease. There was also the time Parcells told Bledsoe in practice to run a red zone play called "84 Red," before pausing and deadpanning that he doesn't even know why he'd call anything in the red zone when all Bledsoe was going to do was throw it to Coates. The QB didn't hesitate. "Well, yeah," he responded. "He always catches it and we always score."

"When you have a guy like Ben, who was uncoverable, it made life very, very easy," Bledsoe says. "If it was third-and-five, I feel like everybody in the stadium knew where the ball was going."

There were growing pains. Coates still remembers Patriots linebacker Vincent Brown, "the Undertaker," drilling him into the grass one practice. He failed to read that the defense was in zone, kept running, and paid the price. But he learned. He always learned. Very quickly, it did not matter what defense Coates faced because he was too big for linebackers and too strong for safeties. Bledsoe had no qualms slinging it to him regardless of the number of bodies around him.

When defenses started to deploy Cover 2, Coates toasted the middle linebacker up the seam, split the two safeties, and Bledsoe accurately delivered it to him in stride. ("I said, 'Shit, OK. You're making it easy for me,'" Coates says.) Without question, his favorite route was the "Y Option," popularized by Dallas Cowboys tight end Jason Witten a generation later. The route seems simple. Coates would run eight to ten yards and turn either left or right. Here, on his couch, Coates sits up straight with a sudden jolt of energy to explain why this route is ruthless in that simplicity and resembles Dennis Rodman in *The Last Dance* explaining the art of rebounding.

His hands twist and twirl and re-create exactly what ran through his brain.

"A safety's going to be out here. A linebacker's going to be here. So, I just have to pick out, who's the slowest? And that comes from watching tape and who's going to react faster. If the safety's sitting out there, maybe I'll run at him like I'm running the seam but I'll hook it up. Now the 'backer can't get here in time. Now, if the safety's deeper and I run to the linebacker and peel it back out? I still know I'm going to beat him."

The most memorable game that 1994 season was a 39–35 loss in Week 1. Coates was always in shape. No boot camp Parcells put his team through in August affected Coates because, each off-season, he'd train in the Carolinas for a full month. He'd squeeze four workouts into a twenty-four-hour day: weightlifting in the a.m., a conditioning test, route running, a four-mile run for a nightcap. It also helped that Livingstone always wore their black jerseys at home which, to this day,

Coates cannot quite comprehend. During this season-opening loss at Miami, his weight dropped from 245 to 230 pounds and he still caught eight passes for 161 yards with 2 touchdowns. His navy jersey a tapestry of mud and sweat and linebacker's tears, Coates contorted his body in the corner of the end zone to fully extend for one Bledsoe lob. Then, against Cover 2, he split the safeties and stuffed one of those safeties (Gene Atkins) into the grass with a stiff arm for a sixty-two-yard score.

Once the ball was in his hands, Coates was a bludgeoning conquistador.

"My mentality as a tight end was 'I'm trying to *hit* you and I'm going to *hurt* you. Because you're trying to hurt me. Don't let me see you—I'm going to catch you before you catch me.' You do it for your team. You do it for the pride you have being a hard worker. Everyone says, 'Man, you dragged two, three guys.' That's just my mindset. One guy's not going to bring me down."

One annual slight always sharpened this edge, too. Coates felt as if the Patriots were perpetually trying to replace him. In his own draft, they doubled up at the position with Randy Bethel out of Miami in the tenth round. Coates was well aware that the CEO of the team then (Sam Jankovich) had also come straight from the same school. He was the athletics director. "Who do you think has the best odds of winning that job?!" Coates says. And even as the kid from Livingstone College made five Pro Bowls—eventually making the NFL's All Decades Team—the Patriots never stopped drafting tight ends: Turner Baur in '92 (tenth round, Stanford), Rich Griffith in '93 (fifth round, Arizona), John Burke in '94 (fourth round, Virginia Tech), both Chris Griffin (sixth round, New Mexico) and Lovett Purnell (seventh round, West Virginia) in '96, and Rod Rutledge in '98 (second round, Alabama).

Coates recites all their names. He rendered them all useless in Foxborough by making himself indispensable. Didn't even take one jab of the cortisone needle, either. "When you know what you can do and how you can do it?" he says. "There's no stopping that person." Once, in '96, he and Bledsoe prepped all week for a very specific blitz from the Dolphins. They waited. And waited. And when the Dolphins finally sent the house frontside in the fourth quarter—"Boom!" Coates says—Bledsoe audibled his tight end out of his vertical route and flipped it out to the right flat. Coates hit the brakes to let a defender comically fly out of frame and rumbled eighty-four yards for a touchdown.

To Bledsoe, this top-end speed was most staggering. Even as Coates beefed up to 260 pounds, he could sprint away from safeties.

"There was really nothing people could do with him," Bledsoe says. "And he was a true tight end. He could block in the running game. He could pass protect. When you put him out as a receiver, man, I know there were some safeties in the league that must've had nightmares about Ben. He'd come down, bounce off of them, catch the ball, and carry them for another twenty yards into the end zone. Ben would've been an amazing tight end for any quarterback any time of his career. If I could've thrown to a healthy Ben Coates my entire career, sign me up. He was an amazing, amazing player. Shannon Sharpe was the other guy around at that time catching a lot of balls, but he was just a glorified receiver."

Publicly, Coates barely said anything. Privately, he was the same guy.

Once he reached the end zone, if anything, Coates threw a half-hearted spike into the grass.

"If you're going to grow up working on a roof with your dad," Bledsoe says, "there's not a lot of time to puff your chest out and talk about how cool you are."

No wonder it's not any of the fifty touchdowns Coates took the most pride in. What he relished most was what resembled hammering nails into a roof: blocking. No house hunters instantly marvel at the roof of a new mansion, just as no fan flipped on TV to watch a tight end seal the edge on a Curtis Martin touchdown. Yet Coates knew that all homes cave in without that roof. Even if nobody cares, he blocked for four different thousand-yard rushers. Martin is in the Hall of Fame. All the one-on-one duels with the likes of "LT" and Smith and White are why he's in such wincing pain today, and he's OK with that because he was drawn to this contour of the football field.

"We're not talking about no backside block," Coates says. "We're talking man-on-man against Bruce Smith, Reggie White, you name all the ones you want to put in there. You've got to want to. Being a Pro Bowl player, an All-Pro player, you say, 'Hell, they put their best on our best. Shit. Cream is going to rise to the top.' So, you have to scratch and claw. You have to do everything. I've seen some phenomenal defensive players. There's not going to be an in-between. You win or lose."

If Kellen Winslow had Don Coryell, Coates had Scarnecchia. He learned that he could not block White the same way he blocked Smith because White was stronger and Smith was quicker. Facing another Hall of Famer every day in practice helped, too. Andre Tippett's hands would move in a million directions and he'd wonder, "What the hell did he just do?" Tippett studied martial arts for more than three decades, earning a seventh-degree black belt in Uechi-ryu karate. Against him, Coates learned that one wrong step, one wrong move, and he could get embarrassed on TV. Still, he never ran from the shameless job requirement. Nor did the Patriots have any problem leaving Coates one-on-one against elite defensive ends.

As a result, his body took a physical pounding. Coates does recall taking Toradol a couple of times but he mostly refused pain meds— rare for his era. Team doctors then handed out pills like Halloween candy. Players were injected with this, jabbed with that, and all along Coates refused to be a test dummy. He feared what the cocktail of meds would do to his insides and didn't want to get addicted. So he gritted through the pain. One game against the Browns still stings. He remembers the team's head coach, Bill Belichick, using both Carl Banks and Rob Burnett as hired hit men to, well, "literally beat the shit out of me." Belichick didn't care about any other threats. He needed to eliminate Coates from the game. Some plays, linebacker Pepper Johnson would even give Coates a third shot.

A typical workday meant blocking a three-hundred-pound end one play and running a seam route the next. All with zero hesitation. Bledsoe knows Coates was a victim of the way he played. "It took an incredible toll on his body. When you're that big, nobody's going to take you on up high. They're going to hit you in the legs and hit you in the midsection. Ben took a lot of punishment." Yet the sincere desire for a Super Bowl ring pushed Coates through it all. In '96, he got his shot and the Patriots lost to the Packers, 35–21. He still believes that if Desmond Howard wouldn't have returned a kick back ninety-nine yards for a touchdown, New England would've won. Don't let the box score fool you. White had three sacks that night but Coates implores all to rewatch the full game. All three sacks occurred in the second half because, he notes, White had to deal with him in the first half. Coates never let him touch his quarterback. With New England forced to play catch-up after Howard's cannon blast, Coates exited the trenches to run routes and White feasted.

Martin sure appreciated his burly tight end. He considered Coates a sixth offensive lineman and says, "without a doubt," Coates should be in the Hall of Fame. One reason Martin got to Canton himself is that both Coates and fullback Sam Gash showed him how to play through pain. Out of the University of Pittsburgh, the knock on him was durability. As a junior, he missed his final two games with a sprained shoulder. As a senior, he missed ten games with a sprained ankle. But in the pros? Martin was an iron man. From 1998 through 2004, he sat out one game. All while grimacing through injuries far worse than anything he had at Pitt.

Those three seasons with the Patriots, '95 through '97, gave Martin an entirely new perspective on pain.

He watched Gash suffer a broken big toe that stuck straight up toward the ceiling. When Martin asked him how in the heck he'd play with this thing, Gash cut a hole in his cleat so the toe could stick out. He saw Coates somehow grit through an ankle that was swollen so bad that he needed to walk into meetings barefoot—no shoe would fit.

When Martin then suffered two high ankle sprains of his own in 2003 with the Jets, he played on. He remembered Coates.

"I didn't even know it was possible to play with that amount of pain," Martin says. "What he and Ben did from a pain standpoint set the course for my career.

"Ben is one of those guys who I always have an admiration for. Even though he might not have noticed it, I'm the kind of guy who'll sit back and watch a person and look at different qualities that I'd like to implement or emulate, and Ben was definitely one of those guys from a toughness standpoint. When I think of Ben, I just think of this utility knife where there were so many things he could do as a tight end. On top of that, he was tough as nails."

Coates stuck a dip of chew in his lip during the week, pancaked players on Sunday, and unfortunately, his body could hold on for only so long. The Patriots released Coates after the 1999 season. He signed with the Baltimore Ravens in 2000, teamed up with Sharpe, and got that coveted Super Bowl ring. He wasn't capable of running roughshod over safeties anymore, but he didn't need to. Coates caught 9 balls on 18 targets in the Ravens' run-first, run-second, run-always offense. His job now was to pave the way for running back Jamal Lewis, who ran for 1,364 yards as a rookie.

No game seems to bring Coates more joy inside his home than Baltimore's 34–7 title smackdown of the New York Giants. That night, he told the offensive tackle to his side, "I got it," and handled future Hall of Famer Michael Strahan solo. Coates can still hear Strahan screaming to the refs that he was holding him and, OK, maybe the gap-toothed sack artist had a point. He was so crafty the officials couldn't tell. Ten years of bruises culminated with a Super Bowl triumph and, as the confetti fell, Coates flipped his hat backward to soak it all in.

"He was trying to finish on a high note and do anything it took to win," Lewis says. "When we're going to run it down the gut, he was going to get in there and be a part of that. Shannon didn't want part of that. We put Ben over there to block Strahan and he held it down. Once Ben Coates got locked in on you, it was a wrap."

Meanwhile, in New England, that coordinator who tried breaking Coates was hired as the Patriots' new head coach in 2000. The linebacker who Coates destroyed more than any other (Lewis) smashed Bledsoe along the right sideline in 2001, and football was never the same again. Bill Belichick and Tom Brady joined forces and delivered six Super Bowl titles to the franchise. Coates never was a part of those duck boat parades through downtown Boston, but he got his ring and retired as the NFL's fourth all-time leading receiver at tight end with 499 receptions for 5,555 yards in 158 games. Only Winslow, Newsome, and Sharpe had more yards.

Over the following two decades, he gradually paid the price for it all.

Coates started off as an assistant coach back at Livingstone College. In 2004, Parcells asked him to intern with the Cowboys to mentor his new twenty-two-year-old tight end, Jason Witten. Coates taught the second-year pro the intricacies of the "Y Option." Running that route with numbing efficiency, Witten finished as the Cowboys' all-time leader in receptions (1,215) and receiving yards (12,977). In 2005 and 2006, Coates coached tight ends for the Cleveland Browns, where both Kellen Winslow Jr. and Steve Heiden had career years. Coates then spent three seasons at Central State University in Wilberforce, Ohio, as the offensive coordinator. The pain in his back, hips, and knees started to set in. He headed closer to home—to St. Augustine College in Raleigh in 2014—and that pain then became unbearable. All the standing was too much. He left coaching.

"I'm like 'Ho-Lee-Shit. This is what it feels like in your forties?' "

As a player, he prided himself on being in control of the violence. Now, all the pain was coming back. In 2019, "all kinds of shit started breaking down." He had the titanium hips put in. He tore his MCL. Yes, he'd do it all over again. Playing tight end was one hell of a ride he wouldn't trade for anything. Coates was always the hitter, never the hittee, which explains why he finds himself pulling up video clips of Mike Tyson these days. He gets a kick out of opponents thinking they had a plan for the heavyweight champ. One thought he could finesse Tyson in the middle of the ring with a sequence of jabs. The bell rang, Tyson walked right up to this sucker and...

"Bam!" says Coates, smacking his hand. "Every guy! I'm like, 'What the hell? What happened to the game plan?'"

His own body still aches, sure, but Ben Coates can live in peace knowing he attacked pro football with the same savagery.

"I'm going to give it to you. I'm going to bring all the pain to you."

He probably should be in Canton. Coates has more yards and touchdowns than both Ditka and Mackey. Like them, he was a willing blocker. He takes a few jabs at other tight ends, saying they cared more about their personal stats. Yet the snub does not bother him because he did not play for a gold jacket.

If he gets the call, great. If not, he vows to never blather on and on about his stats "like some of these prima donna receivers." The fact that he is so resistant to the spotlight is probably a reason he's not in. Fading to the background has faded his legacy.

The quarterback who threw to him all those years calls Coates an all-time great.

"The guys who played against him and guys who played with him do recognize him as that," Bledsoe says. "He wasn't loud. He wasn't going to draw attention to himself. He showed up and went to work. As gifted as he was, he was a lunch pail guy. Because he didn't make more noise about it, maybe that didn't give him the attention he certainly deserved. If you're being honest about it, what you really want is the respect of your teammates and the respect of your opponents. And, man, when you talk about Ben Coates, I'm not sure anybody had more respect from their teammates and opponents than Ben Coates did."

Do not expect a public campaign to get into Canton. Nor will Coates try crossing over into the media in a cloaked attempt to stay on the minds of voters as many have. He knows he's not alone. Coates believes Jacksonville Jaguars running back Fred Taylor absolutely should be in the Hall over Terrell Davis—"Are they going by stats or who's on NFL Network?" Then, there's Drew Pearson. When Pearson didn't make the

Hall in 2020, a video of the Cowboys wide receiver crying went viral. He got in the next year and gave himself a tattoo that reads, "DP 88 HOF 2021 Canton, Ohio." Coates laughs, disgusted. "Are you kidding me? Drew Pearson, hell, I have more catches than he does and I'm a tight end."

And his plea stops there. After all, Dad wouldn't want his son asking for a morsel of notoriety or sympathy. The reason Coates played was the genuine camaraderie built with teammates. He will not be shedding any public tears for sympathy—Coates assures that's the absolute last thing he'd do.

He then lifts himself up, walks to the front door in a slight limp, and heads outside. Those chimes ding in the wind and he gives that front lawn another look.

Yeah, that torn MCL makes all the sense in the world.

The Y Option

The route was not new when Jason Witten started moving the chains with numbing consistency. Ben Coates, Shannon Sharpe, and others rendered defenders helpless running the "Y Option" through the 1990s, but Jason Witten? The sixty-ninth overall pick in 2003 made a living off this route for seventeen seasons.

Of course, something that seems elementary—running eight yards and turning left or right—is anything but. Jason Witten caught 1,228 passes through his career and has estimated that close to half of those receptions came on the "Y Option," a route he mastered like no one in history. Under Bill Parcells, in Witten's first three seasons, the play was called "62 Winston," and hooked at twelve yards. Depending on the defender's leverage, the tight end has the "option" to cut inside or outside at the top of the route. With Jason Garrett calling plays, in a numbers-based system, it became "595 Y Option."

The best way to understand this route is through Witten's favorite "Y Option" catch of his career. In the 2014 wild card round against the Detroit Lions, the Cowboys faced a fourth-and-six from the Lions' 42-yard line. With six minutes left, down three, Garrett called for the "Y Option," and this was the worst possible coverage anyone on offense could've wanted: Cover 2 with man-to-man defense underneath. This meant that all defenders underneath the two safeties could play aggressively. Lions safety James Ihedigbo, the man set to blanket Witten, was ready. He covered the tight end beautifully by trailing his inside hip. While such positioning should trigger an out cut, Witten knew Ihedigbo was anticipating exactly that. He could sense the safety starting to break on that out cut. As if Ihedigbo was laying a trap. So, at the last possible millisecond, Witten instead cut *inside.* He did not discuss this Plan B with quarterback Tony Romo before the snap, yet their reps upon reps of work on the route gave him the same sixth-sense feel.

Romo hit Witten for a twenty-one-yard gain, and soon after, wide receiver Terrance Williams caught the game-winning touchdown.

The route is based on exactly that—a *feel*—that is developed over years. Similar to John Stockton and Karl Malone working a pick-and-roll in basketball, it has far more subtlety than what meets the naked eye.

Parcells traces the roots of the option route back to third-down running backs of the '80s. He cites Tony Nathan, Bruce Harper, Tony Galbreath, and Dave Meggett as a handful who first ran this route best. You wanted to release a smaller, "nifty" third-down back upfield because that was the skill player capable of dusting a lead-footed linebacker. As agility and quickness spread to the tight end position, it only made sense for offenses to release this player on an option route. An extremely larger body—Witten was six foot six, 260 pounds—could also box out that linebacker. Witten had sneaky athleticism in tight quarters, which Parcells notes was a product of Tennessee using him all over its offense at the college level: split wide, in tight and in the slot. He ran every route, too.

Then, Parcells asked his trusty tight end in New England, Ben Coates, to teach Witten the intricacies of the "Y Option."

"When he came to the pros, there were things you could do with him," Parcells says. "You could remove him from the main body and put him out wide, and he could be effective out there. Not too many tight ends could do that. His ability, his versatility, was really what made him such a prolific receiver."

Witten stayed on the field, too. In seventeen seasons, he missed one game.

Football would continue to evolve into a schematic chess match, but tight ends remained proof that the sport—at its best, at its purest—is nothing more than *you vs. me.*

Chapter 8

THE TWELVE-ROUND FIGHT

An imaginary man drove Mark Bruener. From high school to college to the pros, he knew there was someone else on a planet occupied by 6 billion people working harder than him. Inside the weight room, he felt an intrinsic need to slide an extra plate on the barbell, churn out just one more rep, anything that'd push himself to the point of total exhaustion.

In other words, Bruener was precisely the old-school workhorse that the old-school head coach running the University of Washington craved.

Don James didn't merely want tough football players. He wanted "ornery" players. And he told his cantankerous crew ahead of the 1991 season to make sure opponents *remembered* them. Back then, just about all freshmen redshirted. James, however, made two exceptions that season in running back Napoleon Kaufman and Bruener, a tight end who absorbed his words as gospel into the team's season opener. The kid from Aberdeen, Washington, who jokes that he had the same nuns in elementary school that taught his father, would ensure someone on the Stanford football team remembered him.

On a kick return, Bruener's job was to block the "R3," the third man in from the right, and the poor bastard never saw him coming. Bruener completely earholed Ron George, sending him into a somersault. When the Huskies reviewed film of the 42–7 blowout win that ensuing Monday, James said a freshman on the team made a play everyone needed to see. Bruener looked around. "Who's he going to talk about?" he said to himself. "Which freshman?" It was him. Everyone was told to watch his T-bone hit on George and the head coach made it clear, to all, that this was Husky Football.

Fifteen years later, Bruener ran into George.

"Man!" George shouted. "I remember when you knocked me out on kickoff coverage back in 1991!"

Glory at the tight end position isn't always glamorized for the public. For every herculean effort at the Orange Bowl, there are infinitely more memories like this that few beyond hitter and hittee truly appreciate. But from Mike Ditka to Mark Bruener to George Kittle, these small moments persist to serve as the bedrock of the position. To ensure pro football remains a violent game. The best tight ends will not always be gobsmacking creatures whose names and legendary moments roll off the tongue. Bruener caught twenty balls in a season once in fourteen years. He averaged 8.8 yards per reception. In personality and play style, he lived in a different galaxy than Shannon Sharpe, the tight end who supplied the knockout blow to his Steelers in the 1997 AFC Championship.

But immovable objects can last in this league, too. They just need to make sure a defensive player, or two, or three, remember them.

"When you earhole somebody like that," Bruener says, "who has no idea you're coming, it's like that perfect hit where you don't feel much of anything. But then you see the guy and he just goes flying."

That 1991 Huskies team won their next eleven games to go down as one of the best in college football history. They outscored the opposition 495 to 115 and shared the national title with the University of Miami. Three seasons later, the Pittsburgh Steelers drafted Bruener in the first round and he wound up starting on a team that reached the Super Bowl. With this 270-pounder crunching defensive ends, the Pittsburgh Steelers won five division titles and running back Jerome Bettis retired as the NFL's fifth all-time leading rusher. He ensured the ethos of the Iron City franchise endured. When you think *Steelers*, you think pain—Bruener is a reason why. His marathon career passed with marginal fanfare, and that seems to be what Bruener prefers. Sure, he caught a handful of touchdowns near the goal line. What sustained this tight end was life as an extended offensive lineman.

We're more likely to see Sharpe quit his job as a sports commentator and vanish off to a one-horse town than ever utter the following words:

"You really have to embrace the suck," Bruener says. "Your hands are always hurting. Your arms. Your joints. You're never feeling 100 percent. That's part of being one of those guys who's enjoys the toughness and the grittiness of blocking in-line. The best you ever feel is the day you report to training camp. And from then on, your body gradually goes down, down, down, and it takes a month or so after the season until you're back to where you were."

Rookies were not referred to by name in the Steelers' locker room in 1995. Nor did they have funky nicknames. Bruener was "rook." So, when veteran tight end Jonathan Hayes met Bruener, his message was simple: "Rook," he said, "I just want you to know I'm going to be working out every morning here in the weight room before meetings. I invite you to be a part of it." Hayes, a drudge who did the dirty work with Hayden Fry's Iowa Hawkeyes, was in his eleventh season. Once more, Bruener took words from a superior to heart. Every morning, around 6:30 a.m., he lifted weights with Hayes. He was never late and never missed one day because he refused to let Hayes down.

Eventually, it was time to practice where you mostly hoped to survive to see the next day.

While Bruener came of age in college, so did "Blitzburgh," a position group that clearly had time-traveled from the '60s to the '90s. In 1992, the outhouse-built Levon Kirkland complained about his wrist hurting. Greg Lloyd heard him, asked to take a look and...*wham!* A man who'd earn his first of several black belts in Tae Kwon Do the next year karate-chopped Kirkland's wrist as hard as he possibly could. It felt like Lloyd chopped his hand clean off. When the scan showed that Kirkland shattered the scaphoid bone, hell no, Lloyd did not apologize.

Never did, either. The next season, Lloyd couldn't put up with Chad Brown half-assing a drill so, when they squared off, Lloyd drilled Brown so hard that his helmet flew off and his chinstrap detached. Lloyd hovered over his body and sneered, "We come to practice every fucking day around here!"

This was the butcher occupying one side of the Steelers' 3-4 defense. The other was Kevin Greene. When this Hulk Hogan lookalike wasn't racking up 160 sacks on a football field, he was flying horizontal into a pro wrestling ring, ripping his shirt off and throwing his body into seven-foot, four-hundred-pound Paul Wight, otherwise known as "The Giant" and "The Big Show." After passing their initiation, Kirkland and Brown became a pair of mean SOBs in their own right, too.

All the twenty-three-year-old rook Mark Bruener needed to do was stand in the way of these hellions. Every day. Whoever faced Lloyd *remembered* Lloyd, that was for certain, and Bruener was driven to bring the same effect to the field. Midway through that 1995 season, he supplanted Hayes as the starter and lived for what he calls the "twelve-round" slugfest in the trenches. Whereas Sharpe affected a game with three or four dynamic plays down the field, Bruener savored a fifty-play brawl with one specific foe on a Sunday afternoon. CBS cameras didn't zoom in on these body blows, nor did anyone at home particularly give a shit. But Bruener? He lived for these battles.

One archenemy emerged, too. For eight of his nine years in Pittsburgh, Bruener sparred with the same player Belichick commissioned to wear down Ben Coates at the line: Browns/Ravens defensive end Rob Burnett. It got to a point where, even if blocking Burnett wasn't his assignment, Bruener found a way "to get inside of that man's grill."

In their first matchup, Bruener caught a short touchdown, held the ball high with his left hand, and spiked it with authority right in front of the Dawg Pound. Two years later, in Baltimore, Burnett was fed up. He believed Bruener had repeatedly held him in their duels and, finally, he snapped. With both players' arms locked out on each other, Burnett's hands slipped up, knocked the tight end's helmet clean off and he threw a punch to his face. On his way to the sideline, Bruener felt a stinging sensation. "What the hell happened to you?" a teammate asked. His face was sliced and diced like a boxer. Of course, Bruener missed only one play and caught the go-ahead touchdown in the fourth quarter.

On the sideline, TD ball in hand, Bruener shared a warm embrace with tight ends coach Mike Mularkey. Pittsburgh won, 42–34, and Burnett was fined $5,000 for fighting.

"After the game I literally look like I was in a twelve-round fight against Rob because my face was all beat up. I had a swollen eye and everything. And, again, I want to be very clear: Rob was not a dirty player. It was just part of that play. My helmet came off and hands were flying. We were in the middle of everything and, holy cow, that's just how things go.

"A knock-down, drag-out fight."

There were no hard feelings. For Bruener, a stream of blood trickling down the face was inevitable. The essence of the sport itself. Child's play compared to tearing a tendon in his shoulder against the Browns in 2001 (he finished with one functioning arm) or the time he tore the plantar fascia on the bottom of his foot. This was painful, but he wasn't exactly a 4.5 speedster taking the top of the defense, so Bruener numbed it up with a needle and played on. Shots would wear off—and the injury would hurt all week—but the anticipation of a one-on-one matchup was all the medicine he'd need. Be it Burnett or Baltimore's Michael McCrary, Buffalo's Bryce Paup or Jacksonville's Tony Brackens, every matchup was personal. He'd study his combatant's every move. Once the game began, his adrenaline spiked every time the possession flipped and Pittsburgh's offense took the field. Another round awaited.

"You wanted to be the victor at the end of that fight," he says.

Burnett was not alone in his frustration. Bruener's blocking style tended to piss off everyone.

In Pittsburgh, the edge linebackers started calling him the "lobster" because once Bruener got his claws attached, there was no escape. "The lobster got you!" their coach would scold. After signing with the Seattle Seahawks, Brown started facing Bruener as an opponent and declares Bruener's holding both "unabashed" and "shameless." When he'd bitch in his ear, Bruener simply pointed to the turf to note that the officials didn't throw a flag. In a Seahawks win over Pittsburgh Week 3 of the 1999 season, Brown was pushed to his wit's end and kicked the tight end. They've always been friends, but that was how bad Bruener was pushing his buttons.

"It forced me to cross the line," Brown says. "I had to kick the dude."

Brown, like Burnett, was not penalized. He later found a picture of the actual kick and sent it to Bruener for laughs. Because, if he's being honest, Brown was impressed. Bruener had a way of getting those lobster claws on you without making it blatant. The only way to actually get the ref to call holding was to throw your hands up or take a dive. You needed to sacrifice your body in a way that exposed the hold for an official to see for himself. Exhausting as it was to chase Tony Gonzalez and Antonio Gates in the AFC West, facing Bruener was like suddenly getting thrown into a cage fight... if the cage was the size of a coffin.

"A point-of-attack tight end who could beat you at the line of scrimmage," Brown says. "Not many tight ends have that same mentality. In the run game, you knew you were going to have your hands full *all... game...long*. He never stopped. He never let up."

It's bizarre to hear stories of Mark Bruener being such a pain in the '90s when today, as a college scout for the Steelers, at half the size, he comes across as the most mild-mannered gentleman imaginable. There's a total absence of brashness in his voice. Bruener cushions nearly every comment with pleasantries. At the Senior Bowl one year, Chad Brown bumped into his old foe and had a nice chat with a third ex-player who's now in personnel. When Bruener walked away, the other player called him the nicest person he had ever met. Brown agreed before adding, "but he's such an asshole on the field. I hated that guy."

Forget tight ends balancing virtual tightropes in the end zone. Bruener admired different players growing up. Ends like Mike Tice, Ferrell Edmunds, Ron Middleton, Alfredo Roberts, who knew that Priority No. 1 was to block. So, no, he didn't get jealous at the sight of hybrids taking over the position as his career progressed. Bruener's source of fulfillment came in seeing Bettis eclipse one hundred yards in the box score. While other tight ends perfected seam routes and "Y Options," Bruener's favorite play was "38 Boss," an outside run that required him to block the defensive end. If he could seal off a Burnett or a Brackens, then he knew Bettis would gain the corner. What Bruener loved about this play most was that the defense often knew it was coming and still could not stop it.

When Bruener stared the defensive end down, that same end might even call the play out.

"Here it comes again," Bruener would fire back.

The net result in Pittsburgh was every single player feeling a responsibility to dominate their man in the run game. This attitude was essentially implanted into their brains by Mularkey, the tight ends coach and offensive coordinator in Pittsburgh from 1996 to 2003.

Mularkey calls this the toughest position to both play and coach because, frankly, the human body is not always built for what the position demands. You're asked to do what both 320- and 210-pounders do, he begins. That's how he grew up, anyway, as a retro in-line blocker of a tight end himself from 1983 to 1991 with the Vikings and Steelers. As others revolutionized the position, Mularkey's route tree was more of a stump in averaging 10.7 receiving yards per game. To him, the position demanded an element of self-sacrifice for the greater good.

Take the man across from you. Whereas a defensive lineman's mental strain was mild—*Am I attacking the "A" gap or "B" gap?*—a tight end could have "a hundred assignments," he says. Such a light mental workload meant defensive linemen could perfect the act of getting their hands from the ground to a man's chest in a split second. It took a while but, by Year 7, Mularkey realized he should practice the same thing as a tight end from Steelers left tackle Jon Kolb. When Mularkey became a coach, this became a focal point. Before anything else, he put his tight ends through a "quick hands drill."

The position wasn't too complicated to him: Whoever could jolt their hands into the other man's chest when the ball's snapped wins. A craft Mark Bruener mastered.

"If he got his hands on you, you were done," Mularkey says. "I don't care who you were, how big you were, how strong you were, and what position you were. You were done."

He'd finish the play, too.

Whenever the whistle was blown, Mularkey instructed his players to give their man "one violent shove." He wanted them all to get inside the heads of defenders. He knew that if Bruener pushed the envelope, if Bruener played through the echo of the whistle, the defender across the line would quit worrying about which gap he had to plug or which zone he needed to drop into. Because his head was on a swivel. This wasn't something Mularkey merely talked about—the Steelers practiced the "one extra shove" on sleds and humans alike. Understandably, those gnarly linebackers couldn't stand it. "Quit doing that bullshit!" Mularkey remembers them yelling. Barely anyone at home noticed how this was what ruptured an opposing defense for a huge gain, but Mularkey sure did. Bruener's game film was both painful and hilarious because the end across from him—in this twelve-round brawl—was clearly more concerned about getting blasted by the tight end than anything else. The running back would run right by him.

"They couldn't care less where the ball carrier is," Mularkey says. "They were more worried about Bruener finishing them off."

Mularkey ascribed to a philosophy core to the sport's foundation, that *violence* wins over *finesse*. "Every time," he punctuates. "I believed it forever." As a player, under Chuck Noll, his Steelers teams were always in full pads, and he coached with the same attitude. Bruener can still hear his voice. Mularkey was a stickler for technique, because if you're a hair late? A hair off? That defensive end is promptly embarrassing you. A true tight end, to Mularkey, did everything. Not like all these whippersnappers today. He refuses to even call them tight ends. He mocks the tight ends of today as big wide receivers who refuse to block.

"There's a reason for the term, 'tight.' It's not 'split.' He is 'tight,'" he adds. "He's supposed to be down tight blocking big people."

This interpretation of the position so beloved in Pittsburgh was at odds with the tight end redefining the position a few years after Bruener and, uh, it did not go over well. More on that later. Bruener grants that this approach is an acquired taste, but it worked for him. He calls Mularkey one of the best coaches he's ever had. Yes, Mularkey demanded a lot, but he rewarded his players, too. Bruener sincerely wanted to play hard for Mularkey.

This vision for the position stuck in Pittsburgh. As other teams chased pure athleticism en masse, the Steelers continued to lean on the complete tight end. No easy task. As a college scout, Bruener doesn't see any tight ends playing the way he did and, he adds, that's not their fault. The extended lineman is going extinct because spread offenses are the rage in high school. That's the breed of tight end that heads to college. Then, that's the breed of tight end that heads to the pros. Football trickles up. That doesn't mean scouts like Bruener lower their standards, but they do need to project who could learn how to block. If they flash the ability "once or twice" in your evaluation, and they're coachable, blocking is a skill that can be taught. The Steelers rode Bruener until 2003, Heath Miller from 2005 to 2015, and then drafted Pat Freiermuth in the second round of the 2021 draft. The Steelers detected that Freiermuth possessed a desire to block and felt comfortable passing the mantle to him.

They've obviously opened up the offense since the '90s but, as a franchise, still seek a tight end with Bruener tendencies. And why not? He hopes to go down as the hardest opponent defenders ever faced.

"Never a dirty player but someone you knew was going to battle you in a twelve-round fight. And to be that guy—a dependable receiver in the pass game but also a dependable blocker in the run game who could handle a defensive end. Because most tight ends can't handle a defensive end in today's game. They're not asked to. But when you can do that, that really allows the offensive coordinator to expand their playbook in the run game."

Tight ends who can haul in an acrobatic catch but cannot block a lick hurt their offense. If they're lined up on one side of the line, it's fairly obvious the offense isn't running off-tackle that direction. Such is the give-and-take all NFL front offices faced as the evolution of this position sped up in the early 2000s.

The final five seasons of his career, with the Houston Texans, Bruener never finished above .500. He swapped a franchise with an identity decades in the making for one that didn't even exist too long ago. Good luck rummaging for any highlights. In all, Bruener caught fifteen passes as a Texan. When he brought Hayes's morning routine to this locker room, teammates were initially receptive. A handful showed up. But in 2005, as the losses mounted, the bodies started dropping. One by one, in the midst of a miserable 2-14 season, players chose instead to sleep in. It got to a point where the only player to show up was Bruener.

There was no apparent reason to work extra, but he did. Strength coach Dan Riley even said, in so many words, that this season was a lost cause. Why continue? Why care this much when nobody else did?

Mark Bruener's reasoning was simple.

"I don't know any other way."

Mike Ditka asserted himself as the first true "tight end," proving the player attached to the offensive tackle on the line of scrimmage could do damage down the field as a receiver. *Permission and credit go to Getty Images/Bettmann.*

After getting into football almost by accident, Jackie Smith's speed dizzied NFL defenses through a 16-year career. Those who knew Smith best know he was far more than the tight end who dropped a touchdown in the Super Bowl. *Permission and credit go to Getty Images/ Bettmann.*

No tight end before Ozzie Newsome could leap and contort their body at such remarkable angles. If his hands were on the football, he always caught it, too. *Permission and credit go to Getty Images/Focus On Sport.*

True, Shannon Sharpe was a playmaker. But his true impact was felt most off the field, often during the team's prepractice stretches where Sharpe built rare team camaraderie. *Permission and credit go to Getty Images via* Denver Post/*Andy Cross.*

Nothing could keep Ben Coates off the field as the do-it-all tight end for the New England Patriots. He sprinted past safeties, blocked the best defensive ends ever, and today is feeling the effects of it all. *Permission and credit go to Getty Images/Brian Bahr.*

Tony Gonzalez, a Division I football and basketball star at the University of California, forced the league to scout a completely different type of athlete at the tight end position. His dominance ushered in a new level of athleticism. *Permission and credit go to Getty Images/David E. Klutho.*

Make Jeremy Shockey mad, and chances are you would pay. Slights fueled this tight end's game. *Permission and credit go to Getty Images/Jim Rogash.*

When Dallas Clark was a senior in high school, his mother died in his arms. Somehow, the trauma of that night set the course for an impossible rise in college. *Permission and credit go to Getty Images/Andy Lyons.*

Growing up in a group home, Jimmy Graham had to fight for his life on a daily basis. The experience created a different type of monster at the tight end position, one who was always tougher than anyone realized. *Permission and credit go to Getty Images/Wesley Hitt.*

Rob Gronkowski took the authenticity of his idol, Jeremy Shockey, to a whole new level one beer, one spike of the football, one Super Bowl triumph at a time. *Permission and credit go to Getty Images via* Boston Herald.

Born on a "Football Saturday," George Kittle grew into a combination of the tight end greats who preceded him, with a physical brand that would apply to any era. *Permission and credit go to Getty Images/Lachlan Cunningham.*

Chapter 9

EVOLUTION

He wanted to slug his own coordinator directly in the jaw.

Tony Gonzalez had enough. He was ready to take on Mike Mularkey.

The day this tight end great—perhaps the greatest ever—missed out on his one thousandth career reception, mayhem could've broken out inside the visitor's locker room. His confidence had swelled to this extreme. But long before such a breaking point in the twilight of his career with the Atlanta Falcons, before he imagined even playing a down in the NFL, Gonzalez was something much different on a football field.

That's where we start. As smooth jazz plays at Soho House in Austin, Texas, beautiful people are everywhere in perfect tans and designer clothes. This place screams *Tony Gonzalez*. There's an elegance to his gait this afternoon and no limp, no wince in his eyes, no sign— period—that this man played tight end for *seventeen* seasons. In his sleek black jacket with nary a gray hair poking out of his scalp, Gonzalez is fresh off shooting a scene for the TV series *Long Slow Exhale* with actor Josh Lucas.

From a cozy booth, flush with pillows, Gonzalez begins this conversation with one numbing truth from his childhood in Huntington Beach, California. The transformative threat who finished with more receptions (1,325) and receiving yards (15,127) than any tight end in NFL history—and, yes, was ready to throw hands with his own coach—wasn't always this way. He was scared of everything: the dark, ghosts, bullies. Gonzalez was, in his words, a certified "pussy."

The fact that he'd be considered one of the best ever is a miracle. To fully comprehend this miracle, he starts with the first time he tried to play Pop Warner football.

He quit. He absolutely hated to get hit. Always big, always athletic, there sadly was not a mean bone in his body. "I just didn't have it inside," he says. The gladiator nature of the sport was not enjoyable—at all—so Gonzalez constantly skipped practices before, finally, quitting for good. He never had anyone at home pushing him to play, nobody drilling into his skull the life lessons this sport would instill. Gonzalez's biological father wasn't around. His stepdad wasn't much of a sports guy.

When a fellow sixth grader hit him, Gonzalez had no clue how to respond.

"I was the biggest pussy on the team. I didn't even play. I didn't get any time at all. Like, *literally.* No time at all. And there's no dad there to complain, to say, 'Hey, why isn't my son playing?' But I didn't want to play! I remember I wouldn't play and I'd say, 'Whew. Thank God.'"

Anytime he played this sport in shorts, Gonzalez dominated. He was taller and more athletic than his peers. Yet once those pads came on? He cowered. He was a "happy-go-lucky, nice guy" by nature, with zero anger inside. Hit him and he felt zero need to hit back. Inside his garage, friends used to strap on boxing gloves and stage matchups for fun. While everyone else actually tried to knock each other out, he'd laugh, lightly tap his opponent and get decked in the jaw. Meek, weak with the utter lack of "an anger switch," Gonzalez quickly became an easy target for bullies. Eighth grade was the worst. This wasn't stereotypical *give-me-your-lunch-money* bullying—Gonzalez describes it more as "mystical bullying," as "mind bullying." Two ninth graders attending the nearby high school—Bully No. 1 and Bully No. 2 for these purposes—made a point to loiter around Gonzalez's junior high building. By the end of the school year, both were there every day. Waiting. Lurking. Staring him down. As soon as the bell rang, Gonzalez sprinted to his skateboard to zip home and placed himself under house arrest the rest of the day.

Horrified that one of the two would spot him, Gonzalez rarely ever left his home on weekends, too. Nonetheless, they'd find a way to deliver messages to him. One kid in town knocked on his door to relay the message that Bully No. 1 was at a specific location ready to fight. Another kid told him he witnessed this browbeater bust some kid's head open with a skateboard—the threat that he'd be next felt real to Gonzalez. When Bully No. 1 called him, Gonzalez finally asked why he wanted to fight so bad. The kid told him it was because he "talked shit," and the game of hide-and-seek dragged on.

Then, there was Bully No. 2. Gonzalez actually did see him beat a kid to a pulp once. When Gonzalez was throwing the football around in front of his house with his buddy, Josh Holland, and saw Bully No. 2 pull around the corner in the passenger seat of a car, he panicked. He turned to immediately sprint inside, and Holland stopped him. Holland said Gonzalez should hear what he had to say. Echoing Bully No. 1, Bully No. 2 said he wanted to fight Gonzalez because he talked shit. Gonzalez again said that wasn't true, but this ninth grader didn't care. He started to open his car door and...Gonzalez freaked.

"Noooo!" he screamed, running inside his house. Which only emboldened both his tormentors. Which only further damaged Gonzalez's reputation in school because Holland couldn't help but tell everyone.

Looking back, he's certain race was a factor. This wasn't quite the deep south in the '60s with Ozzie Newsome, but Gonzalez remembers racism running rampant through Huntington Beach in the '80s. One bully was white, one was Italian. Gonzalez could *feel* a palpable hatred. He describes the area, at this time, as predominantly white and littered with gangs and wannabe gangs alike. "I think everybody wanted to be in a gang in the '80s." Fights broke out daily in school. The eventual UFC champion Tito Ortiz was in one of his classes. Of his four best friends, two became firemen and two ended up in jail.

He was the exception, a kid who was terrified.

Until his junior high graduation.

As he walked down the line, Gonzalez spotted Bully No. 1 and sped off to hide behind a faraway wall. He was back in that mode of being "scared shitless," he says, "of getting beat up." His family, unsure where he had gone, finally found Gonzalez and the disappointment on his mother's face hurt more than any pain either bully could inflict. Right then, it clicked. Gonzalez made a personal vow to never hide again. He told himself that he'd rather die than be afraid.

Gonzalez never did need to fight his bullies. Success on the basketball court helped fuel his newfound confidence, too. That same eighth-grade year, Gonzalez used hoops as an escape, and this escape gradually helped him feel better about himself. Into ninth grade, Gonzalez decided it was time to tackle his inner demons on the football field and try out for the high school team. His buddy, Eric Escobedo, was the best player on the squad and couldn't believe Gonzalez was giving this another shot. So the *first* day in pads in the *first* hitting drill, he beckoned Gonzalez to the front.

Eric wanted to test him in this one-on-one hitting drill. Gonzalez felt that old fear creep back in. His heart pounded. The two clashed in the hole and...Gonzalez's life was never the same.

"He fucking hit me and that's when we were like two bulls in the ring—just, 'Boom!' We stalemated. All of the coaches went, 'Yeah!' In my head, I'm like, 'Fuck yeah. I got this. I got this.' That *changed* my life. I said, 'I can fucking do this. I got this.' I found that anger switch. I figured out, 'OK, you have to be able to take your mind to a place,' in order to be competitive—that *really* competitive, 'I ain't gonna fucking lose. And when it's time to go, I'm going all the fucking way.' I never had that attitude. I had to build to that."

By his sophomore year, he was called up to the varsity team. At a high school dance, he even ran into Bully No. 1. An anticlimactic encounter, considering Gonzalez now towered over him. Neither of his biological parents are tall—Mom is five foot four and Dad is six foot—but Gonzalez likely got these genetics from a cousin who's six foot six. The offensive coordinator at Huntington Beach High School knew he needed to take full advantage, too. Gonzalez migrated all over the field. Often, he'd split out wide, run as far as he could, and the quarterback chucked it up. His basketball game took off, too.

"Once you get confidence?" Gonzalez says. "Confidence is the biggest thing you can have."

Suddenly, he was a Division I recruit in two sports. He loves his mother, but Judy Gonzalez was too busy making ends meet to offer guidance in sports. He didn't have a father figure, nor was there the typical village of mentors guiding and pushing and telling him how special he was as his star rose. That's a major reason why he ended up in Canton, too. This reality hit Gonzalez while learning about "the Norwegian Way" on HBO's *Real Sports.* In the 2018 Winter Olympics, tiny Norway won an unprecedented thirty-nine medals, eight more than any other country, and how they pulled it off was exactly how Gonzalez was raised. For years, Norway was trounced in the Winter Games. Then, a plan was hatched. All sports become affordable for all youths, subsidized by a gambling tax. If parents went crazy at games, Gonzalez explains, they were kicked out. No scores were kept at any competition level. No awards banquets were held. No national championships. If Norwegian officials got wind of a parent pressuring a coach or a player, they were reprimanded.

The goal was for kids to play for the pure fun of it. They could try any sport they wanted—with zero pressure—and then, at age fourteen, they could zero in on one sport competitively. That's when kids learned about the mental side of it all, received world-class nutrition, and so on.

A light bulb went off. Gonzalez realized his sports life was essentially "the Norwegian Way." He developed a pure love for both sports because there were no expectations. Nobody went to his games. Meanwhile, he saw countless friends get burnt out from a sport they never even liked. On to the NFL, where he played with and against players who hated football. Players literally told Gonzalez, "I fucking hate football." One was a Pro Bowler. Not surprisingly, he barely lasted in the league even though he was supremely talented. This player admitted to Gonzalez that he played only because his dad made him.

Gonzalez points to three of the greatest athletes ever: Wayne Gretzky, Jerry Rice, Roger Federer. They've also said how they were never forced into the sports they later dominated. Their parents weren't overbearing. On the opposite end of this spectrum was the kid Gonzalez shared the region's athlete-of-the-year honors with in 1994. Tiger Woods was practically groomed from the womb to be the greatest golfer ever by a suffocating father and, eventually, crashed and burnt in humiliating fashion. ("Talk about being forced," Gonzalez adds. "Snap, crackle, pop.") While Woods practically lived on a golf course his entire childhood, Gonzalez surfed and hooped and played beach volleyball and kicked a soccer ball. His sole mode of transportation? A skateboard. He's positive that balancing on a board for endless miles helped him at tight end, too.

This was a carefree teen with no dreams of playing in the NFL. Nor did Huntington Beach High School ever send a player to the NFL.

A unique upbringing that he believes created a "perfect storm."

"I was athletic as fuck," Gonzalez says. "Genetically, I am very, very gifted. If other people had it, they would've done the same thing I've done. I did it because I wanted to. Nobody forced me to ever do it. And I think that changed the game for me. That helped me become a student of the game because I loved it."

Granted, this upbringing had a blind spot. Without anyone riding him, Gonzalez showed up to football practices at least thirty minutes late every day. He never studied the playbook. Football was fun but never an activity he took too seriously through high school because he never envisioned the sport actually being his occupation one day. Even on to the University of California, Gonzalez never viewed the NFL as a realistic option, so he carried himself with the same bliss. He was at Berkeley to get a degree, play sports, and party.

Typically, how Gonzalez performed on a game day was a direct reflection of how much partying he did the night before. There were glimpses of greatness in both sports. The last game of his second football season, vs. Stanford, he had 150 receiving yards and he scored twenty-nine points against Washington State the final game of his freshman year in basketball. "I showed flashes," Gonzalez says. "Most of the time, I was shitty." He'd be hungover for basketball practices and games alike, dropping too many goose eggs that freshman year. Living in the dorms was his big mistake because if Gonzalez was ever on the fence—*To party or not to party?*—the choice was always easy. He'd tag along with someone on his hall. It's no coincidence that the Pac-10 Conference didn't acknowledge him on the first, second, third, or honorable mention teams after his sophomore year of football, despite the fact that he was sculpted unlike anyone else on the field. Nor is it a coincidence that Cal went on a Sweet 16 run once he finally moved out of the dorms.

"It's all here," says Gonzalez, pointing to his chest.

One more moment of clarity was needed. He can pinpoint this turning point, too. While partying, he and his friends all headed up to the Berkeley Hills. Gonzalez found a spot on the hill to sit alone and, with his hands around his knees, he stared off into the distance to watch airplanes fly in and out of Oakland.

Says Gonzalez: "It was smacking me in the fucking face: 'Dude, wake the fuck up. You are a fucking idiot right now. Why are you wasting this opportunity?'"

The answer was simple. He was still afraid. Not of a bully. Not of the dark. Not of anything he was conscious of. He realized, in this moment, what he was *subconsciously* terrified of: pouring everything he had into a sport and that effort not being enough. Staring off, he acknowledged this subconscious fear and eliminated it at once. In high school, he could get away with this blissful approach because "99 percent" of the other kids were inferior athletically. Now, he needed to go hard every single play. He needed to stay after practice.

In that same Stanford game, Gonzalez's fumble cost his team a win. He fumbled all of two times in the NFL.

That night atop the Berkeley Hills, it hit him that life is finite. He got into football on his own, but only then did Gonzalez see that if he truly loved football he owed it to himself to go all out. Thinking back, he smiles wide and imitates the literal act of catching a football. He extends for a pass and tucks the ball in. Running routes. Twisting his body in traffic. The "sound" of catching a pass. The "smell" of it. Everything was intoxicating. In '96, he caught 44 passes for 699 yards with 5 touchdowns, was named a first team All-American, and headed to the NFL totally unafraid.

Bullies? Please. Ghosts? Bring 'em on. He overcame this fear, too. After the Kansas City Chiefs selected Gonzalez thirteenth overall in the 1997 NFL Draft, he moved out of his eight-hundred-square foot college apartment and had his mind effectively blown by the manager walking out to the parking lot with him. This quintessential *Berkeley* resident with the long hair and glasses and psychedelic disposition of a man who enjoyed LSD in his day told him it was a real shame what happened to the lady before him in that room.

"What?" Gonzalez asked.

"Yeah, that lady," he said. "We found her. She was dead in there for three weeks."

"Are you fucking serious? Why didn't you tell me that shit!' "

It all made sense. When Gonzalez tried to take a nap, he'd often feel the bed sink as if she was sitting right there. Other times, someone touched his leg. And once, in the middle of the night, he felt hands grip him and physically shake him back and forth. No, Gonzalez wasn't happy with this manager for omitting this minor detail, but it was nice to know he'd survived an actual ghost. He slid into the driver's seat and left college for good. Now it was time to terrorize NFL defenses.

The football field was no place for basketball players in 1997, and that was how peers viewed him his rookie year: as a soft-ass basketball player.

There was no social media then. Most teammates knew that Tony Gonzalez was a first-round pick and little else. The first day he was on the field with teammates, postdraft, veteran defensive end Vaughn Booker stood next to Derrick Thomas and asked aloud, "Who the fuck is this Tony *Gahn-Zahl-Iz*!?" Thomas, who shared the same agent as the rookie, was one of the few players who could point the tight end out a few feet away.

Booker was not impressed. He stared at Gonzalez like he was some stray dog with no business on this field.

"That's him!?" he shouted in front of the whole team. "Hey, Gonzalez! *You* have to block *me*!"

Right then, the fear returned. His heart pounded. He could see a look of bewilderment in everyone's eyes and how it didn't matter what he had accomplished on a college football field. To NFL players, he was a basketball player. As a result, he'd better be willing to get his ass kicked all over again. Especially on Sundays. Right in his own division, the AFC West, resided one of the dirtiest players in NFL history. Volatile linebacker Bill Romanowski essentially became his new bully. Only there was nothing mystical about this. "Romo" *did* smack Gonzalez. At the height of his 'roid rage—he later admitted he took steroids—Romanowski faced Gonzalez twice a year. And the same player who spit in the face of 49ers wide receiver J. J. Stokes and smashed the eye socket of his own teammate in Oakland tried to make Gonzalez's life hell.

One season, Romanowski was fined $42,500 for three illegal hits and a punch thrown at Gonzalez. After one head-to-head collision, Gonzalez told the linebacker right on the field that he'd get fined. To which, Romanowski informed him he did not care.

"He's racist. He's on steroids. He's a cheap-ass player," Gonzalez says. "He's a bad guy. But he was one of those guys saying, 'He's a fucking basketball player.' He'd say, 'You ain't shit. You're a pussy. I'll guard you in my sleep. You got nothing.' My rookie year, he got me a couple times."

Year 1 ended with heartbreak against Romanowski's Broncos. KC lost in the divisional round to Denver, 14–10. Year 2 was a nightmare. Gonzalez's 16 dropped passes led the NFL. Stronger than ever, he felt like "an ox" blocking as a traditional tight end in Marty Schotten-heimer's run-first, "Martyball" offense. But as the drops mounted, he fell into an abyss. He was drinking again, but not in a state of college bliss. Gonzalez locked himself in his room and ripped through Jack and Cokes in an attempt to drink his sorrows away.

Many nights, he cried. Alone.

"A lot of drinking. A lot of self-loathing. A lot of self-doubt. That's such a bad place to be in but it's such a good place, too—if you can get through it. I thought I was doing everything right, which is a really frustrating place to be. I'm thinking, 'I'm doing everything you guys asked me to.' That was the problem. I'm doing everything you asked me to instead of doing what you ask me to do, and what else can *I* do? I never went out to practice early."

It was time to take his dedication to a new level. He started reading more. Gonzalez particularly enjoyed *The Seven Spiritual Laws of Success* by Deepak Chopra and *Winning Is A Habit* by Vince Lombardi. Before each practice, Gonzalez had someone throw him balls in rapid-fire succession. In ten minutes, he could catch one hundred balls. All on routes, too. Quickly, that pure love for catching the ball—the *sound*, the *smell*—returned for good. With no coaches barking in his ear, pressure started to fade. He figured out he learned the tight end position best, frankly, on his own.

Schematically, however, one coach's presence did help. Into Year 3, offensive coordinator Jimmy Raye realized he had a special talent and unlocked the greatness in Gonzalez by migrating him all over the field and feeding him. Often. The tight end's catch rate increased from 57.8 percent in 1998 to 73.1 percent in 1999. And, in 2000, Gonzalez erupted for 1,203 yards on 93 receptions with 9 touchdowns. He was named an All-Pro. The sweetest revenge came against Romanowski. In a 23–22 Chiefs win, the linebacker shadowed Gonzalez and was embarrassed. Gonzalez caught all ten passes thrown his way for 127 yards with a touchdown. This felt like slaying a new bully.

"I crushed him," Gonzalez says. "They were bringing him everywhere I went and I was just destroying him. They finally took him off of me. His own teammates were yelling, 'Motherfucker! He can't guard him!'"

Romanowski was not alone. No linebacker could.

At the turn of the century, Gonzalez effectively basketballified the position. His athleticism put linebackers in impossible one-on-one positions. No tight end in NFL history had ever elevated for acrobatic catches like this before. The way Gonzalez could bend his body in midair was preposterous and, also, no accident. While there were tight ends before who could throw down a tomahawk jam or two in high school, none competed at such a high level. None battled the likes of National Player of the Year Ed O'Bannon or the six-foot-ten Tim Thomas. Severely undersized at power forward, Gonzalez learned how to time his rebounds and get off shots in traffic. He had no choice. Each night, he was giving up five inches. It all fed his athletic muscle memory. When it was time to play football—in the same mano-a-mano battle—catching the ball in traffic was easy. Gonzalez plucked footballs above the heads of six-foot-two linebackers and outmuscled 190-pound defensive backs, and the more he was double- and triple-teamed, the more he says he relished "catching the ball over everybody."

The idea that a tight end is never "covered," that a QB can ignore whatever the X's and O's tell him, started with Gonzalez.

"When I went to the line of scrimmage, it did not matter to me. I don't care who the fuck is out there. You cannot guard me."

Fellow Chiefs tight end Jason Dunn believes Gonzalez's hands were on par with those of Cris Carter and Jerry Rice, adding that his ability to win in traffic rivaled Randy Moss.

"At the end of the game," Dunn says, "you've got to go to him."

The basketball roots helped in one other career-saving way, too.

Gonzalez believes there's "an art" to avoiding injuries. Unlike Mike Ditka, Kellen Winslow, Ben Coates, Jeremy Shockey, Rob Gronkowski, George Kittle, all the tight ends who've opted to seek and destroy, Gonzalez played 270 of a possible 272 games by dodging kill shots. Peripheral vision from basketball helped. If he had an extra millisecond at his disposal, he'd jump back to avoid the kill shot completely. If he didn't, he'd actually fall backward on impact. This wasn't as fun to watch as Shockey barreling through other humans like bowling pins, but Gonzalez knew he was minimizing the long-term physical impact. He actively practiced how to fall. He saw no need to devour a defender along the sideline. Over time, Gonzalez believes he created his own luck. A coach once showed him on film how he was a millisecond away from a tackler blowing out his knee.

Best of all, basketball gave Gonzalez a "sixth sense" to mentally process all moving parts on the field. He could anticipate where opponents were shifting in real time. By 2003, a college basketball player at Kent State who didn't play one down of college football, Antonio Gates, was getting a shot at the NFL.

What happened next, however, puzzles him to this day. Gonzalez had a gift, yet it didn't seem like coaches in the league knew how to use it.

Raye understood what he had in No. 88 but those Chiefs couldn't win, so the coaching staff was fired. In came Dick Vermeil and the famed "Greatest Show on Turf" offense from his magical 1999 season with the St. Louis Rams. Initially, Gonzalez was ecstatic. He saw the Rams light the NFL on fire that season. His new coordinator, Al Saunders, was even an assistant on the "Air Coryell" staff with Winslow. This felt like a new perfect storm. When quarterback Trent Green asked Gonzalez to chat, the first day they met, Gonzalez was thrilled... then Green started talking.

All excitement instantly evaporated when Green informed Gonzalez that his days putting up big numbers were over.

Next, Vermeil brought him in. As an old-school coach who cut his teeth in the '70s, Vermeil's idea of what an NFL tight end was put on earth to do was rigid. Channeling his best Vermeil voice, Gonzalez recalls this conversation, too. Vermeil wanted him to bulk up 255 pounds.

Gonzalez was only twenty-four years old and didn't want to rock the boat, so he didn't push back. Truthfully, he genuinely likes all involved as people. In 2004, Saunders even went out of his way to make sure Gonzalez became the first tight end to ever hit 100 receptions by targeting him 33 times the final two weeks of a lost season. It's not his fault, Gonzalez says, nor Vermeil's fault. This was simply the system and, back then, *players* fit into a *system*—not the other way around. No wonder Gonzalez cannot help but wonder what could've been when he sees coaches go out of their way to feed tight ends today.

"At the peak of my career, the height of my athleticism, they came in for five years and said, 'We're not going to throw you the ball a lot.'"

What those Chiefs failed to understand was that Eddie Kennison and Johnnie Morton weren't quite Isaac Bruce and Torry Holt. Dunn agrees that the offense was more wideout-friendly and based on timing but still loves to tease Gonzalez. "Al Saunders made your career," he'll tell him.

Those Chiefs had one good shot at a Super Bowl. In 2003, they went 13-3 and fell in the divisional round of the playoffs to the Indianapolis Colts. If the Chiefs had any semblance of a defense, Gonzalez believes they would've won it all that season. He calls that the best offensive line ever and believes he and Dunn formed the best tight end duo in NFL history—"We kicked the shit out people"—in helping Priest Holmes rush for 1,420 yards and 27 touchdowns.

Adds Dunn: "When I see all these teams now going two and three tight ends, I laugh. I'm ecstatic and happy for it. The things we did in Kansas City, teams took notice."

After the 2005 season, Vermeil retired and Gonzalez spent the final three seasons of his career in Kansas City catching passes from Brodie Croyle, Tyler Thigpen, and Damon Huard. He told the fringe

NFL quarterbacks to chuck it up to him and his numbers skyrocketed again. Problem is, losing gets old. In the middle of the 2008 season, Gonzalez asked to be traded. The Chiefs were unable to finalize a deal, everyone was fired anyway, and at thirty-two years old he was sent to the Atlanta Falcons in the off-season for a second-round pick. He could not contain his excitement. Gonzalez knew the clock was ticking on his career. This felt like the absolute perfect place to win a Super Bowl with a quarterback on the rise (Matt Ryan), an All-Pro wide receiver (Roddy White), a bruising All-Pro running back (Michael Turner) and, the cherry on top, was a coordinator who played tight end himself for nine seasons. "This is going to be fucking great!" he remembers telling himself.

On Day 1, that coach—Mike Mularkey—told his new star to meet him for a film session.

They sat down. They hit play.

The arranged marriage was doomed.

One thought ran through the tight end's mind as his new coach spoke to him in such a gruff tone. This was their first conversation ever, yet Mularkey sounded...aggravated. As if he didn't even want to coach Gonzalez. For a good twenty minutes straight, the Falcons offensive coordinator played clips of tight ends he coached with the Pittsburgh Steelers in the '90s blocking power plays in the run game.

Again and again, there was Mark Bruener absolutely mauling opponents. Gonzalez could not help but ask himself the entire time: *Why did these guys even trade for me?*

Finally, Mularkey spoke up.

"I know you catch all those balls," he told him, "but this is what we do here. And this is what's going to be expected of you. I just want to make sure you're OK with that."

Again, Gonzalez told his new coach he was on board, but he couldn't believe the Falcons would trade for him if the person calling the plays didn't appreciate what he did best. Honestly, Mularkey had no clue what Atlanta was thinking, either. He had been begging GM Thomas Dimitroff to get him a blocking tight end for a year, and he was not pleased to receive Gonzalez instead. Way back in '97, Gonzalez was the coach's highest-graded tight end prospect. Mularkey even calls him an "unbelievable" blocker at Cal. But Mularkey accuses Gonzalez of simply not caring about this part of the job as his pro career progressed.

To him, this film session was normal procedure. He showed this ass-kicking montage to all his new tight ends. A few, he laughs, looked like they were going to pee their pants watching this series of clips that also included ex-Steeler brutes Mitch Lyons and Jerame Tuman. "Get used to it," Mularkey would tell them.

That was his message here and Gonzalez, he claims, flatly told him that he does not block power plays.

"We did not start off on the right foot," Mularkey says, "because he told me right away that he basically wasn't going to block."

The relationship only grew worse. And worse. Old school collided with new school in spectacular fashion, essentially putting the modern-day NFL tight end on trial right in Atlanta, Georgia.

Neither party was particularly wrong in how they viewed the position. Mularkey represented a lot of what made the tight end position so special, right down to that "one extra shove" at the whistle. What he knew was selfless bruisers, like Bruener, physically beating defenders into submission. Any juror certainly could cast a vote for this. Yet for the tight end to enter a new dominion—to become something more profound—it needed Tony Gonzalez in full. The acrobatics. The ego. He was talented enough to force any coach from any era to change their definition of the position. *Gonzalez* was the reason a guy like Gates even gets NFL workouts and, with the San Diego Chargers, Gates was reeling off eight straight Pro Bowl appearances. *Gonzalez* made it OK for the New Orleans Saints to take Jimmy Graham ninety-fifth overall in 2010. His style of play was so original, so fresh. Scouts began to search far and wide for anything that remotely resembled Gonzalez.

Some teams embraced the change. Others did not. Gonzalez believes that Mularkey was trying to halt this evolution. Mostly because, he says, the coach loathed players with any "glitz," any "glamour" to their game. He claims the OC would mock both him and White in front of the entire offense during film sessions and that he formed an opinion of him before they even got to know each other.

"Because he has that mentality. 'We're grunt work. We're grunters. We don't care about the notoriety. We don't care about that stuff,'" Gonzalez says. "Well, I'm like, 'Motherfucker, I do care about that. I want to score touchdowns.' I had a nice reputation coming in. I had gone to the Pro Bowl ten years in a row, coming from Kansas City. He's like, 'We're not having that here! None of that shit!' OK. You win, motherfucker."

He could play Mr. Nice Guy only so long. Gonzalez started sniping back.

When Mularkey would ask him a question in meetings, he'd reply with a dismissive "I don't know" which only pissed off Mularkey more. The coach's disgust with Gonzalez, the blocker, led to quite a scene after one Falcons practice. Mularkey had one three-hundred-pound blob buried on the defensive line depth chart stay to mash one-on-one into his tight ends. There was no ball involved. Only Mularkey shouting "Hike!" and two players bashing into each other.

"He is literally shortening our necks after practice," Gonzalez says. "I couldn't believe I was doing this shit. I finally stepped out and said, 'I'm done.' He goes, 'You're not going to do it again!? What kind of example are you setting?' I'm not fucking doing it!"

Believing the Falcons were wasting his talent, Gonzalez recommended Atlanta do the same thing the Chiefs did. To go sign their own 285-pound, Dunn-like complement capable of handling the heavy lifting in the run game. That was how the Denver Broncos operated in the '90s, too. They'd run toward Dwayne Carswell or Byron Chamberlain much more than Shannon Sharpe. The Falcons didn't do this, but Mularkey did stop using Gonzalez as a lead blocker.

Both are clearly full of animosity for each other to this day, with

Mularkey assuring there's no love lost between the two. It didn't surprise the coach that Gonzalez didn't invite him to his Hall of Fame Induction. He snipes that the difference between the two of them was that Gonzalez cared about records and he cared about winning. The bad blood was no secret in the Falcons locker room. Wide receiver Brian Finneran enjoyed playing for Mularkey. As an undrafted free agent who overachieved his entire career, he was the sort of nonstar Mularkey likely wishes would've populated the entire offense.

It's not too complicated to him. Mularkey wanted tight ends who both caught passes and blocked, the latter of which was not Gonzalez's top priority.

"Mike Mularkey tried to force it and Tony didn't like being told what to do," Finneran says. "I love the guy. He was a great teammate and a great friend. But he also had that Hollywood aspect to him as well. A pretty-looking dude. Physically dominating. Best at his position in the world. Mularkey just had a mindset for tight ends, and Tony wasn't in the mold of what he had in mind."

The man with the lobster claws himself, Bruener, was not shocked that this union dissolved so quickly. These were two individuals who spent their lives at the tight end position. Both thrived with completely different ideologies. After all those years in KC, dominating downfield, this was a stark departure. "It's like, 'Wait a minute.' This guy's asking me to do something different than what I've done the last twelve years? Thirteen years? I don't know if I really want to do that,'" Bruener says. "Not to say Tony was right or wrong. That was his prerogative."

Everything boiled over in Week 17 of the 2009 season.

Both the Falcons (8-7) and Buccaneers (3-12) had been eliminated from playoff contention. There wasn't much at stake other than Gonzalez being four catches away from hitting 1,000 for his career. Unfathomable for a scared pup in Huntington Beach. Surreal for a rookie nobody took seriously that first day of practice in KC. Gonzalez was dealing with a throbbing calf, but believed he owed it to himself to take some Toradol and play on. This was a chance to go where no tight end had gone before.

By halftime, he got to 999. One dump-off would do it. The officials were even ready to stop the game and give him the football.

"We go into the second half," Gonzalez says, "and this fucker doesn't throw me the ball one time. He doesn't call one play for me. Not one. At the end of the game, he calls it naked for me. Of course, Tampa has three guys on me because they're like, 'You're not getting it against us.' So I don't get the ball. That was the only play for me in the second half."

The Falcons won, 20–10.

Naturally, Gonzalez and Mularkey differ on what happened next.

Mularkey describes a joyous locker room. Yeah, they missed the playoffs, but for the first time in their forty-four years of existence, the Falcons enjoyed back-to-back winning seasons. He can still picture owner Arthur Blank grinning ear to ear. This game wasn't meaningless to him. Gonzalez remembers players and coaches alike being pissed on his behalf. At least Saunders fed him like crazy in that Week 17 game five years prior. At his stall, Gonzalez was livid. He saw Mularkey shaking each player's hand and found that odd. The coach hadn't done that after any other game in two seasons, as far as he recalled. Gonzalez was convinced Mularkey was trying to screw with him.

Locker to locker, the coach inched closer...and closer...and then Gonzalez felt a tap on his back.

There stood Mularkey with an outstretched hand and what he describes as an exaggerated shit-eating grin.

"I go, 'Motherfucker. Get away from me, Mike. Don't fuck with me, dude.' And I've never talked to him like this. Finally, I had it. He goes, 'What are you talking about? We won the game. Aren't you happy that we won the game?' And I go, 'Mike, get the fuck away from me. I promise you, I'm going to beat the fucking shit out of you in front of everybody here.' He goes, 'What is your problem?' And I went after him. I was about to swing and all of a sudden the players jump on me. I'm like, 'You're the fucking worst coach I've ever seen in my fucking life.'"

If teammates hadn't held him, he's sure he would've dropped the hammer.

"We were close. We were close. I was in football mode at that point. I'm ready to die."

Mularkey, in so many words, assures that he was also prepared for such a scenario. He also didn't want to spoil what he deemed a celebratory occasion and says Gonzalez is lying about being held back.

Either way, Gonzalez did apologize to Mularkey, though he made it clear it was bullshit that the coach iced him out. Mularkey started to repeat that he was trying to win the game and the tight end cut him off before taking a deep breath and cooling down so he wouldn't feel like punching his coach again. Miraculously, the two coexisted for two more seasons before Mularkey became the head coach of the Jacksonville Jaguars.

To this day, Mularkey insists that when head coach Mike Smith told him to get the ball to Gonzalez he had no clue why. He even regrets calling that one pass play on the final drive because it got Ryan hit. He contends he genuinely didn't know Gonzalez was stuck on number 999 until he was flying home on the team plane, not that it would've made any difference. "I called plays to win the game," Mularkey says. "I didn't call plays to appease players. I don't give a shit about that." As Finneran notes, Ryan could've thrown a short pass to Gonzalez at some point in that second half, but he was also in his second year. He wasn't about to go rogue. Mularkey is one of his favorite coaches of all time, but even he admits this was a bad moment for the coach. The more Finneran thinks about it, the more he believes it's "bush league."

This is as Darwinian as it gets. The more time passes, the more Mularkey popping in that tape of his ex-Steelers tight ends is akin to Steve Kerr pulling up clips of ex-Chicago Bulls center Luc Longley for the big men on his Golden State Warriors roster. The game changes. To Gonzalez, the evolution of his position is similar to the traditional center in the NBA being replaced by a seven-footer like Kevin Durant launching three-pointers. Without question, the most rapid growth at the tight end position occurred between Gonzalez's first season (1997) and his last (2013). All because he took matters into his own hands.

So much of this position has to do with environment. He cannot help but wonder what would've happened if Rob Gronkowski had been drafted by the Falcons in 2010. "With his big ass!?" Gonzalez says, laughing. No question, Mularkey would've plugged him in as an in-line blocker. Instead, Bill Belichick had a vision for the position, Tom Brady was his quarterback and Josh McDaniels was his play caller. Gonzalez even believes Bruener might've had a chance to shine as a pass catcher with a different coach.

Outside of Raye, he never had the benefit of an offensive mastermind. He took the hard road right down to playing with quarterbacks who shouldn't have been on NFL rosters. And, still, Gonzalez was a first-ballot Hall of Famer. That's why Gonzalez also firmly believes that, regardless of environment, the best tight ends find a way to "get their shit" and keep this evolution moving. Not surprisingly, he had one of the best seasons of his career after Mularkey left. In Year 16, at age *thirty-six*, he caught 93 balls for 930 yards with 8 touchdowns. Former New Orleans Saints linebacker Jonathan Vilma covered Gonzalez that season (and four total) in the NFC South and describes his game as pure poetry. "Like watching art," he says. There were *faster* tight ends, more *explosive* tight ends, but nobody lulled defenders to sleep quite like Gonzalez.

Everything he did was so under control that, before Vilma knew it, he was boxed out. Gonzalez caught everything, too. Vilma never remembers seeing the tight end drop a pass. Whereas Ozzie Newsome tipped the ball to himself in pregame, Gonzalez continued his ritual of getting one hundred catches in.

"Exceptionally great hands," Vilma says. "His hands are super soft, and anything that went his way, he was going to get. Obviously, with the basketball, he could high-point it. So, for me, even if I was covering him, I wasn't covering him. He's like six-six. I'm six-one. So even if I'm covering him, there's no way I can go up and go get him. Because he'd body me out."

Gonzalez's trick was to never explode out of his stance. He instead ran at about three-quarters speed and gave the linebacker a nudge on the hip before breaking out.

"That little split right there is all he needed," Vilma says. "He nudges you on the hip with the elbow and then he bursts full speed for an out route. Now, it's too late. There is nothing you can do. And he'd catch everything with his hands. Imagine trying to come up with a game plan where three of your guys—three linebackers—can't cover him. So now, you're left with the two safeties. So if you do that, how are you going to help with the wide receivers if you're using your safeties on the tight end every time. It was a nightmare dealing with him. He revolutionized that position."

One safety who covered Gonzalez throughout his own eleven-year career speaks in the same helpless pitch. To Donte Whitner, he was the "Tim Duncan of the NFL," because this sneaky rope-a-dope was the football equivalent to the San Antonio Spurs' legend turning around for a twelve-foot bank shot. Defenders knew what Duncan was going to do on the block, but the "Big Fundamental" was too tall, too decisive, too in-tune with the geometry of the play for you to do anything about it.

That was Tony Gonzalez.

He'd run his routes at the same depth and knew exactly what the defensive back was thinking based on leverage.

"It's not flashy," Whitner says. "He wears the same type of tape job every game. He has his buckles up. Same mouthpiece. Same look. Big shoes. But he was a technician. He was all about the fundamentals and the basics. There's a reason he played that long—at that level—that late in his career. He was able to get open because he was a technician and understood the small nuances of the game."

Gonzalez's love for catching a football reached an all-time high in 2012. With a system catering to his strengths and Ryan at his peak, Gonzalez led the Falcons to a 13-3 record and the number one seed in the playoffs. In the NFC divisional playoff round, his nineteen-yard reception set up a game-winning field goal against Seattle. In the

NFC Championship, he caught all eight passes thrown his way. Trailing 28–24, the Falcons drove to San Francisco's 10-yard line, and on fourth-and-four new Falcons offensive coordinator Dirk Koetter called Gonzalez's number on a slant route. A 49ers DB, however, anticipated the play, dropped into that area, and Ryan was forced to throw elsewhere. It fell incomplete.

Gonzalez played one more season, retired, sat out all of 2014, and Tom Brady called.

The greatest ever wanted to see if Gonzalez was up for a catch in Los Angeles. Brady told him to bring his cleats to a practice field at UCLA's facility. This wasn't uncommon—a lot of former players join the QB for throwing sessions. Gonzalez figured Brady was just looking to get a quick workout in. Boy, was he wrong. When he showed up, Gonzalez saw a bunch of nonathletes standing around and no other players. He was the only one catching balls from Brady this day.

Every pass was on the money. Whenever Gonzalez got back to the line of scrimmage, Brady even apologized for not placing the ball in front of him because those extra six inches correlated to three more yards on his YAC. (Of course. Duh.)

When the workout was done, all others in attendance circled Gonzalez like it was an intervention. There was Tom House, the QB's private coach. A nutritionist. A stretch coach. A mental coach. Brady closed in, thanked Gonzalez for the time and asked him a question: "Are you sure you're done playing?" Gonzalez said he was. Brady told him a player can sustain their physical peak until the age of forty-five and that Gonzalez would crush it with Gronkowski in New England. Still, Gonzalez stayed retired. He wasn't keen on the Boston cold but also didn't return out of financial frustrations, out of what was *right* in his mind.

As Gonzalez changed the sport, the salary given to such vanguards stagnated. After that All-Pro season in 2012, he was shocked no team would offer him more than $7 million. He didn't understand it, nor did his agent, Tom Condon. The NFL tight end was asked to do more… and more… and more… all because of him but not seeing a significant spike in pay. Such is life as an NFL tight end. You are forever underappreciated which, on a dime, sends Gonzalez into a state of deep thought here in Austin.

Maybe that's it. Maybe this is why the tight end position has become such a haven for all wild personalities.

"Because we're insecure," Gonzalez says. "Insecurity drives performance. We don't get paid. We were the second-lowest paid position. Isn't that crazy? The second-lowest paid position to fullback. DBs make more than us. Linebackers make more than us. Obviously, D-Line makes more than us. Offensive linemen make more than us. Running backs make more than us. Receivers make more than us. The only position we make more than is a fucking fullback, and a kicker. And we do the most! That's been one of the great struggles in my life, to deal with that. It's so unfair. It's so unfair. I don't fucking understand it."

Tight ends today are made-for-TV characters. Sharpe is a hot-take machine. Gonzalez did a movie with Triple X. Vernon Davis is doing a movie with Morgan Freeman. Put a mic in front of George Kittle's face? "He's on fire," Gonzalez says. Kelce, too. Gronk could be mistaken for a Chippendale. Tight ends have become the true entertainers of the league who never, ever censor themselves. One reason has to be the fact that they are so underpaid. Gonzalez knows that insecurity can drive performance.

In KC, he couldn't understand how cornerback Patrick Surtain made twice as much as him only to get toasted. "He was dog shit. Dog shit!" the tight end snipes. "He got beat all the time."

It's not fair, but guess what? Life isn't fair. All of a sudden, it feels as if we're sitting in a pew of a church, not a restaurant, seeking the meaning of life. Gonzalez is grateful for everything he's been through because playing tight end, he says, forces you to become a better person. The number one criticism Gonzalez receives, of course, is that he wasn't a good blocker. Which pisses him off to this day. He didn't like it then when Mularkey drew that conclusion the first day they met and certainly doesn't like it now when former players make comments on TV. He implores them all, kindly, to "put on the fucking film." Of course, he didn't *like* to block, but he did it.

From Year 1 to Year 17, he had zero choice.

That's the thing about playing tight end. Your route running may be sublime. Your athleticism may be straight out of a basketball highlight. Your hands could be glue. But you also must be willing to inflict and absorb bruises in the trenches.

"It forces you to do some shit you don't want to do," Gonzalez says. "I'm used to grinding it out."

He can still remember getting butterflies in his stomach when the whistle was blown for the nine-on-seven drill to assemble. He'd see wide receivers strut off to their one-on-ones with cornerbacks to another part of the practice field, get jealous, then be forced to deal with those butterflies in a drill that's essentially bodies smashing into each other with a running back finding a hole. Playing tight end, he's certain, forces a man to "grow emotionally" in a moment like this. The very nature of the position forces you to confront *fear* inside, which—it becomes clear—is why Gonzalez was so uniquely qualified to be such a pioneer.

He dealt with that *fear* forever.

"The tight end position represents life," Gonzalez says. "Quarterbacks don't get that. They don't have to hit anybody. They don't have to put on a chinstrap. Tom would not be playing twenty-two years at tight end. No one's ever done it because it's not fun. The shit ain't fun. It's not all glitz and glam. It's getting down and getting your hands dirty. It's a dirty, dirty position that can also be very fun, too. These receivers don't have to fucking do that. They know nothing about our world. They're such prima donnas because they can be. We couldn't do that! We're with the O-Line a lot! They'll bring you back down quick and tell you to shut the fuck up and that this shit isn't going on around here."

That's why it's also no coincidence to him that tight ends make the best football commentators. They're asked to do everything on a football field, so they understand the moving parts at the line of scrimmage *and* what the X, Y, and Z receivers are doing *and* what defenses are trying to do. When Gonzalez gives an example of a typical play call here—and all his responsibilities that'd go into that play—he might as well be speaking Dutch.

He's sure of one other thing, too: Playing tight end makes him a better father. He's applying that whole Norwegian Way to his own parenting style now. He wants his kids to be truly brave for all chaos—all "shit," as he puts it—because that "shit" is inevitable in life. The only way he believes a dad can instill that braveness is by not forcing his kids to do anything. He wants them to find their switch within organically. Like he did. He sees some of his friends trying to eliminate all obstacles for their kids and knows that while this may work for a few years, those are the kids bound to run into a brick wall.

When he's not reading books like *The Self-Driven Child*, Gonzalez is setting aside two hours every day for self-reflection. He sits. He closes his eyes. He thinks. And the fact that he never won a Super Bowl ring doesn't cross his mind. The only regret he has from his playing days is not sharing all his valuable life experiences with younger teammates. He did speak in front of his team once, right before his NFL career ended, and three players came up to him afterward. One was in tears. This player said he wished Gonzalez spoke up sooner.

Today, Gonzalez admits he might've been too selfish through his career, too consumed with being the absolute best player he could be.

Maybe, he wonders, he could've changed more lives along the way.

The truth is, he opened up more doors than he could count.

Finding Gates

Basketball film was all NFL teams had to study. The agent for Antonio Gates sent the footage out to teams and one scouting assistant for the San Diego Chargers thought his higher-ups should take a look.

Truthfully, Jimmy Raye III wasn't sold. The team's college scouting director had seen this song and dance a million times. "Maybe," the son of Tony Gonzalez's favorite coach thought. That "maybe" was enough for Raye to pass the tape along to the team's tight ends coach, Tim Brewster, and Brewster? He saw Charles Barkley in pads. He strummed up a relationship with Gates right away.

"And I'll never forget him saying, 'Jimmy, this guy thinks he can be great,'" Raye says. "So I'm like, 'OK, that's saying something. That's a start.'"

Gates held a predraft workout inside the Kent State Field House where the five teams in attendance had no reason to think he'd ever amount to anything. His body was fleshy, not muscular. He *looked* like a basketball player and ran a pedestrian 4.8 in the 40. A total non-starter. Scouts from the Indianapolis Colts, Pittsburgh Steelers, and San Francisco 49ers were in attendance, as well as tight ends coaches from the Cleveland Browns and San Diego. And Brewster knew something the others did not: Gates had sprained his ankle a week earlier in a basketball showcase.

The two had been talking for two months and grabbed dinner the night before.

When Brewster reported back to the Chargers, he told them they needed to sign Gates as an undrafted free agent and informed Raye that Gates ran a 4.62. "You've got to be kidding me," Raye thought. "We might've really just stumbled across something." Raye ran it up the food chain and everyone agreed to sign Gates after the seven rounds passed. All the rookie wanted was a bump from $5,000 to $7,500 for his signing bonus. Afterward, Brewster visited Raye's office and came clean. Gates actually hadn't run a 4.62. He pulled a 4.83.

"I was like, 'Oh my God. What have we done?'" Raye said. "He loved the kid so much. I'll say this with all certainty. If it wasn't for the relationship Tim Brewster established with the kid and the fact that he was on board with working with Antonio and the belief he had in him—and the belief the kid had in himself—he probably wouldn't have ended up being a San Diego Charger. It was a match made in heaven."

Gates hadn't played football since high school but, at Kent State, the six-foot-four forward averaged 20.6 points and 7.7 rebounds per game as a senior. The year before, he led the tenth-seeded Golden Flashes to the Elite Eight. His timing was perfect. He was offering his athleticism to the NFL right when Gonzalez's trapeze acts were proving to be unguardable in the early 2000s. Raye confirms that Gonzalez's ascent absolutely opened the eyes of the entire scouting community.

In training camp, Gates played with a fluidness that so many other draftable tight ends Raye had studied over the years lacked.

"That innate ability to body people, create separation, catch the ball," he says. "Body control. Ball skills. Most guys just didn't have that. Usually you saw it in the top players. For a guy to be undrafted and have those things, it was like, 'Wow.'"

Still, head coach Marty Schottenheimer wanted to cut him. He thought the Chargers could slip Gates through waivers and bring him back. Raye and company told him Gates had shown too much on his preseason tape for the practice squad to be a possibility—another team would pounce. After some back and forth, Schottenheimer relented. All Gates did from there was play his entire sixteen-year career with the Chargers. He finished with 955 receptions for 11,841 yards and 116 touchdowns, the most for any tight end in league history.

If the Chargers didn't sign Gates out of the draft, Raye knew there was a reasonable chance nobody would have. Instead, he was soon getting double-covered by New England's Bill Belichick. What they imagined would be a three- or four-year project was condensed to one, the result of Gates's "inner confidence." He was unfazed by the game's violence, forever the kid Brewster described to Raye from Day 1. Gates truly viewed himself as the best player on the field, Raye adds, even with LaDainian Tomlinson as a teammate.

He gave the NFL no choice but to continue opening up its mind.

"That's not always the easiest thing to do in scouting," Raye says. "To think 'How do we benefit in taking this guy's skill set and utilizing it with what we do?' Most people were like, 'Oh, basketball players are finesse guys. They're soft. They're not tough. They don't want to get hit.' The next thing you know, Tony Gonzalez became a great player. Antonio Gates became a great player. Jimmy Graham became a great player. People started thinking, 'If you have enough innate toughness and you have the skill level and the willingness to want to be a great player? We're willing to take a chance.' "

Chapter 10

SHOCK TO THE SYSTEM

In storms Jeremy Shockey, right through the front doors of Yard House sports bar in Miami Beach and, honestly, he may as well be barreling down on a defensive back in the secondary.

The man does everything at one hell-bent speed.

Shockey tilts his sunglasses atop his head, points to the other side of the bar—to his go-to stool—and then engulfs my hand with a bear-paw squeeze of a handshake. At forty-one years old, Shockey is a strapping dude. Gone are the blond locks that defined him as an NFL tight end, but the six-foot-five Shockey looks like he still has a dozen snaps in him. The bartender sees him and yells "Hey Shockey!" with a grin. Even though there are a hundred-plus beers on tap, he knows the tight end's poison.

He pours Shockey a vodka-soda with a separate glass of limes.

With one "Cheers!" and one clink of our glasses, he's off.

A conversation with Shockey is akin to an all-out sprint of a marathon if that marathon also happened to be full contact. For two and a half hours, Shockey's brain operates at warp speed with his mouth, miraculously, keeping up. It's stunning how much information Shockey can spit out at an auctioneer's pace. He possesses the unique ability to make a complete stranger instantly feel like an old frat brother in playfully smacking your leg ("Back then in our mini-camp, you hit!") and gripping your shoulder (while quoting a *Caddyshack* line) and pulling your bicep to relive a play and jabbing a hard index finger directly into your chest to explain where he once cracked his sternum.

Arms flailing, Shockey is so animated that the vape contraption in his hands goes airborne and splits into pieces. He's unfazed, too. He retrieves each piece off the floor and puts the vape back together without breaking cadence, moving right along to all his glorious fights over the years. On the field. Off the field. Shockey has been in more brawls than he can count. These days, he's too smart to sock some jabroni at a bar. Litigation and whatnot. However, he is a world traveler, and let's just say Shockey has made his presence known in Brazil.

"I was always a great fighter. Don't you like fighting?" he says, incredulous anyone wouldn't.

He declares himself undefeated in bar fights with the missing knuckle to prove it.

Right there, clear as day, one knuckle is nonexistent. There's not too much science to how this happens.

"You knock someone the fuck out. I broke his orbital bone. I broke his nose. And his jaw. With one punch."

Staring straight ahead, Shockey then reenacts the bloody scene. He was an incoming high school senior when a college kid chucked a beer bottle at him.

"It was like *The Matrix*. I saw it...he threw it...and it was like... *Wooo, wooo, woooo*..."

Shockey ducks his head at the bar with Keanu Reeves dramatics to avoid an imaginary bottle.

This culprit didn't hide. He approached Shockey and...showtime.

"I was like..."

Shockey balls up a fist and punches his hand with a loud *smack!* that's so loud a few patrons at the other end of our bar look over. He connected. He leapt on top of him. He whaled away. When people held his arms back, Shockey started blasting him with his own skull. He continues to relive it all, here, pretending to bang his head on the bar top.

"I tried to kill him and he's out. He's fucking out. I'm still head-butting him and his shit's all fucked up. I'm like, 'Damn, I've got to go to practice in a fucking week.' It was perfect. I avoided the bottle and killed him."

Ironically enough, Shockey's mother worked for the local ophthalmologist. When the guy went to get his face examined, she was the first person to greet him. Luckily, Lucinda quickly connected the dots and covered up her name tag.

He laughs.

What a life it's been.

Jeremy Shockey didn't script a Canton-bound career with records galore, but no offensive player helped return the league to its bloody roots quite like him. He was an unapologetic savage of a tight end who treated NFL defenders like that poor fool's face at every opportunity. For everyone in the sport—teammates, coaches, announcers, fans—it was a foreign sight. No offensive football player in the 2000s played with a defensive mentality quite like this. As NFL offenses justifiably chased the next Tony Gonzalez, right here was a throwback who didn't merely seek contact. He needed it. Like oxygen. Shockey was the closest the sport had seen to Mike Ditka...with a twist.

He didn't hand the ball off to the official and walk back to the huddle. He was in a defensive back's face, spewing F-bombs, daring him to step inside his ring. Shockey pissed people off along the way but, in every sense of the word, Shockey was a *fighter*. The loudest example of why we are so addicted to football. And the way he did it was by taking everything personally. From Ada, Oklahoma, to the University of Miami to New York City to New Orleans, Shockey cultivated as many slights as he possibly could. Utter one bad word about him and, chances are, you'd be cremated.

His work ethic was unrivaled, too. He didn't have time to date. If a woman spent a night with him in NYC, she knew there would be no breakfast waiting for her in the morning. He was obsessed with attacking the sport at this maniacal speed.

In no time, he's back to bullshitting about bar fights.

Shockey doesn't have kids, but the best way anyone can try to picture what went through his mind on the field is by imagining someone bringing harm to your wife, your baby girl, your baby boy.

"You'll go apeshit. Trust me. Apeshit," he says. "It's the same kind of deal. It's very territorial. This is your family. This is your shit. These are my teammates. We've been through a lot."

Start in Ada. One doesn't need a doctorate in psychology to connect the dots. When Jeremy was three years old and his brother was four, their parents split and Dad bailed. For life. Jimmy Shockey never visited, never called, never wanted a thing to do with his boys. Total abandonment at such an impressionable age should activate a lifetime of anguish and bar fights, correct? No wonder Shockey wasn't exactly respectful of authority. No wonder he's so quick to snap. God help Dad if *he* ever was in the same bar as his son. At one point, Lucinda even considered changing her boys' last names, but that would've cost $500.

Bring this very plausible cause-and-effect theory up to Jeremy and he starts shaking his head.

"No, no, no, absolutely no," he says. "If I had a great loving family and my dad was in the picture, it wouldn't have mattered."

He insists he harbors no anger toward his dad and believes he was sincerely born this way.

"I tried to prove myself wrong more than anybody. How far can I push this envelope? How far can I take it?"

Maybe he's right. Grit is in his DNA. When his mother was two years old, in 1959, she sat in the backseat of a car that was struck by a drunken driver and careened into a tractor-trailer. Lucinda's mother, Evylene Pendley, snapped her neck and was forced to live as a quadriplegic. Lucinda's childhood was spent feeding her mother and doing everything she could to get her through the day so, no, she'd never complain about anything and neither would her kids. There was always food on the table, and most of Jeremy's childhood memories consist of fighting with his big brother.

When Jeremy was a newborn, his brother James would get spanked for yanking him off a bed to play. At one and a half years old, no less. At three, James once whipped a belt buckle at little Jeremy's head—and it stuck. Jeremy sprinted after James with a belt hanging from his forehead. Blood poured everywhere, and Jeremy did not shed one tear. His natural instinct was to get payback.

"I think he was even pulling the fucking belt! We were a very physical family. Very hands-on."

It helped that most of Shockey's relatives were nurses and doctors. They were always patching the boys back together. Shockey has zero clue how many stitches he needed over the years. "Pshh...*tons.*" Once, he was walking on a kitchen counter and fell on glass. Another time, when he was three, Jeremy was tackled in the yard by James which, you know, would've been perfectly fine if there wasn't one of those old-school weed whackers with a metal blade laying right here. The blade sliced his leg open.

He was the classic barefooted Oklahoman getting chased by his older brother between trees and through barbed-wire fences every day. When Jeremy was five years old, his mom begged him to take it easy on his body. "You're going to regret it when you're older!" she'd repeat to her son, age five right through age fifteen. Instead, Shockey saw Superman crash through a wall on television and tried to do the same thing himself. He did not compute caution and conditioned his body to handle just about any amount of pain.

"There's always going to be that weird person in the crowd, that person who—'Don't touch that electrician wire!'—and, *Bzzzzz!* You tell him don't touch it and he does. Like me. Trust me. 'Don't do it' and we're going to do it."

That's simply how life is in this pocket of Oklahoma. Thirty miles west of Ada is Pauls Valley, Oklahoma, aka the "noodling capital of the world." What's *noodling?* Shockey's glad you asked. He pulls up a video on his phone and shows locals, posted up in rivers and lakes, sticking their hands in the water to pull up fifty-pound catfish. "Barehanded!"

he says with pride. Shockey didn't noodle quite as much as his friends, but he did learn to always keep an eye out for beavers. They'll find you. They'll attack. "You've gotta get the fuck out. Infection and shit."

Shockey tightens his lips to imitate a beaver with his two front teeth.

"Look at their teeth! It looks like they've been smoking cigarettes for twenty years. Those things are mean. I should have never played football. I should have lost fingers."

Alas, football was the perfect outlet. Not only did Shockey lose a knuckle before his senior year at Ada, he also broke his wrist dunking a basketball. And yet neither slowed him down. He lifted weights with one hand, played on that fall, and learned that football was a perfectly legal way to unload anger. Instead of hurting people in the real world— and risk getting sued—he could do it for free on a football field.

Of course, he wanted to impress the hometown school, too. The University of Oklahoma wasn't interested in this 205-pounder without a true position, so he first attended Northeastern Oklahoma A&M with hopes of catching the attention of Sooners head coach Bob Stoops. This year of suffering at a junior college, he's certain, also made him. Shockey bulked up, caught 33 passes for 484 yards and 7 touchdowns, and compares day-to-day life here with country legend Johnny Cash playing at hole-in-the-wall bars across the country before hitting it big. One night, Shockey's team bus broke down at 2 a.m. Since the bus was so damn hot, he stepped outside to get some fresh air and a sandwich at the gas station. When Shockey went to sit on the ground, there were hundreds of ants scurrying in all directions so he instead decided to lay down on the flatbed of a nearby tractor trailer.

Shockey polished off his sandwich, shut his eyes and, all of a sudden, the eighteen-wheeler started moving. He woke up and leapt off just in time.

If Stoops would've offered him a scholarship that season—at any point—Shockey would've taken it in a heartbeat. Only after Shockey accepted an offer to attend the University of Miami did Stoops seem interested. Shockey told Stoops it was too late, then claims Stoops tried to dissuade him from going to Miami by saying he wouldn't get on the field with the Hurricanes.

As Aerosmith's "Dream On" plays at Yard House, the conversation rings in Shockey's head.

This marked the first major slight he repurposed as petroleum.

"He said, 'If you go to Miami, you're not going to play.' And that's not something you tell a high school kid. You wish him luck. But I understand. It's a recruiting process. It's a game. They have to play their cards. But that one backfired on him, you know? He's probably right 99 percent of the time. I take things personally."

Stoops was not alone. So many friends and family members told Shockey he ought to swallow his pride and stick close to home. Their words only fueled him more. That summer, he lifted weights twice a day and ran three times a day as temperatures crept into the nineties. Most workouts, he puked his guts out. Then, in 2000, Shockey headed to Coral Gables as the perfect personality for the perfect team.

It wasn't an accident.

"When you wake up in the morning and look in the mirror, you can't lie. You can lie to everyone else. When you look in the mirror, you can't lie about that shit."

Swagger was always simmering deep inside Shockey, but with one catch in one moment it all burst out of him—permanently—and his football career was never the same. In his fifth game of the 2000 season, The U hosted top-ranked Florida State and a knee sprain was rendering Shockey useless on the sideline. He could hardly run. Running back Jarrett Payton still remembers seeing Shockey bumming out and got right in his face. "You're *going* to make a play in this game," he told him. With the Hurricanes trailing, 24–20, and 1:37 remaining, head coach Butch Davis asked Shockey if he wanted to go back in. Shockey sucked it up and trotted back onto the field. All drive long, he kept telling quarterback Ken Dorsey he was open.

With forty-six seconds left, Dorsey went to him. Shockey burnt one of the best linebackers in the ACC (Brian Allen) on a seam route, caught the thirteen-yard touchdown, and held up a pair of number ones. The home crowd went berserk. This win officially dawned a new golden era for Miami.

When Shockey returned to the sideline, Payton felt chills. "I told you!" the son of Chicago Bears great Walter Payton screamed. Then, everything changed. That singular moment, Payton says, launched Shockey to "another stratosphere" on campus. He lost track of how many girls wanted to talk to Shockey that night in "the Grove." They threw themselves at him the rest of his college days. If Shockey was at your side, drinks at the Sandbar were on the house.

The morning of October 7, 2000, practically nobody knew who Jeremy Shockey was.

By night, he was a legend.

"He became a rock star, dude. Instant!" Payton says. "It was like, 'Holy cow. Dude, you're in a different lane.' Everywhere he went, he didn't have to pay for drinks. He didn't have to wait in lines. He was *the dude*. People looked at him different when we went into the tavern. There was a spotlight on top of him when he walked around. That wasn't why he was doing it, in my opinion. It wasn't for the spotlight. I think it gave him an opportunity to get out of his shell a little bit. To me, it never changed him in a bad way. It changed him in a way where some people get that stuff and say, 'Holy cow, this is way too much. Let me step back.' For him, he embraced it."

The more co-eds threw themselves at Shockey, the more weights he wanted to lift. The more intense he practiced. And you bet he was pissed the Bowl Championship Series sent Florida State, not Miami, to the national championship to face Oklahoma that season. He would've made Stoops pay. Into next season, he knew something special was brewing. At 5 a.m., during one summer practice, Shockey watched two of the team's heaviest linemen—Bryant McKinnie and Vernon Carey—run twenty sprints of 110 yards and told his coach that they already won the championship. There was no reason to play any games.

"He looks at me funny," Shockey says, "and I said, 'We already got this shit.' I knew it. We got on a fucking roll. It was a symphony. Like Mozart."

Those 2001 Hurricanes remain one of the best college football teams ever, going 12-0 with a laughable margin of victory of 32.9 points per win. They curb-stomped Nebraska in the national title by taking a 34–0 halftime lead and would go on to have *thirty-eight* players drafted into the NFL. Shockey's game was strikingly fresh. He climbed over linebackers, stiff-armed safeties, and kept defensive coordinators up all night. Payton is sure of that. The move he remembers most is Shockey's rapid *"bing-bing"* at the line of scrimmage. To shake off a defender, he'd shimmy his shoulders side to side and be gone.

Above all, however, Shockey brought a swag back to The U. After a seven-year lull, Miami was once again kicking ass and rubbing it in opponents' faces. The attitude was forged in practices, which were a million times more intense than the game. Brawls broke out daily among nineteen- and twenty-year-olds with Shockey almost always in the middle of the mayhem. After getting hit, he'd violently stick his arm into your chest, as if daring you to throw the first punch.

Take the bait? It was on.

To this day, Shockey cannot think of a better atmosphere for any football player at any level. Coaches never needed to scold players because they held themselves accountable for missing any practice, any meeting. They'd load pillow cases up with soap bars and beat each other up—"military shit." On the field, he scrapped most with future Hall of Fame safety Ed Reed and the late, great Sean Taylor. It never mattered if the pads were on. They'd hit. They'd throw punches.

"The amount of pain we put on each other in practice, no NFL fucking team did that. I played ten years, Ed Reed played fifteen. We're weathered. We're good. You can knock my ass out. We'd do seven-on-seven things, I'd catch a pass—no helmet—and Ed would come and fucking..."

Shockey smacks his hand again.

"All day long. We'd get upset. There would be a huge brawl. We'd all hug each other after and say, 'Love you.' At Miami, you'd punch somebody and break your hand. Back then, I felt like the Man of Steel."

Newcomers were typically mystified by the first fight they witnessed on this practice field because these were legit brawls with no apparent rules. Very quickly, they became calloused to throw down themselves, and the reason was Shockey. He set this tone. He, more than anyone, made this an emotionally charged atmosphere.

Linebacker Jonathan Vilma remembers fights literally popping off everywhere on the practice field.

"Jeremy," Vilma assures, "would be the one starting these fights. He got after it. I was like, 'Whoa.' I had never seen an offensive guy get so aggressive. It made the practices so tense. It made everything so lively. He was the catalyst."

This campus celebrity threw a few punches at those bars, too. Vilma was there. Vilma chooses not to delve into the details.

When it came to honing his craft, Shockey couldn't have asked for better defenders to face. At linebacker, Vilma and D. J. Williams both enjoyed long NFL careers. At safety, Reed and Taylor always lurked. All were large, explosive, dying to tattoo Shockey because Shockey could not stop running his mouth. During one inside-run drill, Payton remembers Shockey yapping...and yapping...and it got so bad that the entire defense started walking toward the tight end after the play. The offensive linemen had Shockey's back but weren't happy about it, Payton says, "because his mouth was not shutting up.

"I've never seen that before," Payton says. "Normally, it's one player coming after somebody. Not like the whole defense saying, 'We're coming to get you.'"

During another practice, a horrendous stench filled the huddle. "Dude!" Payton yelled. "Who smells like Bacardí Limón?" He eyeballed the other ten players. Shockey, drenched in sweat, was clearly dealing with a murderous hangover. He continued to party hard in Miami.

Payton won't reveal their wildest night out, either, in case his wife reads this book and asks, "What!?" But what blew his mind those two years was that Shockey's intensity never waned. He'd cut those fingertips off his gloves and go hard. Growing up, people always told Payton about his father's unparalleled work ethic. To him, Shockey had that same greatness inside because of the way he practiced.

The result was a blast to the past.

Like Ditka, Shockey would "run you over," Payton says. Like Ditka, Shockey was "fiery off the field." Whenever Payton watched clips from the 1960s of his father's head coach, the parallels were freaky. He once told Ditka that Shockey played just like him and Ditka agreed.

"The way Ditka changed the game, he set the tone," Payton says. "He was the blueprint, and Jeremy became the blueprint to this day and age, this era of football."

Head coach Larry Coker tried his best to convince Shockey to stick around for one more season, but Shockey knew he was ready. He declared for the NFL Draft and, at Miami's spectacle of a pro day, the man running his workout just so happened to be one of the greatest tight end coaches of all time.

A generation prior, Mike Pope helped mold Mark Bavaro into an All-Pro as the New York Giants tight ends coach. Granted, the personalities of these two tight ends could not have been more different. Anyone lucky enough to get a few words out of Bavaro, Pope says, would think he's a librarian. Yet, the man was also "unimaginably tough" and "cold-blooded." Bavaro famously plowed through seven San Francisco 49ers defenders on *Monday Night Football* in 1986. Nobody in the sport's history emasculated Ronnie Lott quite like him. Teammates called him "Rambo," and for good reason. One training camp, Bavaro refused to say a word about his ill-fitting cleats. Only when a trainer noticed something was wrong, did he ask him to take one off.

The cleat was full of blood.

Pope knew where the position was going. As someone who coached from 1970 to 2016, Pope likens the sport to the Grand Canyon eroding—"It's changing. You just can't see it"—and developed a sense for just how dangerous the tight end position could really be. Before returning to New York in 2000, Pope served as Ben Coates's position coach in New England for his 1995 and 1996 Pro Bowl seasons. The tight end could exploit what he dubbed the "Muggsy Bogues Rule." Get one of these six-foot-five monsters on a smaller defender and it's no contest.

In Shockey, he saw Bavaro. Only bigger. Only faster. At the tight end's 2002 pro day, Pope tried to break him. With NFL GMs and coaches and even ESPN cameras all on-site, Pope made Shockey lay on the ground and pop up quick to catch balls outside his body. All throws in all drills were cartoonishly high or low to the side, and Shockey was a machine. Shockey plucked them out of the sky with ease. Then, came the 40-yard dash. Shockey ran in the low 4.5s, and scouts stared down at their stopwatches in amazement, afraid to say what they registered out loud. At one point Giants GM Ernie Accorsi approached Pope and whispered in his ear to *slow down*. The Giants owned the fifteenth overall pick—Accorsi didn't want anyone else falling in love with the tight end.

On draft day, Accorsi shimmied up one pick to make sure he got his man.

Little did anyone in New York know that Jeremy Shockey was about to render the team cafeteria an octagon.

It's primitive, really.

He did not consciously seek this fight. Something deep down inside him just made this happen. Like Mike Ditka lambasting Ted Karras four decades prior, Shockey inherently needed to let his new teammates know exactly where he stood once he reported to training camp July 30, 2002.

One by one, per tradition, Giants rookies were putting on performances for the veterans at a team dinner. On demand, they were told to stand up on a chair and state their name, their school, their signing bonus, and sing their school fight song. There were also cringy renditions of Neil Diamond, Bobby Brown, New Edition. Tiki Barber's choice back in 1997? The Beatles' "Help!" If the vets didn't like what they heard, they'd force a rookie to sing "I'm a Little Teapot." In terms of hazing, this kindergarten routine was benign. Most rookies played along. Shockey, however, was not most rookies. And Shockey, this day, was in no mood for bullshit. Simply getting to camp in Albany after a five-day holdout was a scene straight out of *Planes, Trains and Automobiles.* The limo driver taking Shockey to camp had one eye and swerved all over the road. He couldn't find the dorms, so they pulled over to a truck station to grab a few hours of sleep.

By the time Shockey sat in that cafeteria, he hadn't eaten in twenty-four hours. He was starving.

Another Giants player happened to be on edge, too: linebacker Brandon Short. In the Giants' most recent practice, Short brawled with tight end Dan Campbell. He can vividly remember his temperament that day—fuming. Such was training camp life back then. Livelihoods are at stake. Tempers flare. It's quite literally, Short says, "one of the most testosterone-filled environments in the world." When I ask if any part of him was intimidated by this wild man from The U, he's insulted. Short grew up in the hardscrabble Harrison Village Housing Project in McKeesport, Pennsylvania, which had one of the highest murder rates in the country. He fought daily. "I'm from a tough fucking place."

A head-on collision was imminent and everyone was on hand. The entire coaching staff. Media members. Co-owners Wellington Mara and Robert Tisch. Even a group of Make-a-Wish kids in the cafeteria this day.

As Shockey chatted with his new quarterback, Kerry Collins, other rookies took turns singing their songs. Finally, defensive end Michael Strahan spoke up.

"KC, looks like you have a rook over there with you."

"Rook," Short chimed in, "you heard the man. Get up and sing."

Shockey informed Short he would not be singing. He wanted to eat.

"Did you hear the man?" Short replied. "You have to get up and sing a song."

"I'll sing it later."

Side conversations started to fade. The intensity in the room elevated and, for a moment, Short let it sink in that absolutely no rookie talks to him like this. He stood up, took one step toward Shockey, and a few teammates grabbed him.

This time, Short was more forceful. "Get up," he said, "and sing a song."

"What do you want me to do, B-Short?"

"Name, school, signing bonus, and sing a song. What's your name?"

"Jeremy Shockey."

"School?"

Shockey mumbled a half-hearted "... Miami ..." then a barely audible "$3.3 million" and, when Short said that players in the back could not hear him, Shockey offered a louder, "This one is for you, *B-Short.*"

That was one too many *B-Shorts.* Short attacked him. The two heavyweights threw furious haymakers at each other in an all-out rumble, crashing to the floor even as head coach Jim Fassel hurled his body into the fray. That day forward, players affectionately referred to Fassel as "Jeff Van Gundy," though Short points out that Fassel got roughed up more than the former New York Knicks coach did clinging to the leg of Alonzo Mourning.

Short describes the fight as something like "alligators" and "lions" rolling around, while Shockey claims Short was upset for one simple reason: "I was beating the shit out of him all minicamp." Barber, howling in laughter, believes a pointed "Fuck you!" from Shockey is what ignited the brawl.

Either way, Jeremy Shockey made one fact clear.

"After that," Barber says, "nobody fucked with Shockey. At all."

Vets instantly appreciated this volatility, especially the man who swapped punches with him. It took Short all of one day to get over the fight because he loved that this rookie never gave a damn. Fassel, too. He was borderline giddy talking about the fight to the press. Shockey? He didn't think much of it. This was any ol' Tuesday in his world. In truth, he wasn't too thrilled about getting drafted by the New York Giants. For a team that made the Super Bowl two years prior, the Giants' offense was, eh, boring. From afar, he always viewed the Giants as a "very bland" franchise. Mom told him not to worry, however, because he alone could change that.

She was right.

Six days after the "B-Short" melee, Shockey experienced a Florida State–like breakthrough as a pro. In the Hall of Fame Game, against the Houston Texans, he caught a short pass, ricocheted off Texans cornerback Jacoby Shepherd, sprinted past safety Matt Stevens—with Stevens tearing at his facemask—and then saved his best for last. Shockey punctuated a forty-eight-yard monster truck mash of a play by lowering a shoulder into safety Kevin Williams. After seeing this, Mara had flashbacks of Bavaro and told Pope he better add a few more tight ends like that.

The tight end's star rose overnight. Again. Accorsi compared Shockey to John Mackey, and teammates genuinely couldn't believe what they witnessed. While all football players are "a little wacky," Short says, offensive skill players tend to be more passive, more cerebral. This single hit gave the entire Giants offense a distinctive attitude.

"To say, 'We're not only going to score. We're going to *beat* you,'" Short says. "I really liked the guy. Maybe some people—because of his mentality—it rubbed them the wrong way. But for me, I loved it. The team needed what Shockey was delivering."

Adds Pope: "Every play with him was you vs. me."

Fassel wanted to replicate what Shockey built at Miami, too, so he'd even encourage Shockey to start fights at practice. Shockey says if there was a lull, if Fassel sensed energy was low, he would tell him to knock somebody out. Each time, of course, he lit right up. "We'd have fights and brawls and it'd be great!" he says. His new Ed Reed was safety

Shaun Williams. Again, it did not matter if the pads were on or not. They smacked each other, threw punches, gained mutual respect.

Nothing was too complicated to Shockey.

"Whatever position you play, you shouldn't take shit from anybody," Shockey says. "You're playing the demolition derby. That's what it is. The strong survive. What do they say in Fight Club? Four people go into a room and only one winner comes out. It's like that. I always tell people, it's like me being locked in a phone booth with somebody. I'm going to be the one coming out. It's like that on a football field. The same exact mentality.

"I take that shit very personally. I played with a defensive mentality. I definitely took out my anger on the opponents."

Within his own locker room, he took on a "prison mentality" because locker rooms are a weird place. It still baffles Shockey how the person right next to him would get cut, replaced, and suddenly there's a complete stranger getting butt-ass naked. There aren't many jobs like this in the world. But through it all, like inside the walls of a prison, one clear alpha that everyone respects emerges. He became that force of nature—Day 1, Dinner 1—because he was so fueled by slights.

Slights always sparked that anger.

Anger that could be released, in all its grandeur, at the tight end position.

His list of victims is long. When David Gibson is reached via email to relive his encounter with Shockey, the orthopedic sales rep was actually in surgery. "Son of a bitch," he told himself. "Shockey!? I have to talk about this guy?" The events of December 22, 2002, have a way of haunting him still. At work, coworkers bring it up. At home, his kids recently played the clip on YouTube for friends. As the legend goes, in the lead-up to the Colts' game against the Giants, Gibson was asked by the local media about the rookie sensation and said he wasn't treating this game any differently. Then came the money quote: "He's no Tony Gonzalez, he's just another player to me."

Those words made their way into an *Indianapolis Star* headline, and

Barber again needed to prod Shockey. He and Collins handed the tight end a copy of the sports section, and Shockey's reaction? Not quite what you'd expect. There was no smoke emanating from his ears. Shockey wasn't fuming at all. He was calm. Creepy calm. Filing it away in the back of his mind. "Which," Barber adds, "is almost worst."

A Colts teammate also handed a copy of the newspaper that Sunday morning to Gibson. He believed his comment was sensationalized but, make no mistake, he certainly wanted to smash Shockey.

"I was tired of his arrogance," Gibson says.

He always viewed himself as a big hitter, too. He enjoyed inflicting pain. This was also a massively important season for Gibson. After backing up John Lynch in Tampa Bay, he requested a trade three weeks in to get some game tape with a second contract looming. Early in this showdown, he even nailed Shockey on a seam route to force an incomplete pass and said a few words he cannot repeat. Basically, he concedes, it was down the lines of: "MF'er, I'm going to be here all day!" Not long after, his world was rocked. At the start of the second quarter, with the Giants leading 3–0, Shockey caught a screen pass from Collins, turned upfield, and spotted No. 26 in his vision. He then lowered the crown of his helmet and, as the tight end poetically puts it, "fucking hammered him." Gibson's arms flailed helplessly as Shockey thundered through him for an extra thirteen yards. The blow sparked a 44–27 blowout win, setting up a win-and-in Week 17 scenario for the Giants.

Gibson credits Giants offensive coordinator Sean Payton for this gem of a play design that got Shockey stampeding downhill. One Colts cornerback also took on a block with the wrong shoulder, which blinded Gibson's vision. Shockey arrived and it was too late. Gibson insists he actually did not feel a thing and didn't realize how bad this was until his wife told him over dinner that it looked horrible.

"It looked like I was trying to grab every ounce of fiber I could to get him on the ground after he trucked me," Gibson says. "Essentially, I was hoping I'd grab on to his legs and let him fall over top of me. Well, I wasn't as low as I should've been and, yeah."

ESPN replayed the collision many times over with the play defining Shockey's historic rookie season. And no, Gibson never did get that coveted second contract with the Colts. He believes this one play was a factor, too. He played one more season in Tampa and was done.

"One mistake can haunt you for the rest of your life," he says. "When your career ends in the NFL, it's tough. It's like a death. So, it definitely took me a while to get over that and try to find a new passion in life. It happens. You've got a fifty-fifty shot. Kill or be killed."

Personal feuds were everlasting. The next week, with a playoff berth at stake, Shockey's leaping touchdown grab over Philadelphia Eagles safety Brian Dawkins was the game-winner. The two tumbled to the ground and a nodding, smiling Shockey told the future Hall of Famer, "I got you this time!" This score was revenge for a teammate. Wide receiver Ike Hilliard's season ended with a Dawkins cheap shot earlier in the season. Ahead of the ensuing wild card matchup at Candlestick Park, 49ers linebacker Julian Peterson said on a conference call with Giants beat writers that, OK, Shockey has a lot of confidence but that it also hurts him. "He'll get frustrated," Peterson said, "and then blow a couple of plays." In the second quarter, Shockey caught a pass at the 9-yard line and was drilled by safety Zack Bronson who, of course, was instead trampled himself. Shockey spun free. Shockey eyed Peterson at the goal line. And rather than score an easy touchdown, he entered a new address into his internal GPS to totally change course and lower his head into Peterson.

Shockey was stopped short of the goal line, but have no fear. Two snaps later, he caught a touchdown.

Things would take a turn for the worst. That day the Giants also suffered what was then the second-worst postseason collapse of all-time. At one point, Shockey lobbed a cup of ice into the stands without looking and the ice struck two kids. Shockey apologized to the family in the locker room afterward. Yet even after signing a football for the kids—and sensing that the family had accepted his apology—the father of the kids ripped him in the press.

That was why Shockey later told *Sports Illustrated* he'd "do it all over again" and that he feels sorry those kids had to be raised by a father like that.

From the cafeteria brawl in July to the airborne ice in January, this hell-raising tight end made it abundantly clear in Year 1 that nobody would tell him what to do or what to say. New York City loved him for it. To this day, people tell Shockey that he's the reason they became Giants fans. He was Reality TV before Reality TV—you never knew what he'd do or say next. The hair. The snarl. The tattoos. Nobody looked like him, either. When the Twin Towers were attacked on September 11, 2001, Shockey told himself that if he ever got a tattoo, it'd be America themed. New York drafted him, and it only made sense to get a bald eagle draped in the American flag on his right bicep. The art took twenty-one hours over three days to complete. Shockey always cherished this country's freedom, too, another reason he never thought twice about spouting off. During training camp in 2006, Shockey called head coach Tom Coughlin an asshole to the press. When one teammate asked Shockey, point-blank, why he said that, Shockey didn't miss a beat.

"Freedom of speech. First Amendment. I pay my taxes."

And he walked away.

Says Short: "We were laughing like, 'This dude's crazy.' "

Crazy enough to reveal his sexual fantasy to a magazine. Crazy enough to interrupt a teammate's interview session after a blowout loss in Seattle to scream, "We were outplayed and outcoached. Write that down." Nothing was off-limits. He blurred private and public behavior like nobody before him, and everyone got drunk on his authenticity. To many, he was beloved. Shockey's jersey sales ranked number one in the NFL. A teen from Western New York named Rob Gronkowski even wrote him a letter. To critics, he was a carnival act. But even in this pre-Twitter age, both groups could not look away. Shockey agrees he probably did blaze a trail of individualism in the NFL and, for a moment, wishes social media existed then.

He then pauses and scrunches his face as if he just gnawed on those limes. "No, I don't wish that. That's all fake."

He partied with fellow bachelor Derek Jeter all the time and threw drinks back with New York Yankees pitcher David Wells. New York tabloids linked him to a string of actresses and models. To the outsider, it might've seemed like Shockey was unhinged. All this, however, masked the reality that Jeremy Shockey was uniquely obsessed with the sport.

He wasn't married. He didn't even have a girlfriend. His day-to-day life was extremely regimented. During a game week, he woke up at 5 a.m., stayed at the facility until 5 p.m., and was usually in bed by 8:30. He'd refuse to give himself more than those three hours each day. The only night he'd go out during the season was Monday—and only if he wasn't training hard on that off Tuesday. "Seriously," he says. "Everyone called me a hermit. I had a military mentality." Shockey loved studying the science of recovery to take care of a body he was treating like a piñata. He had regular acupuncture sessions and helped popularize hyperbaric chambers in the NFL.

Even when he did drink, guilt tended to seep into his conscience. It was common for a drunk Shockey to bang out seventy-five to one hundred push-ups at 3 a.m. because, to him, this was no different from Ed Reed doing push-ups at Miami after dropping an interception. He needed to punish himself. No wonder he took it another level when one bid for revenge failed. Against the Dallas Cowboys, Shockey badly wanted to make Jerry Jones pay for drafting safety Roy Williams when the owner told him he'd be their pick at eighth overall. He played poorly in a Giants win. So after everyone else headed home, Shockey hotrouted to the weight room to squat four hundred pounds.

This became a common postgame sight and why Barber calls him a "maniac" and "a foxhole guy." And why Pope describes the football field as Shockey's personal "glory land," adding that the tight end flatly had trouble understanding why others weren't wound as tightly as him. He lived hard. He worked harder. The logic was simple to Shockey: "I'm here to win fucking games and go on my way. I'm not here to do all the extra shit. I'm not here to get along with the media. I'm not here to get along with teammates that don't want to win."

Shockey could not understand how teammates balanced professional football with a family life.

Kids? Marriage? None of this made sense to him.

"Because I gave all my shit to football. I'm thinking in my mind, because I'm so selfish, I'm like, I hear them on the phone talking about their wife, cheating on their wife, and I hear about their shit and their kids and I'm thinking if they didn't have that shit, how good would they be? If you didn't have that bullshit, imagine how good you'd be."

Once, Shockey was blunt with running back Reggie Bush when he later played for the New Orleans Saints. He told Bush that he'd be in the Hall of Fame if he wasn't dating Kim Kardashian. Just because Shockey was spotted with a model in NYC doesn't mean the two were spending quality time together. The toast of the city says he never actually dated anyone those six seasons. That would've served as a 5 mph construction zone along his frenetic warpath to Sundays.

Sex with a model in NYC was one thing, he assures. Dating is quite another.

"I didn't go to her house one time," he says of one relationship. "It was very simple: Play football. Don't have any of the headaches. It makes life very simple. I love kids. But you see it with a lot with guys out of college. They have a baby mama and have to pay, pay, pay. If they didn't have this problem, how successful would they be? . . . I was good at getting girls. Ain't nobody sleeping over and I ain't going to your house. It ain't like that. Sorry.

"I just feel like I had to be responsible for the whole locker room. So if I'm worried about this or a girl I got pregnant, how the fuck am I going to remember my plays? It's impossible. Like I said, it was something that was always instilled in me. When I was fourteen, my mom gave me a box of condoms and said if I wanted to have sex to use a condom. At fourteen! So, it's very common sense."

There was no trapping Shockey into a windfall. Over the years, a couple of women tried tricking him into child support by claiming they were pregnant when he clearly wasn't the father.

Those three free hours per day were spent taking care of his body because Shockey was putting himself through Ditka Era punishment. The second Shockey learns what Gonzalez thinks about his play style, he flashes the exact thin smile Barber describes. The comment is innocent and truthful: Gonzalez believes Shockey could've lasted a hell of a lot longer in the NFL if he wasn't trying to demolish opponents all the time. While harmless, the comment still gets lodged into Shockey's brain...and he refuses to let it go. He stores it and sporadically brings it up throughout our conversation.

When it comes to blocking, he pokes fun at Gonzalez and says those KC and Atlanta offenses ran away from him. He claims it was never his goal to play fifteen years, adding that he would've played longer if he didn't have any Super Bowl rings. He brings up the fact that Atlanta went to the Super Bowl *after* Gonzalez retired and adds that Gonzalez "never sniffed a championship ring."

"So, I don't know why you play. I love the game but if I'm not winning any games, if I'm not going to the fucking championship, I don't give a shit. All the Pro Bowls. All the money I make. I know it's all about timing but, fuck, winners are winners. From college to the pros and even high school. I can't imagine not being competitive."

Most of all, he stands by his violence. He says that this is the way he was raised while Gonzalez, "being a basketball guy," was not.

Whereas Gonzalez understandably couldn't believe one coach had him doing blocking drills after practice, Shockey made a point to lock horns with Strahan during pregame hitting drills. "Hey, big boy," he'd taunt with a snarl.

"I had to work at that shit every day. The people who already have it, who are already that fast and that big and that strong, they usually don't make it. Strahan, that's how I learned my blocking. It took a lot of him beating me, me being upset, and me whacking him. Cheap-shotting him! The next thing you know, he's upset. It's a big brawl."

As a receiver, Gonzalez left Shockey in the dust, but Barber also eclipsed 1,200 rushing yards each of the five years he played with the tight end. In 2004 and 2005, he went over 2,000 total scrimmage yards. Barber knows Shockey's presence was a major factor why, too. When Shockey flexed out, he lured a linebacker with him. Then, when Shockey was asked to block? He headhunted.

Linebacker. Defensive end. *Defensive tackle.* It did not matter. Shockey would blindly beeline toward his assignment.

"Every. Single. Play. That's why I loved the dude, man," Barber says. "He was such a great athlete but he was physical! A lot of these tight ends now are basically wide receivers. Jeremy Shockey would earhole a 280-pound D-Lineman if you asked him to, and would not be afraid to scrap it with him. He was old school."

Adds Short: "He took it beyond just trying to catch passes and just trying to block. He wanted you to know that he was better than you. He made a point to kick your ass just because you were lined up on the other side."

In breaking others, he broke himself. Gonzalez wasn't wrong. Gibson wasn't wrong, either. Shockey made four Pro Bowls but never parlayed a 74-catch, 894-yard rookie season into the Canton-bound career many predicted because he showed zero care for his own physical well-being. He never played a full season. The broken sternum comes to mind first and, yes, he sticks a finger right in your xiphoid process to explain where he got drilled against the Seattle Seahawks. It felt like his heart fell right out of his chest.

Countless games, his feet were plastered with blisters by the end of the first quarter and his cleats filled with blood. When Shockey broke his ribs, it hurt every time he sneezed. He suffered concussions. A sports hernia. Turf toe. Every body part you can think of. He's not hurting nearly as bad as Ben Coates, but there are mornings Shockey wakes up and wonders, "What is this?"

He can't help himself.

"Tony never got hurt, did he? That fucking guy must pray more than me."

Before games, Shockey loaded up on Toradol and, for a brief period, a pill called Vioxx. Not many people know about this anti-inflammatory drug because it was pulled off the market in 2004. The medical journal *Lancet* estimated that 88,000 Americans had heart attacks from taking Vioxx, with 38,000 of them dying. Here, Shockey reenacts his NFL mornings, first pretending to be sprawled out in bed. Stiffening up, he says he felt like "Mr. Freeze." Once he could get out of bed, the pain was unimaginable. Shockey gingerly lifts himself off the bar stool and tiptoes around Yard House. Those first three, four steps, Shockey felt like his body would completely shatter.

Shockey certainly justified the existence of public relations officials associated with the New York Giants. Yet, Wellington Mara always understood that this, right here, was the real Jeremy Shockey. The warrior who could hardly get out of bed and, without blinking, lived like there was no tomorrow the very next game. At practice, Mara would watch on from his sideline chair and, afterward, "cattle prod" Shockey for dropping a pass. Shockey loved it. In the middle of an embarrassing 45–7 loss to the Saints in 2003—when Shockey was injured, goofing off on the sidelines—Mara came right down to reprimand him in front of teammates. Barber couldn't believe the sight, the raw disappointment in Mara's face. This looked like a father scolding his son.

The bond was so special that before Mara died in 2005, the owner's family requested for Shockey to see him in person. Right there in a packed room of kids and grandkids was the tattooed loose cannon from Ada. Two years later, on December 16, 2007, Shockey's career in New York effectively ended when wide receiver Amani Toomer fell into him at the end of a running play. Shockey broke his left fibula and injured his ankle. Thinking back to that night, his temper boils once more. He doesn't believe Toomer had any malicious intent, but Toomer wasn't exactly apologetic.

"I'm sitting there in the motherfucking training room, and he comes up to me and says, 'That was your leg I fell on?' I'm thinking in my mind, 'Calm yourself, Jeremy. Don't fucking grab him and fuck him up.' He took a block, it was a run play. And it is what it is. He was lazy. He didn't do his job correctly and he broke my leg. He's a Michigan guy. I'd never come up to a guy and say, 'Hey! Is that your leg I broke?' It's like the old Rodney Dangerfield. 'Your boat scratched my anchor!' I was pissed off."

Those 2007 Giants went on to shock the undefeated New England Patriots in the Super Bowl, at which point the relationship between Shockey and the Giants was broken beyond repair. John Mara wasn't the same as his father, Shockey says, and gone was the GM (Accorsi) who drafted him. Shockey was reportedly upset that the team would not let him watch the Super Bowl from the sideline in crutches and, as the game neared, he vacillated on whether or not to attend. When he decided to go, he paid his own way to the game. Things only got weirder when Shockey was the lone no-show at the Super Bowl parade and both the White House and ring ceremonies.

He's proud of that ring and the lifetime of sweat that went into it. The reason it was so hard for him to attend the Super Bowl was that Shockey had a staph infection in his lower leg.

After the game, from a wheelchair, he went straight to Dallas for another surgery.

"I damn near lost my fucking leg. Did I tell the media that? No. It's none of their business. The media didn't know that. The Giants didn't even know that. It's my body. It's not theirs."

By "leg," he specifies that it was the foot area, calling this a "ski boot break." He never went public with how close he was to losing his foot, either, because he wanted zero sympathy. ("I'm good on the sob stories.") Into that 2008 off-season, Shockey was depressed. He loathed the fact that most everyone was labeling him jaded and jealous. ("Being jealous of my teammates? I love that ring. Are you kidding me? I put in six hard years for that fucking ring.") At twenty-two years old, he didn't mind the paparazzi following him. The Giants hired a security detail for Shockey and he hired one himself. But no longer did he bask in that

NYC spotlight. There was no way he could play one more down for the Giants.

The pressure was too much. The messy exit clearly still bothers him.

"Shit, what else could I have done? I guess I could've made six all-star games in six years but I only made four. I tried my best. New York, I love the city, I love the people, I love the sports fans. But it was different. When you put yourself on that pedestal and try to do good and try to treat people right—but they build you up just to kick you off?—it's like, 'Motherfucker. You built me up just to write a terrible story about me.'"

If the Giants weren't going to trade him, Shockey was leaning toward retiring for a season to let his body and mind heal. He's still convinced it wouldn't have gotten this bad if Wellington Mara were still alive. The Giants did eventually deal Shockey to the New Orleans Saints in July for second- and fifth-round draft picks. He had one more sweet moment of redemption in him, too. Reunited with Sean Payton, he won another Super Bowl. This time, Shockey played and caught the go-ahead touchdown in the fourth quarter of a 31–17 triumph over the Indianapolis Colts.

No paparazzi stalked him in New Orleans. He hit it off with guys like offensive guard Jahri Evans and enjoyed himself on Bourbon Street in peace. The stress level in the Big Easy was considerably lower. About the only incident Evans can think of is when an unconscious Shockey was carted away due to dehydration at the Rehab Pool Party in Las Vegas. A slew of Saints players were present—it was scary. Otherwise, it was the same Shockey. He called for the ball, but Drew Brees was running such a well-oiled machine that nothing Shockey said caused any drama.

As an Eagles fan growing up, Evans saw Shockey go full heel tormenting his team. And he loved it. He started talking trash himself on the offensive line.

"He was a gladiator," Evans says. "What people see is what they really get with Shock. He didn't allow people to disrespect him."

No amount of backlash ever changed Shockey. Vilma loved him in Miami and, from afar, thought his old college teammate got a bad rap in New York simply because he was outspoken. When the two reconnected as teammates in 2009, he was thrilled. Shockey wasted no time asserting his "prison mentality," too. When the Saints held joint practices with the Houston Texans in 2009, Vilma heard a raucous cry on a separate practice field—"Rar-rar-rar! Break it up! *Boom! Boom! Boom!*" he relives—and, of course, Shockey was the one who incited the riot. After an incomplete pass, Shockey said something, linebacker DeMeco Ryans shoved him, Shockey shoved him back, and the two threw punches on their way to the ground.

This felt like being back in Coral Gables. In his best Shockey impression, Vilma assures this all started with the tight end yelling, "Man, these guys can't cover me, man! These guys suck!"

Too often, football is made out to be quantum physics when it's more like dodgeball in a high school phys ed class. At its core, the sport is ultra-primitive. It's a tough game played by tough people and, more than any tight end since Ditka, Shockey understood this. No wonder those Miami coaches let fights break out and, on to New York, Jim Fassel would tell him to start a fire. His energy was contagious. It'd come in a package of F-bombs and flags and a stench of liquor, but your entire team would be nastier.

"You want those types of guys on offense," Vilma says, "because if you're in the heat of battle, who are you going to go to? Who's going to set the tone and fight back?"

The emergence of another player from Miami ended Shockey's Saints career after three seasons. In 2010 third-round pick Jimmy Graham, a dual-sport player in college, Payton saw the potential for his own Tony Gonzalez. Payton told Shockey that Bill Parcells told him this was the best pick in the draft, and Shockey confirms that Parcells was absolutely right.

Practically no one will remember that Shockey spent the 2011 season with the Carolina Panthers.

With one major exception.

This NFL career ended with one much different scene in the team cafeteria.

Back at the Panthers' stadium during training camp, Ben Hartsock was eating pork tenderloin when, suddenly, he started choking. Time slowed down. First, he thought drinking water would be a swell idea—*Plunge it like a plunger!* he told himself. That only made it worse. Hartsock started walking to the bathroom before realizing nobody would be in there to help if he collapsed. Luckily, he made a weird sound that grabbed everyone's attention. Hartsock gave the thirty or so teammates in the cafeteria a universal "I'm choking" signal and, first, a three-hundred-pound defensive lineman came to the rescue. Well, not exactly. Hartsock describes this as the worst Heimlich maneuver attempt in human history. "It felt," Hartsock says, "like he was spooning me. As if you were doing the Heimlich in a way to not offend somebody."

That's when Shockey coolly walked over and signaled thumbs-up or thumbs-down. With a thumbs-down, Hartsock let him know this was not working. Shockey brushed that D-Lineman aside.

"Just shimmies him out of the way," Hartsock says, "and gives me one big hammer drive. One big 'Boom!' That was it. It was over. I'm fine. Red-faced. Breathing. Trying to status-check everything. And Shockey, just as casually as he approached, casually sits back down and acts like he does this two or three times a week."

Right then is when the athletic trainers sprinted in with a defibrillator and tracheotomy kit. If Shockey hadn't saved the day, they would've cut Hartsock's throat open and shocked him back to life. Hartsock wasn't sure what to buy the man who has it all as a thank-you gift. He was done having kids but told him that if he did have a child, Shockey could name the baby. Hartsock settled on the most expensive bottle of Johnnie Walker he could find.

Damn right he loved everything Shockey represented. This was "Gronkowski 1.0."

"He absolutely showed up to practice sometimes, like, 'Whoa. Shock, rough night?' But when the helmet went on, he was ready," Hartsock says. "He knew the playbook, and the guy played his balls off. He sold out for the team. Shockey was a guy who could live the *Playboy* lifestyle and still be a Pro Bowl–caliber player, and an awesome teammate. He played with his heart and soul and laid it all out there. Football players have a great ability to see through BS. Football players can smell fake a mile away, and Jeremy Shockey was absolutely authentic. He owned it."

The kid who got this whole football thing started by using his fists to fight Ed Reed at The U ended it balling those fists up to save lives.

After that 2011 season, he was done.

He got his rings. He didn't need the money. But, in March 2012, it sure seemed like Warren Sapp assassinated his character in labeling Shockey the "snitch" in the Saints' Bountygate scandal. No team signed Shockey that off-season but, once more, Shockey took the high road. Nine years later, I bring up Sapp, and Shockey points out that it wasn't long after this accusation that Sapp was caught with a prostitute and lost his job at NFL Network. He never saw a reason to sue Sapp for defamation because Sapp had no money. That same year, Sapp filed for Chapter 7 bankruptcy and, according to the *Tampa Bay Times*, had only $826.04 in his checking account and $339.31 in his savings account.

"What am I going to take? His sneakers?" Shockey says. "I feel bad for him. I'd say all kinds of crazy stuff, too, if I didn't have any money left. Actually, I would not. I'd get a job like a normal person."

Right here is Shockey's true contribution to the Great American Tight End: unabashed authenticity. When any tight end—hell, any NFL player—has the guts to spout off today, they undoubtedly have Shockey to thank. He's no chameleon. He doesn't tweak his language for a target audience or consult with handlers. Teammate. Coach. Book writer. Anyone could be sitting right here on this bar stool and he'd tell the same story, slap the same thigh, and order another round of drinks. Nobody lights up a room like him. When the Giants had a Super Bowl reunion a few years ago, Shockey headed right to his old coach, Mike Pope. At Pope's side was his wife, who also happens to be twenty years younger and, in Pope's words, looks like a runway model.

Shockey took one look at her, then at his coach, then at her again.

"Ms. Pope," he said, "what are you doing with that old man there? You need to come with me. You're too young for him."

The room went dead quiet and Shockey wrapped Pope in a bear hug.

"Well," he told him, "I gave it my shot!"

As passionate as he was with football, there's no amount of money a network could pay Shockey to talk about football. If anything, he'd like to broadcast a completely different sport because it'd be fun. Fame means nothing to him. He doesn't need to massage a public image to feel warm and fuzzy inside. Instead, Shockey is bringing his prison mentality to the business world. He makes more money in real estate and investing than he ever did playing football. When a buddy invested $50K in one crypto company, Shockey put $50K in with him. In a three-month span, the stock skyrocketed 200 percent. When he took over one person's loan and could tell a banker was full of BS, he cussed him out like this was an NFL Sunday.

"I still don't take shit from people," Shockey says. "I'm Irish, dude. I'm going to fuck their whole family generation for the next one hundred years. The Irish curse."

Speaking of Ireland, he's been there six or seven times. Once at the Guinness factory, he claims he and his buddy drank forty beers. Each. He's still drinking, still jet-setting the world at warp speed and still loving every second of it while—he kindly points out—never getting arrested. That's the way he was raised. Mom would've never bailed him out.

Shockey takes a quick look at his phone and pops upright. It's time to run. He needs a haircut.

He slides those shades back on, says bye with a dap that's more of a bear hug, and hustles off to his mode of transportation outside: a scooter.

"Don't make fun of me!"

And just like that, poof, Shockey is gone.

Chapter 11

"BE WHERE YOUR FEET ARE"

The surge smack-dab in the middle of this career is striking. In 2007, Greg Olsen was drafted in the first round by the Chicago Bears. He headed to this position's holy lands, where the shadow of Mike Ditka lingers more as an eternal overcast over Soldier Field. Straight out of The U, Olsen was good as a young pro. Not great. Like every tight end who had played for the Bears since Ditka departed.

The front office shipped Olsen off to the Carolina Panthers for a third-round pick in 2011.

His first half decade in the pros, Olsen averaged 48 receptions for 504 yards per season.

What came next was one of the best five-year runs in tight end history. With the Carolina Panthers, from 2012 to 2016, Olsen's production doubled to an average of 77 receptions for 969 yards. He became the first tight end ever to string together three straight thousand-yard seasons and was the go-to guy on a team that went 15-1 and reached the Super Bowl.

None of this was an accident.

Because forget football. Everything in his *life* changed in May 2012, when Olsen and his wife, Kara, headed in for a routine sonogram at the eighteen-week mark of her pregnancy. They were having twins and, this day, planned to learn the gender of their babies. Never did they expect to get news like this: their son, T. J., had hypoplastic left heart syndrome, a congenital defect that limits blood flow to the heart. That

October, T. J. was born with one side of his heart severely underdeveloped, and he'd undergo three open-heart surgeries before the age of three. Hospital visits, surgeries, and real life now clashed with practices, film sessions, and a game. Yet after T. J. was born—and the sleepless nights mounted—Greg Olsen's football career skyrocketed.

"It's not a coincidence," Olsen says. "You draw a lot of perspective from those tough times. You draw a lot of resiliency and toughness and ability to compartmentalize and focus on what's important in the moment. I always look back at that run of my career and everything we had going on—on the field and off the field—and those things fed each other."

These days, as a retiree, Dad's voice is heard each Sunday. As a broadcaster, he's a natural because (like Iron Mike) Olsen displays a knack for narrating the sport with an endearing bluntness. He dissects its complexities in a digestible way. This also is no coincidence because tight ends, by nature, relate to the everyday American. They have, as Mark Bruener said, embraced the suck. They have, as Tony Gonzalez said, been forced to grow emotionally. All in the name of chasing a dream.

That's why the reverse is also true: Americans can relate to tight ends.

It's difficult for the factory worker to comprehend what Tom Brady is possibly thinking at the line of scrimmage as safeties and corners try to disguise a coverage. Or how Randy Moss high-pointed a bomb in the middle of three defenders. Or the amount of centrifugal force it takes for Aaron Donald to humiliate the 320-pounder in front of him. We cannot begin to relate to such interstellar feats of body and mind. But that everyday fan glued to the NFL all Sunday who then hears an alarm at 6 a.m. the next morning to change diapers, put a pot of coffee on, take a shower, get dressed, and head to work? This fan can see themselves in the tight end who cradles a short pass and fights for extra yardage. For some, it's conscious. For many, it's likely subconscious. But Olsen knows that people appreciate "the work, the grind, the toughness" that goes into playing the tight end position.

And that is what then makes the electrifying play so much sweeter. The tight end is still capable of being the single most entertaining player on the field any given moment.

To Olsen, this was a calling. A running back through his youth, he sprouted to six foot four as a sophomore. His father, the head coach at Wayne Hills High in New Jersey, realized there wasn't a future for this tall, skinny kid at running back. Nor was he a burner. So, Chris Olsen shifted his boy to tight end. With Dad as coach and his older brother at quarterback, Greg lived every teenager's high school dream. Neither father nor son will forget the hug they shared walking off the field as state champs. Greg initially followed his brother, Christian, to Notre Dame but transferred to Miami before playing a down. He saw what Jeremy Shockey was doing in Coral Gables and believed a new genus of tight end was propagating. From Miami to Chicago to Charlotte, what Olsen loved most about this position was its ubiquity. He was forced to tap into different parts of a brain that could never call timeout. Olsen would join the linemen for their run installs during the week…before cracking his knuckles and accruing a constellation of bruises on Sunday. He'd saddle up with the wide receivers the same week to make tweaks to the route tree based on specific matchups… before then juking a linebacker at the top of his route to make a key third-down catch.

"I embraced that challenge," Olsen says. "Not only physically, but mentally."

General manager Marty Hurney orchestrated the trade for Olsen during training camp of the 2011 season. The Panthers, with new head coach Ron Rivera, had an organizational plan to utilize Olsen in ways that the Bears did not. By then, offensive coordinator Rob Chudzinski had cemented his status as one of the position's greatest teachers after coaching Bubba Franks, Jeremy Shockey, and Kellen Winslow Jr. in Miami and then Antonio Gates in San Diego. After facing Gates every day in practice as the team's defensive coordinator, Rivera understood a six-foot-five weapon like Olsen could both pretzel defensive schemes into knots and make life a lot easier for rookie Cam Newton. Carolina had already signed Shockey, so two from The U seemed better than one.

There was no wasted time. Right away, Olsen's "magnetic personality" stood out to Rivera. How he was shockingly blunt. How no topic was off-limits with his new teammates. The first three weeks, backup tight end Ben Hartsock found Olsen too in-your-face, too New Jersey. "My Midwestern delicacies," he says, "were like, 'Why is this guy so abrasive?'" Once he was able to bust through Olsen's thick outer shell, Hartsock found him to be one of the most loyal teammates ever. Through his ten seasons with five teams, Hartsock never saw anybody this side of Peyton Manning who cared about football as much as Olsen. That has always been what Rivera looks for in the players he scouts. He researches what their parents did for a living. *Were they in the military? Were they teachers? Was there a coach in the household?* The fact that Olsen's father coached four decades told him this was most certainly a veteran who could help his rookie quarterback.

It's hard to imagine how the 2011 Panthers offense could've functioned without Olsen, too.

Inside the huddle, whenever Newton started to call a play, he wasn't able to verbalize Chudzinski's wordy play calls. He stumbled and bumbled and hit every second or third word. "And then," Hartsock says, "we'd all look at Greg and he'd fill in the cracks. It was a regular occurrence. You'd get the first pass at it with Cam, and then Greg would give the last little bit. In unison, we'd all look at Cam and then look over to Greg." Once a play was called and the ball was snapped—like Ben Coates did for his first overall pick of a QB—Olsen was an instant security blanket for Newton.

The quarterback struggled calling the plays but knew where to find his big tight end.

"And Greg," Rivera adds, "would always be there."

Olsen became the pied piper for this team on the rise, the veteran who took groups of players out to dinner the night before games and always picked up the tab. He didn't plop a credit card down as a flex. Teammates could tell that he genuinely wanted to spend a couple of hours getting to know them.

He loved to talk, too. Like, a lot. On the team flight home from games, Olsen would migrate from the back of the airplane to the front. Win or lose, his adrenaline pumped too fast to sleep. Let alone relax. Rivera remembers one such flight in 2012 vividly. The Panthers had just beaten the Chargers to improve to 5-9, and the coach's wife actually boarded this massive DC-10 with the team for the four-and-a-half-hour flight east. The Riveras sat in the very front of the plane, with Olsen seated in the very back. After a while, Stephanie Rivera couldn't hold it in any longer.

"I keep hearing the same voice," she said. "From the back of the plane. Someone's been talking for three hours."

"It's Greg," Rivera said. "Don't worry. It'll get louder. As the players fall asleep, Greg just moves up to the next guy to talk to."

By the time the plane touched down in Charlotte, Olsen had reached their row. Nobody is shocked that Olsen's star is rising on television.

"Greg is an orator," Rivera says. "He loves to tell stories. He can't help himself. From the time we took off to the time we landed, Greg never stopped talking. Football. Current events. Life. He had an ability to intermingle with whatever group it was."

To cultivate real relationships with teammates, Olsen and the offensive line started "Fellowship Thursdays." Right after practice, Panthers players would meet up to bare their feelings. Absolutely nothing was off-limits. Political, social, football. You could vent on any issue without anyone in the room taking anything personal or any words in the room getting out. Players felt like they could cleanse their souls. And considering an NFL locker room consists of every type of player from every type of background—with testosterone at maximum capacity—these sessions helped shatter any lingering tension. The result was organic team chemistry that fueled four playoff appearances in five years.

The quarterbacks started coming, then defensive players. Even Rivera and one of the strength coaches joined in. It was cathartic for all.

"You would get in," Rivera says, "and you could gripe about anything."

T. J. and Talbot Olsen were born on October 9, 2012, at Levine Children's Hospital in Charlotte, North Carolina, with Mom and Dad fully aware of the challenges ahead. From the beginning, Greg and Kara chose to let the world in on their struggles. They started the "HEARTest Yard" fund at Levine to help families experiencing the same pain and, when T. J. turned two, they sat side by side for a tear-jerking interview. At one point, Fox's Jen Hale asked Kara where she drew her strength. She credited her husband because not one day went by that Greg, she said, didn't "look at the positive in every situation." They had no clue how long T. J. could survive with half of a heart then. Greg vowed to enjoy every day they had with him because they didn't know what tomorrow would bring. To this day, Olsen's fortitude amazes Rivera. They sat down for several talks through the hard times. Rivera repeated a line he heard from Dr. Kevin Elko, a mindset coach who has consulted with several NFL teams: "Be where your feet are." Whenever he needed to be with his son, Rivera told him to get out of the facility, to not even think about football at all.

What shocked everyone was how Greg Olsen locked in when it was time to practice. To say he compartmentalized doesn't do his performance justice. Olsen's game reached a new level that 2012 season. "God, how does he do it?" Rivera asked himself. That edgy New Jersey native wasn't afraid to show his vulnerable side to everyone. "Gutwrenching," says Hartsock, thinking back to the most emotional conversations they shared. Remarkably, he can't remember Olsen taking veteran days off to collect himself mentally. His need to practice was too strong. Philosophically, he was always someone who refused to relinquish practice reps. Sitting out meant that coaches had an opportunity to fall in love with his replacement, a cause-and-effect he would not allow. Beyond this, the field was now a safe haven.

His feet were on a football field, so his focus as an NFL tight end reached an extreme.

A level he had never reached before.

"The biggest thing," Olsen recalls, "is to appreciate when you're at practice and you're at the games and you're in your element doing what you love to do. You appreciate it because you know when you leave that world, you're back to the real world. You're back to real-life struggles. You're back to real-life adversities. You're back to things that really matter. Football during those times was a reprieve. I could go escape for a few hours and get my mind on something that I really enjoyed doing, knowing that at the end of the day, when I checked out, it was back to the real world and back to real-world problems and being a dad and a husband and a son. Having that approach allowed me to be where my feet were."

His feet were rarely on the sideline, too. Olsen played at least one thousand offensive snaps five years in a row, a total of 5,164, from 2012 to 2016. He wouldn't change a thing because Olsen believes this is what distinguished him from the greats of his era, but looking back? No question he shaved potential years off his career. In 2016, especially. Against Washington in Game 14 of that season, Olsen broke his elbow and probably should've shut it down with the Panthers out of playoff contention. Olsen, however, was also only seventeen yards shy of a third straight thousand-yard season and hadn't missed a game since September 16, 2007.

Sliding on injured reserve, to him, would've been akin to quitting on both his team and himself.

So, that week, trainers fitted Olsen with an arm brace that made it seem like Olsen was trick-or-treating as Frankenstein, not playing a football game. The elbow was so bad that he needed a brace that prevented him from fully locking out his arm. At the top of the second quarter, he hit the milestone. He safely stepped out of bounds and roles reversed. Now, everyone else was talking his ear off for an assembly line of hugs. No embrace was more heartfelt than the one from Newton.

The Panthers were clobbered, 33–16, by the Atlanta Falcons that day. But even after making history, Olsen didn't pop the shoulder pads off and grab a water. He kept playing with that swollen elbow. Forty snaps in all. In the season finale one week later, he played another forty-six meaningless snaps.

The elbow was "uncomfortable," he says, "awkward." In both games, his brain shifted to a survival mode that completely locked Olsen into each and every snap. Olsen wasn't really able to enjoy making history.

"You train yourself that 'This is what's expected of you, this is what you do,'" Olsen says. "You figure out a way to do it. There were times where, yeah, you hurt. Things don't feel great. But you've got to roll. At that point, it's pride. Pride can be a dangerous thing, but pride can be a great motivator."

Like practically every tight end before him, Olsen needed to be pried off the field. Debilitating foot injuries eventually did him in—but not without a fight. Late in Olsen's career, even as Rivera begged him to take a day off, Olsen kept practicing.

That's how everyone will remember him. The lack of an off switch. It's no surprise that—at Olsen's peak—the Panthers were also one of the toughest teams in the NFL. As a coach, Rivera knew there was only so much he could say. Players listened to the vet talking their ears off because this vet backed it up.

"He refused to not practice," Rivera says. "There were times he'd say it out loud in front of the young players on purpose to shame them into understanding how important it is to practice. If a rookie missed any time, the first thing Greg would say was, 'Wow, man. When I played, if you were a rookie, you never thought about taking a day off. You showed up with a broken leg. It didn't matter.' I think that sent some good messages to the young guys, how important it was to get out and practice."

His sixty-three career touchdown receptions were not viral hits. Olsen gets that other tight ends were more exhilarating. But he was a force of consistency that just kept pushing the play button, right into his final season with the Seattle Seahawks in 2020. He took pride in any fan out there scanning the numbers at the end of a season—at his number of catches, yards, snaps—and saying, "Holy shit!"

At the tail end of summer in 2021, right when the scent of freshly cut grass could be a siren song luring Olsen back for a fifteenth season, I ask Olsen if he feels that urge to hit play just one more time. He admits there's something special about the anxiety this time of year. Those butterflies. But then he wakes up in the morning, takes his kids to baseball practice, and he's good. He relishes this next phase of life as a broadcaster and, above all, *a dad*.

Eight years after T. J.'s birth, his modified heart started to quit.

Dad announced to all on Twitter that the heart was "reaching its end" and T. J. went on the transplant list.

Eight days later, their prayers for a miracle were answered: T. J. found a match. Families can spend months on a waiting list for a new heart. In Seattle, for example, the average wait time is six months. The Olsens don't know where the heart came from, only that the sobering reality is most accidents happen around holidays and T. J. received his new heart after Memorial Day Weekend.

T. J. thanked everyone for their prayers on his dad's Instagram page and rang the bell at the hospital. That exact moment, it felt like the entire country wept tears of joy. The Olsens became the country's adopted tight end family.

And Olsen, the tight end who couldn't stop talking, is still talking.

He just has a new audience each day.

Chapter 12

IOWA MADE

This is the most relentlessly optimistic tight end on the planet. The man sitting here in his pickup truck—live from Livermore, Iowa (population 381)—tells stories for four hours straight. With a coffee in one hand and a water jug in the other, Dallas Clark rockets from one tale to the next. So, when the conversation shifts to the worst moment of his life, initially, he is a man composed. He reimagines the events of May 14, 1998, with poise.

Until, abruptly, the trauma paralyzes him in his tracks.

His lip quivers. His eyes well. His words come to a screeching halt and he would very clearly like to think about anything else.

On that day, Clark was a senior in high school. He returned home from baseball practice two blocks away to find both his mother, Jan, and his aunt, Judy, cleaning up the garage. In four days, Clark was set to graduate with the other thirty-one seniors at Twin River Valley High, a school that no longer exists. He told Mom about his opposite field home run at practice and headed inside to eat dinner with a pep in his step. The finale of *Seinfeld* was airing this night, and he couldn't wait. He can still hear Green Day's "Good Riddance" playing from the episode because that was right around the time Aunt Judy let out a haunting shriek in the garage.

He sprinted toward the sound and found Mom collapsed on the ground. She couldn't breathe.

Clark dashed back into the house to call 911, returned, and tried to resuscitate her with CPR. He never took a CPR class in school but frantically tried to remember everything he had seen in the movies and... nothing. Mom was unresponsive. It felt like forever for the medics from the hospital in Humboldt ten miles away to arrive. A doctor told Dallas that his mother had died instantly from the heart attack, that there was nothing he could've done. She was forty-nine.

Here, he is skeptical. He still believes they told him this just to make him feel better.

Nothing could change the fact that Mom died in his arms. That PTSD stays with a person forever. Clark, now forty-two, grabs the drawstring of his hoodie with his left hand and stares ahead in a trance. His voice cracks.

"And I just wish I...well there's a lot of wishes of how...so, yeah. It's tough."

That's when a tear drips down his cheek. It's too painful to revisit those emotions, so he replays the good times. Her infectious laugh (he can still *hear* it). Her smile (he can still *see* it). Her beaming positivity (he's a spitting image). Clark admits he probably wasn't the easiest kid to deal with in sports because he loathed losing. Through it all, Mom was solid as a rock. As a parent himself now, Clark has deep appreciation for her way of assuring him everything would be OK without dousing him in what he calls *"You're great!* bullshit." Both his parents smoked cigs. Mom didn't live the healthiest lifestyle, but how could she? Jan was too busy working her ass off to take care of her three boys.

Dallas chokes up again.

"She had no time," he says, pausing, "for herself."

This all happened at a fragile crossroad in her son's life, too, a few months shy of college.

He remembers the temptation to scream "Screw you, God!" and quit religion, quit believing in anything. Instead, he went the opposite direction. He told himself that we're all here for a reason and that

Mom's was to get her three boys through high school. Thinking this way gave Dallas peace in his tenuous state. Of course, it doesn't remove the pain. He still finds himself asking "Why?" and once more thinks of everything Mom missed. How he would've given her "every frickin' dime" he made after becoming an NFL player. How Mom loved Jeeps. Hell, Dallas would've bought her fifty of them. That hurt most as he rose from total obscurity. She deserved to tell anyone who'd listen in Livermore and beyond, "That is my son."

He pauses again.

"She's doing it in heaven. She has the best seat in the house."

His spirit could've deteriorated for good and, truth be told, he was driven to his wit's end on two occasions specifically at the University of Iowa. Yet, each time, he pressed on. He felt an indefinable energy source inside. Lawns were cut. Newspapers were delivered. Appendixes nearly burst. Dallas Clark knows better than any tight end that it pays to be brave for everything life throws at you.

When Mom passed, he vividly remembers having a choice. He could continue to chase his dream or pack it in.

"That's what life is—response," he says. "How do you respond?"

Before he knew it, there was 3:57 left in the 2006 AFC divisional playoff round. It was third-and-five. Clark lined up in the right slot with his two feet right above the "A" on the Ravens' logo at midfield and took off on a twelve-yard out. When he stuck his left foot into the ground, cornerback Corey Ivy actually broke before he did to cut underneath the route. Peyton Manning threw the ball anyway.

The living legend trusted his tight end with the Indianapolis Colts' season on the line.

Thinking back, Clark cannot shake one thought from his mind. He doesn't bring this correlation up often—to anyone—because it's a sensitive one. It also opens up old wounds.

"Do I make it as far as I make it," he wonders, "if Mom doesn't pass?"

As a teenager, his dream was quaint. All Dallas Clark wanted was a letterman jacket. He didn't even need to star in the middle of a defense like his older brother Derrik at Iowa State. Dallas was perfectly content walking into a big-time university as a linebacker, emitting endless buckets of sweat and...maybe...one day...if he was lucky...having the opportunity to blast off on special teams. Anything it took to wear that jacket through the quad.

"I was like Uncle Buck," he shouts, "with the five-year plan!"

He was a talented quarterback and linebacker in high school, but no Division I schools cared. Only one college coach even called Clark through the heat of the recruiting process. For baseball. "My door," he says, "wasn't getting knocked down." Clark didn't own an email address, so he did the only thing he could. He made a personal VHS highlight tape with the help of his other brother Dan, who played and coached at D-III Simpson College, and hand-delivered it to schools. He was already traveling to all of Derrik's Iowa State games, so he made a point to get his footage to schools they played.

The only road Dallas saw toward that coveted letterman jacket was the one paved by his older brothers. As a linebacker. The defensive coordinator who originally recruited Derrik to Iowa State and moved on to the University of Pittsburgh was interested in Dallas—this was his only recruiting visit—but Larry Coyer couldn't get the school's head coach to sign off on a scholarship. Clark gets it. He jokes that it would've been career suicide to give a scholarship to a country bumpkin from the cornfields of Iowa. Dallas didn't bother sending a tape to Iowa State because he didn't like how the new staff jerked his brother around as a senior. Holding an emphatic *one* with his index finger, Clark says the only school that responded to his tape was Iowa. And he's pretty sure the only reason was to stick it to the in-state Cyclones. One of their assistant coaches wandered into his high school basketball practice and, even then, special teams coach Mark

Hendrickson probably only stopped in Livermore on his way to see "a real athlete."

Clark didn't care. This was his sliver of a chance. His face lit up at the sight of this man in the black sweater with the tiny Hawkeye logo stitched above the breast. Hendrickson had a briefcase in his hand and his eyes on the court. Where, of course, Clark was a damn maniac.

"That dude, walking into our small gym to see me?! I was just buzzing up and down the court."

Whatever Dallas did that day was enough to warrant a chance to walk-on. His world was then rocked with Mom's death in May.

The boys' parents were separated, so they lived with Mom in town while Dad—"Doug," they called him—lived on a farm in the country. After the heart attack, Dan came home to stay with Dallas through the summer inside the home Jan had rented. The next domino to tip in Clark's life actually occurred on the baseball field. He broke his collarbone. While playing shortstop on the school's baseball team, the 203-pounder bashed into a second baseman. Just like that, he figured his best shot at a letterman jacket was to buy one at a thrift store. As Clark punched in the phone number of Iowa's linebackers coach, Bret Bielema, he expected the chat to resemble a breakup. Why would Iowa even waste its time with a walk-on who shattered his collarbone? Water coolers were more valuable.

To his shock, Bielema could not have been nicer. He told Clark that the school would take care of him. Clark put the collarbone in a figure-eight brace to let it heal naturally, blasted through thirty or so movies from Blockbuster and—considering it wasn't healing quickly—Bielema recommended Clark grayshirt that fall to join the team in the spring. Clark obliged. And since he couldn't do anything with the football team, bored out of his mind, Clark signed up for a Tae Kwon Do class. He loved Bruce Lee movies and couldn't even touch his toes out of high school so, hey, it couldn't hurt. Within months, he was doing splits and worked his way up to green belt with a blue tip. "I was like, 'What the hell is happening here?'"

Iowa went 3-8. Hayden Fry retired. Kirk Ferentz was hired as the new head coach, and Bielema—"Thank God," Clark says—was retained. Someone was still on staff to make sure he wasn't completely lost in the weeds. Still, Clark wasn't good enough to even warrant his own jersey number the spring of '99. While all the scholarship kids had fancy screen-pressed numbers, the Hawkeyes held Clark in such high esteem that they wrote "142" in Sharpie on his gear. Again, he didn't care. Clark was eventually given No. 90 but even this crappy uniform hardly fit over his shoulders. He felt like a second-class citizen. After spotting a hole in one of his socks, he stepped in line to grab a new pair from the equipment guys. The All–Big Ten cornerback in front of him got a new pair, no questions asked, but when Clark asked? One was incredulous. "What?" he sneered. "Just because the scholarship kids get new socks, you think *you* need new socks?!"

Clark showed him the hole. A new pair was tossed at him in disgust.

"Like he's reaching into his own dresser drawer and pulling out a pair of *his* socks. That was the bullcrap you had to put up with." He threw them at me, like, 'Here! Ugh. Geez. You pain me. I can't believe you breathe the same air that I breathe!'"

Not that this walk-on was exactly knocking his coaches' socks off during practice. That first spring was ugly. One indoor practice, a mammoth Iowa offensive linemen pancaked Clark, grabbed his facemask, and bounced his head against the old-school, concrete-soft Astro-Turf. "Bam! Bam! Bam!" Clark recalls. "Smashing it!" Honestly, this player was simply executing what so many other upperclassmen were thinking. Everyone was fed up with the *Rudy*-like runt trying too hard every snap. Clark knew he was annoying the hell out of everyone, but whatever. He was wired to go balls to the wall in everything, be it a football practice or a bus stop. When his college roommate dared him to jump a brick wall that was at least four feet high, he drilled his shin and finally cleared it after three attempts. Only later that night did Clark notice he was bleeding profusely. The next morning, he got it stitched up.

Clark had nothing—*nothing*—to fall back on when the freshman year wrapped up. His mom was renting, so after she passed there was no use hanging on to that house or returning to Livermore. Both brothers were off chasing their own football dreams. Iowa City became home. All summer, for $7 an hour, Clark woke up at 6 a.m. to mow the athletic fields for the school's grounds crew. His boss, groundskeeper Larry Putney, was the archetypal "old crusty man" spending too much time at the VFW, too. Clark did whatever he said and could give the man known as "Larry Legend" hell right back. "Are you going to be able to get up, old man!" he'd laugh.

This put food on the table. There was also never a dull day.

One morning, a groggy Clark fell asleep at the wheel inside Kinnick Stadium and tore a two-foot rip into the heavy padding that wrapped around the field *riiiight* where Larry could see. The good news? Larry didn't stroll into work until 8 a.m. There was time to cover up his crime. The bad news? The padding covered a heavy piece of plywood that was eight feet long and weighed 150 pounds. He needed to drag it across the length of the entire field. Taking several breaks to catch his breath, Clark eventually found a good hiding spot and patched it together with electrical tape that held up for one rain.

"I was like a mouse, when you lift a bale of hay and the mouse says, 'Oh shit, The whole world can see me!' I'm carrying this across Kinnick Stadium. It's 6 a.m., but in my head I feel like there's seventy-one thousand there. I'm just, '*heh-heh-heh-heh*,'" he says, panting nervously. "You're scurrying across like you're trying to find another bale to hide under. I needed that job."

It took a full month for Larry to find that damaged pad and, yes, he tore into Dallas good.

Such was walk-on life. He had no choice but to take on every job he possibly could to pay his way.

One winter, Clark delivered the student newspaper, the *Daily Iowan*. While all his friends slept in, Clark woke up at 5:30 a.m., grabbed the stack of papers outside his dorm room, hit play on his Discman, and traveled all over campus to the beat of Third Eye Blind's iconic debut album. For a while, he worked in a parking lot booth where people constantly gave him double looks. Not because Clark was a football player, no, he was just far too happy for such a miserable job. People shot him a puzzled glare as if to say, "You're supposed to hate the world. Why are you saying 'Hi?'" If there was an ad in the newspaper offering students any amount of money, Clark took it. He was a puppet for dentist students, convenient because he sure didn't have dental insurance. For $50 and free cleanings, he did whatever they said. Psychology students always needed subjects for case studies, too. For $25 a pop, he'd help them figure out why people pick red M&Ms.

"I had no choice. I needed to eat."

He didn't live the Jeremy Shockey life on the weekends, no. He couldn't afford to let loose. Clark didn't want to give the new head coach any reason to dump him. Instead, he became obsessed with Iowa's conditioning program and hit it off with Ferentz's new strength coach, Chris Doyle. Inside the weight room, each player had an index card with their max lifts written on it. Clark soon lived for seeing that number go up by five pounds on the squat rack. He killed himself in sprints. He says he attacked every day like the crazed Lattimer in *The Program* screaming "Place at the table!" Gradually, coaches couldn't help but notice. The best day of Clark's life, to that point, was when Bielema randomly showed up during one conditioning session and yelled, "Can anyone catch Clark?!"

"I could've died," Clark says. "Stuff like that? That's it. Making tackles in Kinnick, that wasn't even... it was *THAT* moment."

He took on an obsessive focus with whatever task was directly in front of him. If he was running a sprint, that was all that mattered. Then, the cold tub. Then, the shower. Then, dinner. He didn't have the luxury of a meal plan like everyone else, so he cooked. His go-to? A big tube of Pillsbury "Grands!" biscuits with a can of baked beans. Then, it was time for homework. Then, sleep.

He woke up, and it was back to following the lead of Doyle and Ferentz. They became his family.

"If those dudes told me to bury a body," Clark says, "no questions asked. I'll put my fingerprints all over it. I'll put my blood on it. I'll say I did it. I owe them. Football was all I had."

The fall of 1999, Clark was a seventh-string linebacker. But he didn't care. Special teams was his ticket to getting that letterman's jacket, and he expected to dress for Iowa's season opener at Nebraska. Two weeks before the game, his exuberance backfired. During a walk-through, Iowa ran an onside recovery drill and coaches warned players not to leave their feet. Nobody was in pads. This wasn't live. Clark, of course, forever ignored such red tape. He pogoed high into the sky for the ball and crashed hard on his bad shoulder. An X-ray revealed that the collarbone had healed in awkward fashion, as if forming a joint, and it's curved to this day. Clark missed two weeks, returned and… something wasn't right. He felt like shit. When starting outside line-backer LeVar Woods—Clark's idol on the roster—asked what was wrong, Clark admitted he felt terrible but gave Woods strict instructions not to say a word to the trainer. He couldn't miss one practice, one rep. Keeping a close eye on the kid, though, Woods eventually had no choice and alerted head trainer Russ Haynes, who gave Clark some Tylenol and sent him back to his dorm room.

At around 11 p.m., Clark felt like he wanted to crawl into a hole and die. He headed immediately to the emergency room across the street, where the doctor looked at him with concern.

"Your appendix is about to blow," he said. "You need to go have surgery."

Clark had an emergency appendectomy and, even from his hospital bed, he tried to maintain an edge. Determined to put on weight, Clark had Doyle send him cases of protein shakes. He watched Iowa's lone win that season from a wheelchair in the press box and decided to redshirt. He got the collarbone surgery, once and for all, and another college football season went up in smoke. Just like that.

The kid bursting with positivity was inching closer…and closer… to a breaking point.

Mom's death. No money. His own health issues. Stressors were adding up and Dallas Clark didn't have much support from "Doug," either, who passed away in 2014. Son doesn't want to smear the dad who brought him into this world, and true, there are life lessons Clark took from him. As a kid, he actually wanted to play basketball at Indiana University because he liked Bobby Knight, and the reason why was that Dad cussed him out all the time. The three boys always feared the drive home from games more than anything a coach said in the locker room—he means this in a good way, too. "It was, 'Why weren't you hustling back?' It was never about a coach, a teammate, an opponent. It was about 'you.'" There's also no denying that Dad's financial problems became his problems. After Doug's sports bar ("Double D's") failed, he owed a boatload of taxes and ripped through his boy's graduation money atop the refrigerator (about $1K–$2K) in addition to most of the life insurance money from Mom (about $9K–$13K). Dallas was sent to college with literal nickels. Doug promised to pay his son back, never did, and Dallas can only shake his head today. "What did that buy you? A day? It would've bought me a semester."

If Dallas returned to Livermore, he didn't visit Doug for long. Once, Son asked for his own Social Security number—he needed the digits to apply for grants and loans to stay in school—and Dad refused because he was trying to stay off the grid. Luckily, Dallas hit it off with who he calls "Angel No. 4 or No. 5" in his life, a man named Bob Upmeyer, who worked in the school's financial aid department. ("I'd bury a body for that guy, too.") Back when he was "Dallas Clark Nobody," he told Upmeyer that his dad wouldn't give him his Social, and Upmeyer offered him extensions to buy time. Eventually, Dallas pried that number away and stayed in school.

All this weighed on Clark until he finally cracked. Twice. The first time, in Year 1, Derrik came to get him for the weekend. Or, as he puts, his big bro pulled him "out of the tank." Dallas's car had broken down, so he couldn't leave himself.

This transition to college was overwhelming and Clark sincerely began to doubt himself. There were more kids in his freshman class than all of Livermore. He felt alone in every conceivable way. Derrik was still chasing his own football dream with the Iowa Barnstormers of the Arena Football League. Dan, the oldest, was coaching D-III football. All three boys were at critical moments in their lives. All three were still coping with a horrific tragedy. Yet, they weren't talking to each other, a silence that led to a raw "loneliness." Dallas wondered if this whole football thing was worth it, if he could keep going. Maybe it was best to just stick with his classes and become a teacher. During that one-hour, forty-five-minute drive from Iowa City to Des Moines, he cried and cried and asked questions that didn't have answers.

Then a discovery: Derrik was hurting just as much as him.

"We were all floating. That foundation was gone," says Clark, lip quivering. "They were all I knew and could trust and could love. Derrik was pivotal at that moment to lean on, and I'm sure if you asked him, he was probably about as shaken and lost as I was. Being that outlet of support, that will never be forgotten. That's what brothers do. There's nothing better than a brother's bond when it's met in the middle. That's really what Mom's death did. It forged that bond between the three of us."

The second time he was pushed to the edge, Clark went on a bike ride to an empty Kinnick Stadium. The gate was open, so he walked inside, lay down on a bench in the student section, looked up into the sky, and talked to God. "What am I doing?" he asked. "Does this have a point?" In that moment, he lost his finite focus. He was looking too far ahead.

Dallas Clark needed a break. A sign. A reason to keep pushing. He was No. 44 now, taking linebacker Raj Clark's old number. Iowa didn't even need to switch out the nameplate. That third year, 2000, Clark finally got onto the field. The first game of his career was the "Eddie Robinson Football Classic" against eighth-ranked Kansas State at Arrowhead Stadium. Clark was so jacked to play that he puked his lungs out before kickoff, hatching a nasty habit. He'd go on to puke before every game into his rookie year of the pros. Eventually, he realized this "It's on!" ritual wasn't healthy. This day, it felt like 110 degrees on the field. As a blocker on one punt return, his adrenaline out of control, Clark mercilessly bench-pressed the long-snapper into the sideline. He's not necessarily proud of it, likening this to beating up your sister. But, holy hell, did it feel good to unleash two-plus years of patience by taking this poor sap "to the shed." To Iowa's sideline, too. Not even his own. "I could've been nice enough to drive him into his sidelines," he says, "so he could've gotten up and got a drink."

The flight home was a blur. Upon returning, Clark vomited again and hooked up to two bags of IVs to return his bodily functions to some sense of normalcy. When he stepped on a scale, Clark was shocked. One game of special teams dropped his weight from 235 to 220. He's not sure how he didn't burst into flames. One person ran through his mind that day: Mom.

"I came to life," Clark says, emotional. "It was a big moment."

All season, Clark knocked heads around on special teams. He was happy. When it came to playing linebacker, however, he was still a fourth-stringer. He couldn't read and react, almost always swallowed by the clutter. "I sucked," he admits. Which made Clark quite a puzzling case for Iowa's coaching staff because, in the weight room, he was a world-class athlete. Doyle loved calling him "Roy Hobbs" because he felt Clark was just like The Natural. To this day, Doyle believes Clark could've become a pro golfer or baseball player if he desired. His explosion. His hand-eye coordination. His cutting ability. "He came out of nowhere," Doyle says. "Nobody knew about this kid. This is an NFL player that nobody knew about and literally just knocked on our door and walked in." These three years created a monster. But Ferentz couldn't understand how the same Roy Hobbs–like athlete who sent other human beings airborne, who latched onto a block forever, who wasn't merely good on special teams—rather, phenomenal—was so bad on defense.

Says Ferentz: "We're all watching tape, like there's a disconnect. I'm not the smartest guy in the world but I was thinking, 'Maybe we have him out of position.'"

Meanwhile, Iowa was bad again. Ferentz's record dropped to 4-19 in two seasons. Unable to lure four- and five-star recruits, the head coach started to move players to completely new positions at a rate unheard of for a Big Ten school. At so many of these one-light towns in the Midwest, the best athlete played quarterback out of necessity. Schools like Twin River Valley with thirty-some kids in a class simply give the ball to their best player and get out of the way. Quickly, Ferentz gained a sixth sense for signing these players and finding them a new home. Chad Greenway was a high school quarterback in South Dakota who also played basketball and ran the high hurdles in track. Ferentz made him a linebacker. Greenway would retire as the Minnesota Vikings' fourth-leading tackler of all time. Brandon Scherff was a 275-pounder who started off as a sophomore quarterback in Denison, Iowa. He also grabbed a school-record 613 rebounds and won the shotput title in track and field in high school. All Ferentz did was mold him into an offensive guard and Scherff became a perennial NFL Pro Bowler. When Ferentz's Hawkeyes upset Nick Saban's LSU Tigers in the 2005 Capital One Bowl, seven of his twenty-two starters were former high school quarterbacks.

Ferentz was a realist. He knew the five-star recruit typically takes a flight right over Iowa City. By truly *developing* players at new positions, he transformed Iowa into a power. No coach has stayed with one school longer through the twenty-first century. This tends to be a hungrier bunch, too. "If you find the right guy," Ferentz says, "it can be a blessing." And this magic touch has its roots in that 4-19 start when Ferentz first turned a pair of 245-pound tight ends (Bruce Nelson and Eric Steinbach) into his best offensive linemen...and when he moved a lost linebacker named Dallas Clark to tight end. He'd see Clark play catch with his roommate, starting quarterback Kyle McCann, and he made it look easy. Granted, Clark resisted when Ferentz first approached him about the move. He was still determined to follow his brother's footsteps. "Stupid," Clark says, sickened, taking a sip of coffee. "I was stubborn and still that walk-on thinking, 'I'm calling my shots because you're really not doing anything for me.'" So, Ferentz was smart. He presented the idea to the Clark brothers and, most important, McCann to get everyone in Clark's inner circle telling him this was best for him.

It was strange hearing everyone banging the same drum as 2001 spring ball closed in. Ferentz sat Clark down one final time to convince him, Clark caved and Clark instantly realized this was destiny. This was the sign he had been looking for all along. He loved being a Swiss Army knife capable of inflicting damage in an infinite number of ways, just like one of his favorite TV characters as a kid: Angus MacGyver. In the backyard, he was always the all-time receiver for his quarterback brother. And whenever friends rallied together for games of pickup—tackle, never touch—it always took a good two or three bodies to bring him down.

"I loved that feeling of, 'All right. Try to tackle me,'" says Clark. "That challenge was already engrained in me. Like, 'You're not bringing me down. I'm not going to let just one guy bring me down.' I unlocked all of that into this position. Like, 'Holy cow.' I'm back in Livermore. 'All right! Tackle me! Let's go!'"

That walk-on mentality now had a new long-term mission: Become the best tight end imaginable.

Everywhere Doyle looked, someone was throwing Clark the ball. Learning tight end consumed Clark "twenty-four hours a day," the strength coach says. All along, Ferentz could sense Mom was on his mind. "He really wanted to make her proud," he adds. "He attacked it a hundred miles an hour like he does everything." In the spring game, Clark caught a touchdown and worked diligently with McCann all summer long to master the playbook. As a linebacker, Clark always wore gloves, but now he hated how sweaty his palms got in the heat. One day, he ripped them off and loved the feeling of that Wilson leather smacking his bare palms. It was beautiful. The ball stuck, he says, "like glue." Gloves off, he felt like a true receiver. Faster, even. Gloves on, he was back in an "I want to kill somebody" linebacker state of mind. Clark slid wristbands on to absorb the sweat and never wore gloves again.

In 2001, Clark caught 38 passes for 539 yards with 4 touchdowns. Iowa went 7-5. The following year? Both he and the program busted onto the national scene. Clark had 43 receptions for 742 yards with 4 touchdowns as Iowa went 11-2, quarterback Brad Banks finished second in the Heisman voting, and the Hawkeyes earned a trip to the Orange Bowl. One play particularly grabbed the NFL's attention, too. Against Purdue, Clark cradled a short pass in the left flat, high-stepped over a defender's diving fingertips, and tore ninety-five yards to the end zone. On the same field he was mowing a few years prior, Clark held a left arm high into the sky and the home crowd went bananas. Indianapolis Colts offensive coordinator Tom Moore recalls general manager Bill Polian watching this exact play on film and declaring, "Wow. That's our guy."

Clark had one more year of eligibility but—after everything—it was time. He made a quiet promise to Mom to earn his college degree in the future, held a press conference announcing he was turning pro, and dropped out of school to basically stuff his face with food for two months. At Iowa, Clark beefed up from 203 to 245 pounds. But in his mind, there was no such thing as a 245-pound NFL tight end, so he guzzled NCAA-approved protein shakes that tasted like puddle water and pounded two medium-sized Totino's party pizzas before bed and ate . . . and ate . . . and pounded more weights. In his mind, Clark had no choice but to eat nonstop because (a) he believed all NFL tight ends were 275-pound goliaths, and (b) he had freakish metabolism. "Like *Days of Thunder*," he calls it, "stuck in frickin' high gear." Even into his forties, when pot bellies are a rite of passage for all dads, Clark is able to polish off a jug of ice cream every night before bed and it turns to muscle. His training, under Doyle, only intensified ahead of the NFL

Combine with Doyle dissecting all drills down to a science. The 40. The three-cone drill. There was still nothing Clark loved more in life than having a plan and attacking that plan at full tilt. By the time he stepped on the scale at the Combine, he was 257 pounds.

With the twenty-fourth overall pick, Polian got his man in the 2003 NFL Draft.

Years later, it hit Clark. All the success he had on a football field— in college and the pros—can be traced back to one simple virtue. He needed to trust Ferentz and Doyle.

"That trust is the foundation of making things happen," Clark says. "Because I never once questioned our workouts and said, 'This is too much. This is too little.' I get to the Colts and all Polian preaches about is one voice. He's like, 'Listen to Coach Dungy. Don't listen to the outside world. Don't listen to your mom, don't listen to your dad, don't listen to your cousin, don't listen to your brother.' Everybody right here in this room is all it takes.' "

If Clark had stayed stubborn, if he'd told Ferentz one more time he was a linebacker, then he knows he'd currently be an elementary teacher. That was his major. Yet through his education classes, one concept stuck. Clark was fascinated by the psychology behind *Nature vs. Nurture*. The nature, in his life, is undeniable. All the grit and sacrifice in Mom's genes were part of Clark's DNA. But the more he thinks about his rise at Iowa, the more he realizes external factors shaped who he is, from Doug blowing through his savings to mowing Kinnick to all those tubes of biscuits that he swears made for the best possible meal. All these experiences made Dallas Clark, especially the one that started it all: Mom's heart attack.

"Would I have made it this far if I didn't do this stuff? If I had my school paid for, if I had a warm meal to go home to, I don't know. I do know I had a choice. It was either 'do it' or 'get out.' Get a job, get money, survive.

"If I'm from a home with loving parents and we're well off, I don't know. It's a fair question, right?"

Part of Dallas Clark didn't believe the voice on the other end of this phone call. When Polian called to inform him he was their pick, two words crossed his mind. *Who? Me?* The GM told Clark that owner Jim Irsay would be flying in to pick him up in a couple of hours. *Come again?* And he then asked Clark what number he wanted to wear. After conceding that he probably couldn't keep 44 because it's a fullback number, Clark said he'd double it up and take 88. There was a long pause on the line. Polian told Clark that the Colts already had a No. 88, wide receiver Marvin Harrison. "Forget it," Polian told him. "You'll be 44. We'll figure it out." Indy got around the rules by listing Clark as a tight end/fullback on the roster, and even as John Madden roasted the rookie for wearing a number in the 40s during an exhibition broadcast, the number stuck.

He took Polian's advice and absorbed Tony Dungy's pearls of wisdom. At least once a week, as a dad today, Clark finds a way to weave Dungy's "Perception vs. Reality" message into a life lesson for his kids. Exactly as everyday life isn't nearly as glamorous as Generation Z makes it seem on social media, the NFL was always far more cutthroat than what the average fan saw for three hours each Sunday with a beer in hand. Clark was ready for this cutthroat world, too, even if he had no clue. The first time he stepped into the huddle, in minicamp, the tight end looked around. He saw Peyton Manning and Edgerrin James and Reggie Wayne and Marvin Harrison, and he couldn't help but wonder, "Why the hell am I here? Should I get them water?" Then came a hazing for the ages, compliments of the offensive coordinator Moore. A fellow Iowa alum, "a crusty old hawkeye," Clark calls him, Moore ran the rook into the dirt. Clark lined up at every alphabet letter possible in an NFL offense. Out wide ("X"), in tight ("Y"), in the backfield ("H"), in the slot ("Z"). With his signature scowl and growl, Moore wouldn't give Clark a break while the team's starting tight end, veteran Marcus Pollard, chewed on a protein bar from the sideline. The only moment

Clark detoured that direction was to puke into the garbage can. Nobody else flinched, either. He missed one play, rinsed his mouth out with water, sprinted back into action.

"Nine guys out of ten would've told Tom Moore to fly a kite," Clark says. "He put me through so much that first minicamp. I mean, they put me everywhere. 'Yes sir. Yes sir.' Doubting? Questioning? No! No, no, no, no. It was just, 'Yep. This is what I've got to do.' And it was beautiful. I loved it."

Moore saw right away that this was a young man undaunted by hard work. Whereas most players sort of rolled up when they fell to the ground, he noticed that Clark "splattered" like a bug on a windshield. He'd kid Clark that he had to be the dirtiest kid on the block back in grade school. "Being great," Moore says, "was very important to him."

The Colts already had a special offense brewing. Manning, the first overall pick of the 1998 draft, had led the Colts to 13-3, 10-6, and 10-6 seasons. A matchup problem at tight end, Polian figured, could supply another element of unpredictability. Yet even though Moore had the right idea, migrating Clark all over that practice field, this role didn't crystallize overnight. For starters, Clark broke his leg in grisly fashion ten games into that rookie season. New England Patriots cornerback Ty Law drilled him in the knee and, after helicoptering through the sky, his ankle twisted on the landing. A herd of teammates gathered around for support as Clark's entire leg was tucked into an air cast and he was taken off on a stretcher. A day before this chat, he watched the replay of this game on NFL Network with his twelve-year-old son and his son could not stop laughing.

To him, the image of Dad spinning in midair was hysterical. "Like he's watching a video game," Clark says.

Funny thing is, this offense soon mirrored precisely that. With Manning calling all plays at the line of scrimmage, this was a pixelated juggernaut.

One does not earn a doctorate in this quarterback's offense by pulling an all-nighter, either. The pressure was palpable. Manning would tell everyone exactly where to be and when. "He told the water boy where he had to be," Clark says. So, Clark took baby steps. He'd study the daily play sheet with his position coach, Chris Foerster, a good thirty minutes before every practice. Clark made sure Manning never needed to tell him the same thing twice. The kid who was afraid to even slug a beer as a walk-on in college refused to screw up this opportunity. Nobody was mistaking Clark for a Los Angeles Laker—he couldn't bully cornerbacks like six-foot-six Kellen Winslow. Nor could he snare the ball from the tops of their helmets like Tony Gonzalez.

At six foot three, Clark needed to find something else. His edge was everything he had just been through for five years.

"My walk-on mentality fit so well in this offense," Clark says. "You couldn't afford to say, 'I just didn't have it today.' No! There was nothing worse than screwing up and coming in the next morning and having to watch that play with Tom Moore and your coach and Peyton. You wanted to go out and prove everyone right. That's the perfect environment."

Very quickly, Manning and Clark realized they were kinfolk. Manning wasted no time that rookie season taunting Clark for holding a press conference to announce he was "leaving" Iowa. With a drip of sarcasm, he informed the rookie that nobody does this. You release a written statement to minimize the blow, and that's that. How could he be such a tease? "Peyton is good like that," Clark says, "giving jabs." Over time, Clark jabbed him right back. Even though this quarterback was instantly the most competitive person Clark had ever met, he was competitive himself. When he couldn't get open during games and Manning shot him an icy glare, Clark shot him one right back as if to say, "Don't tell me! Let's do it again!" Off the field, they became ball-busting accomplices. If a rookie on the team was getting too cocky for Manning's liking, the duo would fill a fifty-five-gallon garbage can about halfway with water and lean it outside of his door in the middle of the night. Clark would knock, speed off, and whoever opened from inside soon had their room flooded with water. Timing was crucial. They'd do this the last night of camp because that probably meant the person inside had their luggage resting near the door. After pranking a new PR assistant to make him feel part of the team, Manning heard a frantic "Help!" inside the room. A cry so loud that it almost sounded like the poor sap was drowning.

"You think he's OK?" Manning asked Clark.

"Yeah, he's fine."

Players also had their own golf carts at camp to get around campus. Of course, Clark helped Manning execute his master plan of putting a teammate's cart on a raft in the middle of a pond.

On the field, the two treated a practice in Terre Haute, Indiana, no different from a frigid night in Foxborough with seventy thousand crazy fans, Clark adds, "wanting us to die." That's where Manning's forty-five game-winning drives with the Colts started because the intensity at training camp never waned. Honestly, though? The rapport between Manning and Clark stretched back further than July. For three months prior, quarterback and tight end ran routes together. They didn't climb up Don Coryell's route tree, one through nine, like most all QBs do with their receivers in the off-season. They'd instead drill two specific routes for twenty-five reps on any given day. Manning would declare, "OK, today it's slants and fifteen-yard sideline comeback routes" and the two locked into game mode for as long as needed.

If something wasn't right, they'd stop, discuss, repeat that route until it was perfected to the inch.

"Dallas was wired the same way," Manning says. "I'm one of those guys, if I missed a throw, I'd say, 'Let's get another one.' If Dallas dropped a pass or he and I were just off, we'd get another one. The receiver has to run another route. That's fifteen yards. He was like, 'Absolutely. Why would we move onto the next one before we have this one right?' The fact that he loved to work, that's when I knew he was going to be a part of our offense. He asks questions: 'What are you looking for on this defense?' He was a football rat. A junkie. Even when he was a first-round pick with the Colts. It wasn't like he said, 'I made it.' He kept working like he was still a walk-on."

Polian told Ferentz, a couple of years in, that Clark is such a football junkie that he thinks the tight end loves getting his ankle taped. Getting on Manning's intellectual level wasn't so much about book smarts or even football IQ as being a tireless worker who cared about the game on a deeper level. This QB pushed and pushed and Clark could not get enough. He realized he had earned Manning's trust for good when he dropped a pass against the Denver Broncos and Manning went right back to him on the same route in the same game—and *he* became the variable that made an excellent offense historic. As it turned out, Clark never needed to inhale all those pizzas. Within an all-gas, no-brakes offense, the tight end position evolved into something Clark never envisioned. There was no bashing into three-hundred-pound ends here. Instead, the Colts released Clark downfield like Harrison, like Wayne, and he served as the triggerman in this scheme.

If defenses went to nickel, subbing in a defensive back for a linebacker, they'd run the ball Clark's direction and he'd piledrive that 190-pounder downfield. If the defense stayed in base personnel, they'd flex him out where he'd draw a linebacker or strong safety in coverage. The real key? The Colts didn't need to substitute a new player into the game. Manning could keep the offense's cruise control set at maximum velocity.

Manning puts it best. Defenses had no choice but to ask themselves one question each week: "What's our plan for Dallas Clark?"

This was no longer a plucky walk-on. Whenever players did box jumps, it was as if they couldn't stack enough on top of each other for Clark. "It got to a point," Manning says, "where it wasn't a 'wow' thing anymore." This athleticism is why Moore compares Clark to Ozzie Newsome, the tight end he faced twice a year as a Steelers assistant in the old AFC Central. Yet even though Moore had coached in this sport since 1961—the year Mike Ditka became the first modern tight end—he never used a specific player as a blueprint for Clark in devising this offense. Clark was "intrinsically motivated" in a way he rarely saw.

"I always refer to him as my R&R guy—results, not recognition," Moore says. "All he cared about was results. A lot of people want to be good, but do you want to put in the time, the effort, the work, the study habits? He was always going to be prepared. He wanted greatness."

The slot became Clark's self-described "happy place." What a feeling it was to see that play clock tick 6...5...4...and know Manning would still get the Colts in an unbeatable play. He loved peering inside toward his buddy and the two seeing the exact same soft spot in a defense. Coordinators tended to shade an extra defender over the top of Harrison and Wayne and could use the sideline as an extra defender. But Clark, *inside*, had all sorts of wiggle room. "I have this chump safety," he'd say to himself. "Let's run the ball and I'll drive this guy back ten yards," or "They're buzzing a linebacker out? All day. Let's throw the ball." Each play called had complexities, layers, checks, nuance.

One mistake could get a player benched. Dallas Clark thrived under this pressure and, by 2006, it was time to shine.

Instead of frantically scrambling to sign a wide receiver as Brandon Stokley battled injuries and ended up on IR with a torn Achilles, the Colts plugged Clark into his happy place. All sweat, all heartbreak, all sacrifice led to one defining moment in the AFC divisional round of the playoffs at M&T Bank Stadium in Baltimore with those three minutes and fifty-seven seconds on the clock. The Colts led, 12–6, with the ball at the Ravens' 45-yard line. One more first down would inch the Colts into Adam Vinatieri's field-goal range and punch their ticket to the AFC Championship.

When the Colts stepped up to the line, Manning couldn't quite decipher Baltimore's alignment and called a timeout. It was a rough night for the QB. At this point, he was 14 of 29 with 2 interceptions.

Frustrated, Manning trudged over toward the sideline to chat with Moore. Ravens defensive coordinator Rex Ryan was either sending an all-out blitz or playing some form of Cover 2 with man-to-man underneath. The Colts opted to call a play that worked vs. both. If Manning felt like the blitz was coming, he'd bring in the other tight end to block and send Clark on a sail route. In man coverage, he was confident Clark could burn his defender. The Colts lined back up and—anticipating a blitz with the play clock at "5"—Manning quickly jolted back into the shotgun.

Only, it was a ruse. The Ravens didn't send the house. Thankfully, they were still playing man-to-man.

Cornerback Corey Ivy was in perfect coverage, and as Ivy broke out of Clark's route before he did, two words crossed the tight end's mind: "Oh shit." Immediately, he wished the Colts had called an in-breaking route and assumed Manning threw it elsewhere. To his shock, in came the ball. This was no perfect spiral—the ball wobbled as it cut through the sky—but the timing? The ball placement? Sublime. These two had worked on this pattern more times than they could count. Manning had released the ball before either player broke outside, so it was exactly where it needed to be. It grazed *juuuust* past Ivy's outstretched left hand and into Clark's arms.

"I reached out to get anything on it. I mean...the football gods," says Clark, closing his eyes. "That ball rolled up my arm and I still don't know how I caught it."

Adds Manning: "That just shows you the trust I had in Dallas."

As safety Ed Reed signaled incomplete, Clark held the ball up high and Manning shook his head in disbelief. The Colts melted some clock, tacked on a fifth field goal and, to this day, Ryan brings this play up whenever he runs into Moore and Manning.

One week later, it'd only get sweeter.

For a half, the Colts were slapped around by the team that had owned them. When Manning's pass outside to Harrison midway through the second quarter was intercepted by cornerback Asante

Samuel and returned for a touchdown, the Patriots appeared primed to beat the Colts in the playoffs for the third time in four years. At the half, trailing 21–6, Dungy barely raised his voice. Whatever the opposite of a Vince Lombardi speech resembles, this was it. He told the Colts they didn't need to change anything. They'd score, stop New England, then score again. He was right, too. That's exactly what happened. And after the Patriots went back ahead, 28–21, Manning dropped a deep ball in the bucket to Clark for twenty-three yards. Somehow, he tapped both feet down. The Patriots went ahead again, 31–28, and Clark hauled in a fifty-two-yarder with 7:35 to go. His zigzag after the catch sent Artrell Hawkins diving into no-man's-land. Vinatieri knotted it up at 31–31.

The cherry on top of Clark's 6-catch, 137-yard title performance? On third-and-two, he flattened a defensive back as Joseph Addai crossed the goal line for the game-winning touchdown. As teammates mobbed the running back to celebrate, No. 44 was a little late. For good reason. He was retrieving the game ball for Addai.

"That game was our Super Bowl. To frickin' knock off those guys?" Clark lifts his hand to his cheek, still visibly relieved. "They were it for us."

In a rain-soaked Super Bowl, the Colts had no problems with the Chicago Bears.

Not only did Dallas Clark earn that letterman jacket, he was now a Super Bowl champion.

At the Colts' ring celebration that off-season, the tight end made his way over to Moore. He's sure the coach was a few drinks deep, so the timing seemed right to wrap this non-hugger in an all-time bear hug. "Coach Moore!" Clark said. "Thanks, man!" And in a very grand-fatherly way, Moore put his arm around Clark's shoulder. "Dallas, I just always wanted you to do your best. That's why I was always on you." Up until then, he had no clue what Moore really thought of him. This was another moment Clark will treasure forever.

From there, his career took off. After the 2007 season, he signed what was then the richest contract ever for a tight end, a six-year deal worth $41.7 million. In 2008, he broke John Mackey's franchise receiving record for a tight end with 848 yards. And, in 2009, Clark finally earned that elusive Pro Bowl berth with 100 receptions for 1,106 yards and 10 touchdowns.

A season that put his life's work on public display.

That index card at Iowa marked up with his weight gains? On the very first play of a *Monday Night Football* game in Miami, Clark toasted a linebacker up the seam, stretched out for the catch and trucked safety Gibril Wilson for an eighty-yard touchdown. That "finite focus" to only worry about that lawn to mow, that paper to deliver, that meal to cook? Against the Houston Texans, Clark somehow hung on to the ball knowing full well he was about to get Tasered by Houston Texans safety Bernard Pollard. Those Tae Kwon Do classes? Against the Ravens, he extended for a one-handed touchdown in the corner of the end zone with breathtaking flexibility. A catch that jumped Clark ahead of Mackey on the Colts' all-time receptions list.

Even when he became the big man on Iowa's campus, Clark loved winter training more than the actual games. He savored the painstaking process of *becoming* a great player more than actually *revealing* that greatness in front of a packed stadium. Exactly as he treasured his seventy-two catches for first downs in 2009 more than any touchdown. Third down, to him, is what makes the sport special. The defense calls its best possible play. The offense reaches for the ace up its sleeve. He stares into the eyes of the defender in front of him and, channeling his best impersonation of Moore, Clark barks, "Two men in a phone booth! One comes out!"

All those summer sessions with Manning paid off most in 2009, too. The route they simulated more than any other was a seam against Cover 2, a throw Manning says he could've completed to Clark with his eyes closed. He knew the exact angle Clark would take and could tell by the linebacker's back when Clark would stick his right foot into the ground and move toward the middle. Manning didn't so much fake a handoff to a running back as wield a pistol from the holster to decimate defenses with this play. There's a tendency for all offenses to unwrap brand-spanking-new plays in the playoffs because you think the defense will have your best plays blanketed. And that is the mistake, Manning explains. Into a divisional round rematch with the Ravens, on the first play of the second drive, Manning didn't care that Dannell Ellerbe hardly bit on the play fake. He whistled the football right past the linebacker's earhole to Clark up the seam for nineteen. Indy won, 20–3.

"You know that's frustrating for the defense—'Wait a minute. We worked all week on stopping that. How did they complete that?'" Manning says. "That's the reps. You spent all week stopping that. We spent the last six years perfecting that route. So, we're going to win that battle. I don't care what defense you play."

After dispatching the New York Jets, the Colts returned to Miami for the Super Bowl. In town early to partake in Pro Bowl festivities, Manning and Clark snuck in a weightlifting session at the Miami Dolphins' facility when the team's executive VP of football operations sauntered in. "This guy," Bill Parcells said, pointing at Clark, "is a pain in the butt." The Colts fell short in this Super Bowl, to the Saints, and this wild ride of a tight end life began to off-ramp. He and Manning were rolling again into 2010. They didn't even need to say a word or flash a hand signal, instead adjusting routes with what Clark calls subtle "eye looks." But six games in, Clark tore three ligaments in his wrist against the Washington Redskins. The doctor who performed the surgery said that he typically only sees this injury in snowmobile and ATV accidents when someone holds on to handlebars tightly and the rest of their body shifts upon a violent stop.

His season was over. When he returned in 2011, something was missing: his quarterback.

After starting 227 straight games for the Colts, Manning missed all of 2011 and underwent four neck surgeries. Indianapolis went 2-14— "a shitshow," Clark says—and a team that had won ten-plus games in eleven of twelve seasons dismantled. Rather than pay Manning's $28 million option bonus, the Colts decided to blow up their operation and drafted Andrew Luck first overall in the 2012 draft. Clark spent one season in Tampa Bay and another in Baltimore, and gosh, it sure felt strange to actually call plays in a huddle. "From feeling invincible," he says, "to being in another person's pants." After the 2013 season, it was time. Clark signed a one-day contract with the Colts. And, no, not a soul could mock him for holding this goodbye press conference.

It was emotional. Clark spoke with his head down, hunched over the lectern, because looking up at his family and his teammates in attendance for too long brought tears.

The same tears that resurface in our conversation whenever Mom comes to mind. Clark still misses her like crazy and is hesitant to connect her death to his success. It feels wrong. Borderline cryptic at first. But there's no reason to dance around the tragedy because the trauma from that day instilled a profound life perspective. He lives in the moment. He does not waste a second. Not in a "desperate" way, he explains. He's no daredevil checking wild feats off a bucket list. Rather, he possesses an extreme appreciation for life.

"I'm always going to try to find the good," Clark says, "because when you go to the place that Mom's death took me and you hang around there a little bit, it's not a good place.

"If you get knocked down, you've got to get back up."

In size. In style. In demeanor. Dallas Clark believes he and Tony Gonzalez are polar opposites. When the two met once, it was ... awkward. He thought the All-Pro was looking down on him. But when Clark starts talking about life, he sounds just like Gonzalez. We're sitting back in the pews of a tight end cathedral. Clark delves deep—really deep—into the meaning of life. The volume of his voice spikes at the thought of the lemmings who wake up in the morning, let out an aggravated sigh, punch in, punch out, eat, sleep, and repeat.

Treat any job as a mundane nine-to-five and the net result will be exactly that: dull, unfulfilling.

Clark knows everyone is put on earth for a specific reason.

"And it's our job to find it. I see so many people just go through life. Like, 'Yeah, this is it.' Bull. Shit. You want to slap 'em. No! No! You really think this is it? I'm talking about having value. Having self-worth. There's nothing better than seeing somebody feeling valued. If you're not, then you better be on your path toward finding that because if you haven't found your self-worth and you're just in cruise mode? You're going to have a rude awakening and look back like, 'That's it? That's my life?' Well, who else is there to blame? You."

The tight end position itself guided these two players to the same state of bliss and purpose. Neither chose the position, rather the position naturally chose *them*.

Mainly because both are more alike than they realize.

Clark, too, sees an inherent insecurity to the position. To him, a tight end is the "redheaded stepchild" on an NFL roster. Offensive linemen don't like them because they step on their feet and need help as blockers in the run game, and tight ends get to score touchdowns. Wide receivers hate tight ends because they steal targets away from them. You're forever an unwelcomed intruder who looks to your left and your right, as Clark does here in his truck, thinking, "I'm making everyone mad." That was why he gravitated toward the specialists in Iowa and Indy. They always seemed so happy.

Clark, too, fell in love with the sport organically. Not at some snazzy five-star camp or even a high school football game. No, it was during all those pickup games with his buddies when there were no parents or coaches present. When the sport was stripped down to its essence—to how Ditka shaped the position itself in the '60s, to how Gonzalez overcame his inner fear in that hitting drill at practice—Clark simply could not get enough.

"You either got beat or you beat somebody," Clark says. "You either cried and took your ball back home or you stood up to it and fought back. So many lessons were learned on those fields with no parents around. Now, you have parents doing a lot of that fighting for their kids. There's something about being a kid and *you* have to figure it out."

This very real love for a sport is how a kid loses fifteen pounds in his first collegiate game before projectile vomiting. And how Ben Coates plays through constant pain without thinking twice. And why Jeremy Shockey does push-ups in the middle of the night because he's feeling guilty from drinking. And why Gonzalez feels the need to go toe-to-toe with his own coach. People give Clark eye rolls when he says this, but he believes the tight end position is the absolute best position for anyone to play because you literally need to do everything.

He reached this point of discovery, like Gonzalez, via all of life's ups and downs.

As a father, he's no snowplow parent for his sons, Dane and Camden, and his daughter, Hazel. He'll never actively remove obstacles that stand in their way because Clark knows they'll need to encounter that same shit Gonzalez harps on. Hard times are needed for the soul. Hard times help you grow. Clark never wishes what he experienced the night of May 14, 1998, on anyone, but that night spawned his intense zest for life. He never viewed those shifts as a parking attendant or all the a.m. lifts with Doyle as a burden. Each day was an opportunity.

After that emotional farewell to the Colts, Clark could've set a map on a table and literally moved his family to any city in the country. But he knew he needed to pass this virtue on, this idea that nothing good in life comes easy, so the entire Clark family moved right to Livermore. To the site of unspeakable sadness. He never ran from the trauma. It made him. He built a house about a mile and a half from the family farm where he now tends to corn and oats. It's more hobby than profession. At the time of this chat, he was fresh off an exciting midlife crisis. One day, Clark decided to research the Iron Man Competition online and discovered that people who compete can raise a ton of money through sponsors. He decided, on the spot, to raise $1 million for the

Stead Family Children's Hospital in Iowa City. Then, he took it a step further. He texted Manning to see if his old pal was still doing work with the children's hospital that bears his name in Indianapolis. He was. Clark decided to raise $1 million for his hospital, too.

People told him this sounded like an impossible goal. Fine by him. This was the sort of thing that'd make Mom proud. Jan had every reason to complain, and never did. She raised three boys on nothing but love and hard work—paycheck to paycheck—and he'll never forget her sacrifice.

When Clark drives home from sports games with his kids, he doesn't ask why they didn't hit the ball or how they missed a big shot. He thinks big picture.

He asks one simple question: "How are you going to respond?"

The response is what's most important in life. Always.

Chapter 13

KNOW YOUR WORTH

He knew this was the biggest decision of his life. Jimmy Graham fully grasped that reality in the spring of 2009.

After putting the finishing touches on a rollicking collegiate basketball career at the University of Miami, it was time for Graham to decide what to do in life. He could've followed the path of just about every other talented six-foot-seven forward before him by playing professionally overseas. He had offers in Spain, China, and Russia. One team even offered him half a million bucks. Enticing for a kid who quite literally could not afford anything when he was homeless.

The NBA was intrigued, too. With nine tryouts lined up, Graham could've tried clinging to the barren depths of a roster. And if he was lucky? If he filled water bottles for a season or two? Perhaps he'd earn a ten-day contract and claw his way into the rotation.

He could've put his degrees in business management and marketing to use. Graham graduated that spring with excellent grades. The school president, Donna Shalala, raved about his smarts at his commencement ceremony that spring. He could've joined the military. Plan B was always to sign up for "BUD/S," a rigorous six-month Navy SEALs training course. For the longest time, Graham viewed the military as his fate since so many family members served. His stepfather was in the Eighty-Second Airborne Division and became a drill sergeant. He felt an urge to push both brain and body. The country was still at war in the Middle East and, deep down, Graham felt a "real yearning" to be part of a brotherhood that he completely missed through his childhood.

Then, there was football.

Both Shalala and the Miami Hurricanes' head coach, Randy Shannon, told Graham he should stick around campus for a year as a graduate student to play football. This echoed what two Hurricane assistants kept saying any time they bumped into Graham. Both Joe Pannunzio and Clint Hurtt would yell to Graham throughout his hoops career that he needed to flip over to the football team and make real money. Next thing he knew, Graham was hanging out with one of the school's best quarterbacks ever: Bernie Kosar. At a random barbeque in someone's backyard, the two threw a football around and chatted. Kosar relived some of his wildest stories as the Cleveland Browns' quarterback for a good thirty minutes before finally turning serious. Kosar told Graham that he could be a playmaker in the NFL. *What*, Graham thought to himself, *is this old man talking about?*

He's not sure why, but that same spring the New England Patriots reached out. Somehow, they got word that Graham was thinking about football and sent assistant Matt Patricia to Miami to put Graham through an NFL tryout. He liked what he saw in these agility drills— the size, the strength—and the Patriots offered Graham a spot on their practice squad to basically redshirt for a year. Anyone with any inkling of an NFL dream, of course, would sell their soul for a chance to be in the presence of the greatest coach and greatest player ever. This, too, was unbelievably tempting. Graham couldn't believe the Patriots even knew he was considering football. "It was honestly insane," he says. Yet, Graham also didn't want to show up completely cold—he knew he wasn't ready. So instead, he interpreted Belichick's interest as hope.

And with practically everyone telling Graham he'd be nuts to turn down the lucrative overseas deal and the NBA tryouts, he did precisely that. He returned to The U that 2009 season. Not only that. He'd play *tight end*, the position that Bubba Franks and Jeremy Shockey and

Kellen Winslow Jr. and Greg Olsen made so famous here. Word spread. And right when his confidence started to sprout, Jimmy Graham will never forget what happened next.

He was mocked, taunted, called "soft." One person laughed right in his face.

"This is a man's sport," this person told him. "Grown *men* play that sport."

Who exactly said this? Graham only grins. It was someone everyone would recognize and Graham promises to reveal this person's identity the day he dons a gold jacket in Canton, Ohio. ("I've been saving this one.") Tony Gonzalez basketballified the position with a play style the sport had not seen, but Gonzalez had also excelled at high-level Division I football. That person laughing at Graham had every reason to be skeptical because it was also true that Graham hadn't even strapped on the pads since his freshman year of high school. He knew practically nothing about football. To all outsiders, this was a twenty-two-year-old in No. 00 dunking and fouling and blocking shots.

But Graham also knew where he was at eleven years old.

An orphan. In the back of a van. Getting his face beat in.

He was ready to play football.

———

Pain. He only felt pain in that van. When death is imminent, coherent thoughts do not pass through the mind.

This day, the kids at his group home were heading to the movies. And once the driver parked to head into a store, these fourteen- and fifteen-year-olds took turns pummeling Graham. They stomped him, punched him. It became impossible for Graham to breathe. He was suffocating.

"I could feel the bones in my face breaking," he says.

His spirit was crushed. His face was bloodied. His eyes were swollen shut. But he was still able to speak. In tears, Jimmy Graham called his mother that night to explain what happened. He begged her to come get him—ASAP. And what did Mom do? She hung up the phone. She left her son alone and, for a month straight, he cried himself to sleep. There would be more beatings, too. In fact, Graham says here that many things happened to him as a kid that he'll never share with anyone because those events are too dark, too traumatizing. The sad reality of his childhood is that nobody wanted him. Graham was constantly given away by the people who should've been nurturing him.

"Dropped on the side of the road," he says, "figuratively and literally."

First, his biological father abandoned him. He thinks he was three years old. The only memory he has is Dad leaving the house in his fatigues and being told he was off to war.

That left Mom to raise Graham in this dirt-poor pocket of Goldsboro, North Carolina, and she displayed zero interest in doing so. She had already tossed her daughter into foster care. When Jimmy was nine years old, she reached an agreement with the boy's ex-stepfather—a man who Graham admired deeply. While the word "love" wasn't used by anyone, Graham most certainly loved his stepfather. This was the man who showed him how to tie his shoes. Yet when the stepfather discovered that Graham's mother was still getting $98 per week from Graham's biological father in child support, he was livid. He believed that money should've been delivered to him, since he was the guardian. Mom refused. So the stepdad drove Graham to social services, dumped him off, and told the mother to come get him. The one person Graham loved as a kid, his stepdad, effectively showed him how much he was worth right then and there: ninety-eight dollars.

Living back with Mom was hell. Not only did she treat him like he didn't exist, but her new boyfriend was physically abusive toward him. Graham lived in fear that his mother would throw him into a group home, like his sister, because he saw what five years behind those walls did to her. When he visited once, a girl held a knife to his sister's neck. Another time, he saw that the other girls had apparently taken scissors to her hair. They cut an inch off here, a foot off there because they thought their boyfriends were checking her out.

When Graham had a feeling his time was coming, he tried running away.

He leapt out of the second-story window, backpack on, and ran. "Just ran," he says. He spotted cops down the street and considered approaching them. Maybe they'd help. Maybe they wouldn't. He wasn't sure and he really had no reason to trust any adults. So by day, he instead grabbed food at a buddy's house from the back door. Brian Foster gave him food, kept it quiet and, to this day, remains the only friend Graham held on to from his childhood. By night, he lived in a massive tree outside a nearby church. Seriously. The extra-long branches were "hella comfortable." Part of him actually considered making this his new life but two weeks after running away Graham returned home. Mom coaxed him into the car. He fell asleep. Upon waking up, he freaked. Realizing he was at a group home, Graham locked the car doors and screamed. He became so apoplectic that the police needed to be called in.

None of it changed his mother's mind. She yelled for Jimmy to get out of the car and dropped his clothes off in black garbage bags. Again, Graham was told how much he's worth.

That first night, a herd of kids jumped him. "Beat my ass," he says. There was no running away, either. Kids who fled could get hit with misdemeanors because running onto any private property was technically trespassing. This massive white house in the middle of nowhere, Kennedy Home, mostly housed troubled kids then. Kids who were caught using drugs, selling drugs, on the brink of doing much worse. The website for Kennedy Home may seem "pretty and beautiful" today, Graham explains, but don't be fooled. There were fifteen kids living under one roof with two staffers when he arrived, and Graham refers to himself as the only true orphan on-site. Programs like this would receive funding from the government to serve as a second chance for juvenile delinquents.

That sounds swell on paper. For Graham, it was hell. Surrounded by fourteen- and fifteen-year-old offenders, he was an innocent eleven-year-old. A biracial kid in the south with a budding red afro and a stuttering problem.

That day in the van was the norm. A "weekly occurrence," he says. Graham learned quickly he needed to get hard.

"They were savages," Graham says, "and to survive in a place like that, *you* have to become a savage. You've got to fight. I wasn't big at the time. I'm not going to sit there and let them beat on me, talk down to me, it was almost like a hierarchy. Prison-ish. Guys would make guys fight each other. There were brawls like that. Everybody would circle up, and I remember this guy named Danny. He was in my same room. They had to move me because of this nasty fight we got into. Things got pretty violent. When you're eleven and twelve—and you're almost fighting to the death—because I'm so little at the time, I remember fighting trying to kill the guy. Because I'm worried that I might die.

"It was one of those kill-or-killed type of places. You've got to get to that level. You've got to fight for every breath. Especially when you can't breathe."

During the day, he'd head to school, where sixth grade was "fine" and "dandy" and "cute," and it was back to the group home. Back to fighting for his life. On the back of the patio—where he was forced to fight—Graham got sick of it. At eleven, maybe twelve, he beat a kid down with a broomstick.

Whereas the other kids were here by court order, he was here because of his mom. He made a personal vow to be nothing like them whenever he could gain control of his own life.

After nine months, his mother took him back. Nothing improved, of course. It was around this time that Graham started visiting Abundant Life Fellowship Church in Goldsboro. He needed the free food that church supplied and made a point to stick around for Bible study class on Wednesdays. Graham rarely said anything, but the church's youth leader, Becky Vinson, couldn't ignore the fact that Graham was wearing shorts and a tank top in twenty-degree weather. She started driving him home and, at age fifteen, Graham finally let his guard down to the entire group at church. When it was his turn to ask for prayers, there was an urgency to his voice.

Graham asked all to pray for him because he was terrified he'd be ejected back into the group home.

Vinson had enough on her plate as a twenty-six-year-old nursing student raising a six-year-old daughter, but hearing this was heart-breaking. She needed to do something. She needed to take Graham in. Inside a trailer, on her $12,000 salary, the three didn't even have functioning heat. During the winter months, Vinson would crank the oven up and everyone would wear as many layers of clothes as they could. Graham was still working through anger issues, still getting Fs on his report card. But he finally had a family and someone, in Vinson, who showed him love. "Unbelievable human being," Graham says. His adopted mother had the same demons. Vinson had been kicked out of her own home at sixteen years old and was homeless for two years.

Almost overnight, Fs flipped to As. She taught Graham how to believe in himself and, soon, Graham learned something else about himself: He was ridiculously athletic. It was always in him. He could hardly function on the eighth-grade basketball team but, man, could he jump. At five foot eight, Graham dunked. With two hands, too, since his hands were still too small to even palm a basketball. Now, the kid who needed to run five miles to practice had some support at home. He played only that one year of high school football, on the freshman team, but estimates he had close to twenty sacks. Cycling through three different high schools, Graham never had a vision for his future. He simply dominated at the ABCD Basketball Camp and through the AAU circuit to become one of the top 100 recruits in the nation. Forty scholarship offers poured in, and why not? Graham owned a forty-five-inch vertical leap. Even as he grew to six foot seven, he could land handsprings in the front yard.

Miami was the choice and Miami sure was fun. Initially, this former president of the science club in high school was a chemistry major. After a year and a half, Graham ditched the crazy lab sessions to ramp up the partying because, hey, rules are rules. All twenty-year-old athletes in Coral Gables are required to take full advantage of the gorgeous sights and sounds. Shockey set the standard. Never a prolific scorer, Graham was still one of the most electric players on the basketball court. His blocks were more like Greg Focker–style volleyball spikes. His two-handed jams were even more violent. Graham fouled out once, and Shalala first put the bug in his ear. "Jimmy," the school president said, "you know you're playing the wrong sport." By NCAA rules, since he did not redshirt, he had a year of eligibility to play another sport after graduating.

Football it was.

He chose a year on the gridiron with the 'Canes over the Patriots, the NBA tryouts, the overseas offers, the SEALs. Beyond his final stat line that 2009 season—13 games, 17 receptions, 213 yards, 5 touchdowns—Graham cites moments of "extreme growth." Like his first practice. With pads on for the first time in eight years, he might've been utterly clueless in the huddle. But most certainly not afraid. Not for a second. A 31–7 blowout loss to Virginia Tech helped. The rain, the cold. He didn't even catch a pass that night, but experiencing the sport in the elements for the first time helped. Then there were the training sessions with UM's Andreu Swasey ahead of the draft that began at 5:45 a.m. each morning. Like that track star in Kentwood, Louisiana, decades prior, Jackie Smith, he added fifteen pounds while simultaneously getting faster. In training, Graham ran the 40 in 4.48 seconds and hit 40.5 inches on his vertical...all at 260 pounds.

One coach who grasped the essence of an ever-evolving position sensed greatness. Bill Parcells—the man who coached Mark Bavaro, Ben Coates, and Jason Witten—was now running the Miami Dolphins and, as luck had it, his staff was coaching the South team during Senior Bowl

Week in Mobile, Alabama, ahead of the 2010 NFL Draft. Practices tend to mean more than the actual all-star game through what's essentially a weeklong job interview. Scouts and coaches from all thirty-two teams packed the bleachers and sideline with eyeballs glued to this peculiar basketball convert. And, all week, the Dolphins didn't exactly test-run Graham to see if he could be their own Tony Gonzalez 2.0. No, Graham believes this Dolphins staff went out of its way to strategically hide him. Bury him. *"Embarrass"* him. The Dolphins plugged this avatar of an athlete in at fullback for two days of practice, even though the only human being to ever play fullback at this size was probably "Turley" in the *Longest Yard* reboot. It was rough. One drill, Graham served as the lead blocker on a toss sweep and viciously collided with USC's hard-hitting safety, Taylor Mays. "This dude comes from thirty yards deep and knows it's a toss," Graham says. "He's running as fast as he fucking can. Me and him detonate. *Boom!* Both of us hit the ground and I'm like, 'I'm not going to survive this shit.' "

When I ask Parcells if he was trying to throw other teams off that week in Mobile, he says he cannot remember that far back. Fair enough. Graham's memory sure is vivid. During one receiving drill, he remembers a different South player dropping the football and a coach—standing right next to him—screaming "Jimmy Fucking Graham!" in a strange attempt to smear his name to anybody in listening range. Perhaps a scout was paying half attention and would give the tight end a demerit. Game day arrived and Graham got excited when the South team drove from its own eighteen-yard line to the North's nineteen in only four plays at the end of the first half. One route, one catch, one touchdown would show those thirty-two teams what he could do in the pros. With seven seconds left, the South dialed up a seam pass to the tight end...but not for Graham. He was kept on the sideline as Alabama tight end Colin Peek scored.

That being said, all week, Parcells and GM Jeff Ireland followed Graham everywhere he went.

Miami wanted him. Yet as the draft neared, Graham expected a completely different team to draft him: the Baltimore Ravens.

This team's offensive coordinator, Cam Cameron, put Graham through the worst workout of his entire life. Lined up everywhere from H-back to receiver to the slot to tight end to split end, Graham ran a hundred-plus routes for a QB Cameron brought with him. He couldn't even walk for three days after. Cameron later told him this was the hardest workout he put *anyone* through this side of Ben Roethlisberger. "He tried to kill me," Graham says. What's crazy is Cameron took the brunt of it. On the fifth of twenty sluggos—slant and go routes—the tight end broke the coach's leg. Cameron was lined up as a pseudo defender, Graham needed to react off him, and...*bam.* The tight end ran him over. Cameron needed to wear a boot for several weeks and assured his bosses back in Baltimore, which included GM Ozzie Newsome, that Graham was legit. He tried to break this hooper and Graham could not be broken.

Cameron told Graham the Ravens would draft him, and the team even sent him a playbook. Half the building viewed him as a basketball player, the OC said, half as a football player. He knew 100 percent of the building would be convinced when they saw the same *Jimmy Graham* he did.

"Cam said they were guaranteeing they were going to draft me," Graham says, "I was going nowhere else. So I started studying the playbook."

It was right then that Graham also started to realize his rough upbringing prepared him for this new world. The willingness to dive for a football fully knowing you'll be walloped by a safety across the middle? "Hard times," Graham adds, "create tough men."

There was just one little problem for the Ravens, Dolphins, and Patriots.

Another team was hot on the trail.

The coach who long viewed Parcells as a father figure was also intrigued. The week following the Senior Bowl, Sean Payton's New

Orleans Saints were preparing to face the Indianapolis Colts (and Dallas Clark) in Super Bowl XLIV right at the Miami Hurricanes' facilities. While they geared up for the biggest game of the season, the Saints multitasked by asking UM coaches and trainers which of their players was the most pro ready. The answer, constantly, was the tight end who caught all of seventeen passes. Up close, they watched this behemoth train. "A big tree running," as Graham puts himself then. This was also where Graham first met Shockey. The brash tight end was chilling in the cold tub. The two hit it off.

After winning the Super Bowl, after all hangovers from Bourbon Street wore off, it was time for the Saints to learn more about Graham. One of Payton's best qualities as the head man was how much he valued the opinions of his scouts. This was no different. He went right to his area scout in the southeast, and there's a good chance Jim Monos knew Graham's game better than Graham himself. Monos offered his ringing endorsement. On game days, Graham looked like a robot counting his steps. Monos remembers thinking the kid had no clue what he was doing. But inside the red zone, the potential was clear. His speed. His leaping. His catch radius. There was nobody like him. Other scouts might've been turned off by the drops, but Monos knew better. He watched Graham enough in practice to know those hands were glue. And the first time Graham got extended snaps in a game, against Duke, he caught 5 balls for seventy-two yards. "I remember thinking, 'OK, this is what this guy's really capable of,'" Monos says. Meanwhile, the Senior Bowl didn't deter him. That was where he got to know him as a person. Monos, a Maryland basketball fan, loved telling Graham that Terps great Greivis Vasquez owned him on the court.

The Saints continued to learn as much about Graham as possible, bringing him in for an official visit.

There's also a very good chance Parcells let his guard down and talked up Graham to Payton, too. They were that close.

Draft day arrived, and the big decision was whether or not to draft a different tight end in the southeast: Florida's Aaron Hernandez. He was clearly a first-round talent, but Monos couldn't sign off. "He was just terrifying," Monos says. "You didn't know what was going to happen, but you knew he lived a hard life." After the scout's word of warning, Payton called Florida head coach Urban Meyer for intel. Meyer never called back.

Elsewhere, both Miami and New England still coveted Graham—on their terms. He remained quite a gamble. A year after Belichick offered him that practice squad spot, Graham heard the Patriots were going to take him in the fourth round. New England drafted Arizona tight end Rob Gronkowski in the second round. Baltimore took a more conventional tight end, Oregon's Ed Dickson, seventieth overall. Miami took offensive lineman John Jerry seventy-third. Then, New Orleans had their shot at ninety-fifth overall in the third round. The best decision-makers, like Newsome, pour endless hours into stacking a draft board and then stick to that draft board. They refuse to let emotion poison the decision-making process. This time? Payton told the room he had a vision for Graham and made him the pick. He didn't care that other players were rated higher.

He beat legends Newsome and Belichick and Parcells to the punch by stealing Graham a round early.

Thirty seconds after the pick, Payton received a phone call. It was Parcells to congratulate him. He knew he shouldn't have waited.

"I thought that was a good move on his part," Parcells says. "Especially because Sean utilized the tight ends in the more modern way. He used them in different positions and out, away from the main body. Kind of like satellite players as well as the in-line players. Graham could do all that."

In the fourth round, the Patriots got around to completing their master plan on offense by selecting a second tight end 113th overall, Hernandez. One selection later, so did the Ravens. They took Dennis Pitta where they likely would've drafted Graham.

Graham was thrilled to head to New Orleans. His mind immediately raced back to the first NFL game he saw live. Before taking his plunge into football, on October 12, 2008, Graham watched the Saints spank the Oakland Raiders, 34–3, from a suite high above. His college roommate was dating a girl who had season tickets. Midgame, Graham let his mind wander.

"I always wonder," he said aloud, "what would've happened if I stuck with football."

Two years later, he was playing in this same stadium.

There's really no other way to put it. On the field, he was a leg-breaking machine. But Jimmy Graham completely BSed his way through interviews with NFL teams. The night before his fifteen-minute meetings with teams at the NFL Combine in Indianapolis, he frantically crammed jargon into his mind to sound smart. He was essentially a high schooler the night before a big test, memorizing phrases on flash cards. His agent, Jimmy Sexton, told him exactly what to say.

Graham coolly referred to two-safety looks as "2-high" and one-safety looks as "1-high." When a team asked what his favorite run play was, Graham puffed his chest out. *"Power,"* he said, lowering his voice an octave to sound tougher.

What a hilarious façade. He was green as grass.

"I remember showing up and I don't know anything," he says. "I mean, nothing. Legitimately. I really wasn't ready to play football."

More accurately, to quote former Saints coach Jim Mora, Graham knew *diddly-poo* about this sport. Physically, there had never been anything quite like him, but if looks alone guaranteed success in pro football, Arnold Schwarzenegger would be meeting Dolph Lundgren in the A gap. Very quickly, Graham did resemble an elixir of a tight end. But it wasn't by accident. On to the NFL, Graham desperately needed— and received—the right expertise from the right people. It all started during one of his first practices when he screwed up a route, dropped the ball, and moped back to the huddle with his head down.

Jeremy Shockey took one look at the rookie and was disgusted.

"Bro," he told Graham. "What are you doing? We're from The U. We have a different fucking standard. I don't want to see you dropping a ball. I don't want to see you messing a route up. Every time you score on somebody, you let 'em know. Every time you run somebody over, you let 'em know. It's not about football. You represent The U now. Everything you do from now on, you have that fucking attitude."

The rookie took these words to heart. As memories replay today, an evil smile flashes across his face.

"From then on," Graham says, "I was an asshole."

He was always tougher than anyone knew, but after this pointed message from Shockey, he started playing with a brazen cockiness that'd stun an outsider watching a Saints practice. Each Friday, Payton let the starters on offense face the starters on defense for six scripted plays. As Graham's star rose, there was a recurring scene during this period. First, Graham would do exactly what everyone saw on an NFL Sunday. He'd steal a touchdown over a helpless defender's head. But then? He'd take that football, spin his fingers onto the laces, turn toward the defensive sideline, and missile a fastball as hard as he possibly could at the head of one, Gregg Williams. The defensive coordinator avoided one head shot but did get drilled in the back once. With a pair of middle-finger salutes, he'd snipe back, "Fuck you!" and chuck the football back at Graham. The game within the game was on. Williams would start doubling Graham with a pair of defenders in a "vise" technique that he actually started using on Sundays, too. (And other defenses copied.)

If Graham still managed to score, he'd fire the ball at a player on that sideline, that player would return fire and, chances are, a fight would break out.

Williams loved Graham's heel turn. He knew such asshole behavior gave any team an edge. The bombastic DC once watched a practice at The U in the early 2000s—with all those glorious fight fests—and called it one of the greatest things he ever witnessed on a football field.

"I'm not afraid of getting people hurt," Williams says. "Learn to fight." So, this became the scene in New Orleans. Shockey traded haymakers with Ed Reed at The U and, here in New Orleans, Graham's nemesis was cornerback Malcolm Jenkins.

"He and Malcolm would get into it every…single…day," Williams says. "When I talk about true forms of competition, are you a competition-aholic? If you are, that's about winning an argument. That's about winning a staring contest. That's about a talking-shit contest. Everything we do is about competition. And if you're afraid of that? Get out."

A fake apology tended to turn feuds into fights. Graham would flatten Jenkins and give him as sarcastic of a "You're not as tough as you think you are"–style apology to make him feel soft. Then, it'd get ugly again. Graham estimates the two fought at least twenty times. If a fight turned into WWE wrestling, Payton would step in, but he rarely played referee. Usually, Williams and Payton watched on from afar. "Smiling," Williams admits, "and not letting anybody see us." A respect was earned. Everyone on the Saints defense viewed Graham as one of them.

When the Bountygate scandal ended Williams in New Orleans, Steve Spagnuolo was hired as the new coordinator and swiftly broken in. After his first touchdown against the coach, Graham gave him a little chin music. It was a close call. The ball whistled inches past Spagnuolo's temple.

Afterward, Spagnuolo asked what the heck this was all about.

"Coach," Graham told him, "you can't let me score. Every time I score on you, I'm going to launch the ball at your face."

Spagnuolo looked like he saw a ghost. He had no clue what to say.

Attitude alone wasn't enough. Graham needed to learn the sport, too, because there's no way to con your way through a game at a position that requires you to do everything. That's where the team's other veteran tight end, David Thomas, helped out. Only later did Thomas tell Graham that he thought he was an idiot his first month in town. He was shocked Graham knew so little about the sport. Basketball was all about flow and feel, not set plays. Thomas helped teach him the position. Wide receiver Marques Colston taught him how to run routes. Two weeks in, Drew Brees pulled Graham aside. The quarterback told Graham that he wanted to work with him every single day after practice. He had good reason to be this vested, too. Brees informed Graham that he could be equal to or better than Antonio Gates, his ex-teammate in San Diego. "I'm telling you," Brees said, "you have that ability."

Brees believed in Graham before anybody.

One breakthrough that 2010 season came on *Monday Night Football.* A win in Atlanta, and the Saints were in the playoffs. There was only 3:28 to go. Trailing 14–10 on third-and-three from the Falcons' 6-yard line, they called timeout, and Payton asked Brees what he wanted to do. "I want to throw it to the big kid," he said. Initially, Graham had no clue who he was speaking of. He looked around—at Colston, Shockey, Reggie Bush, Lance Moore, Robert Meachem—and realized that was him. Lined up wide right, he ran a slant, boxed out the safety, and caught Brees's pass as linebacker Sean Weatherspoon whisked past his facemask.

Next came a 360 dunk with that ball over the crossbar.

And this came one week after Graham played against the team he'd expected to draft him. During pregame, Cameron told Graham he wished they took him and to show the Ravens what they're missing. "You're going to be a superstar," he promised. Graham caught two touchdowns. One was a torso-twisting one-hander. The other, at the goal line, left Ray Lewis in the dust. After both scores, he flexed his biceps. Like his mentor, Shockey, he played with an air of vengeance. Like Tony Gonzalez, he hated the insinuation that he was a soft basketball player.

He wanted to make the teams that passed on him pay.

"I'm a very driven person," Graham says. "I'm an aggressive human being when it comes to my goals. If you tell me, 'This is how you feed yourself,' I'm going to do it better than everybody else. Because I'm a pretty hungry person and I know what it's like to not have food."

That ensuing off-season, Shockey took Graham out to eat and told the youngster that his own time in New Orleans was coming to a close. The writing was on the wall. "This is your team now," said Shockey, who then offered all the advice Graham could ever need. To this day, Graham feels indebted to Shockey for this chat. Through the NFL lockout that off-season, Graham reconnected with Swasey to train and, in 2011, authored one of the best seasons in tight end history with 99 receptions for 1,310 yards and 11 touchdowns. Early on, Graham broke one route off because he was covered and assumed Brees was throwing elsewhere. He thought wrong. Brees threw a pick. On the sideline, Brees told his tight end to never quit on a route. Even if there were two or three bodies hanging on the tight end's limbs, he'd give him a chance.

"I realized then, it's not about being wide-open," Graham says. "This dude, in big moments, is going to just toss me the ball."

That, he did—149 times, to be exact. To this day, Brees and Graham text "TDB" to each other, short for "Throw me the damn ball." Brees loved lobbing 50-50 balls to his six-foot-seven tight end. The only player whose catch radius rivaled his was Detroit Lions wide receiver Calvin Johnson. His lack of formal training as a receiver almost seemed like a good thing. His game was more spontaneous than polished. No two catches were ever the same. At Carolina, with safety Charles Godfrey draped all over him, Graham was able to cradle a tipped ball on his descent to the grass because his right arm was so long. He then topped this catch in the Week 17 rematch. Backpedaling downfield, he kept linebacker Jordan Senn at bay by shoving his left hand into his chin. With his right hand, he casually let the ball roll up his arm and pin against his body. What happened so fast to everyone else on a given play unfolded in slow motion to Graham.

So, the records fell.

That season, Brees shattered Dan Marino's single-season passing record. Into Week 17, Graham and Gronkowski both were primed to break Kellen Winslow's thirty-one-year record for receiving yards by a tight end (1,290). Graham set the record with a ninety-seven-yard day against Carolina, but it didn't last long. Minutes later, Gronkowski broke Graham's mark late in a 49–21 win over Buffalo. No, Graham has not forgotten that the Patriots allowed backup quarterback Brian Hoyer to lob a twenty-two-yarder to Gronkowski with ninety seconds left. This competition drove Graham more than Gronkowski could ever know. Throughout his Saints career, Graham pinned Gronkowski's No. 87 jersey up on his wall. Week to week, he'd compare their stats.

"I was so obsessed with trying to beat him in everything," Graham says. "It used to eat me alive."

America was robbed of the ultimate Tight End Super Bowl that year, too. This Saints team seemed destined to host the New York Giants in the NFC Championship after Graham's best play of the season. With 1:48 to go in the divisional playoff round, at San Francisco, Graham lined up in the left slot and got a half a step on All-Pro linebacker Patrick Willis. It was all Brees needed. Neither quarterback or tight end cared that safety Donte Whitner had a clean shot to terminate Graham at midfield. Graham torqued his body midair and caught the ball at its highest point right in front of Whitner. On his way to the end zone, he stiff-armed Carlos Rogers to give the Saints a 32–29 lead.

Graham took up so much space that Whitner couldn't even see the ball.

"He's that big of a guy. Do I go for the ball? Do I go for the man?" Whitner says. "It's a difficult thing to think in such a short amount of time. He was a physically dominant guy who was just bigger than everybody out there. When you see him on the field, he was so much bigger than you actually think he is. When you see him in his football uniform, he's huge!"

Unfortunately, another tight end's heroics rendered Graham's touchdown a footnote in history. Vernon Davis, the sixth overall pick in 2006, caught the game-winner with nine seconds left on the ensuing drive.

As Tom Brady and Gronkowski built a special rapport in Foxborough, so did Brees and Graham. In 2013, Graham's sixteen touchdowns led the league. He had fun doing it, too. Violently slamming the football over the crossbar became Graham's trademark celebration...until he couldn't do it anymore. In 2014, the NFL instituted what became known as the "Jimmy Graham Rule," declaring that dunking a football was akin to taunting because the ball was being used as a prop. The No Fun League might've had a point here. Twice before, Graham's dunks knocked goal posts askew. Of course, Graham didn't care. He immediately defied the rule bearing his name in an exhibition game and was fined $30,000.

He would not comply to age-old norms. That same off-season, Graham tried taking on the league when it came to a much different matter.

As Tony Gonzalez noted, one reason tight ends are so different personality-wise is because they've been so woefully underpaid over the years. Despite being asked to do a pinch of everything, a tight end's salary hovered just above kickers and fullbacks. Graham, in 2014, took a stand. After playing out his rookie contract, he told the Saints he wanted $1 more than Gronkowski. That was it. Instead, they gave him the dreaded franchise tag. At a tight end's rate, that was good for $7.053 million. Knowing he was mostly a wide receiver in this Saints offense—and being a "headstrong human being"—Graham filed a grievance to be declared a wide receiver. The season prior, Graham lined up in the slot or out wide 67 percent of the time, and that tag was worth $13.132 million. In an unprecedented twelve-page ruling, arbitrator Stephen Burbank declared that Graham was a tight end. One key reason, to him, was that Graham was still being defended as a tight end by safeties and linebackers. While the ruling prevented Graham from earning an extension on par with the game's top wide receivers, the Saints did make him the richest tight end ever with a four-year, $40 million deal.

The good times, however, did not last. The Saints went 7-9 and shipped Graham (and his contract) off to the Seattle Seahawks with a fourth-round pick for center Max Unger and a first-round pick. What should've been a historic QB-TE connection broke up after only five seasons. If the Saints hadn't shipped Graham off, longtime guard Jahri Evans is certain Graham would've gone down as the greatest tight end in NFL history. Williams cannot agree fast enough, too. The rapport between him and Brees was that special. The Saints would get maddeningly close to reaching the Super Bowl three more times with Brees, from the "Minneapolis Miracle" in 2017 to Nickell Robey-Coleman's uncalled pass interference in 2018 to a divisional playoff loss at home to the Tampa Bay Buccaneers in 2020. Graham is convinced his presence would've put the Saints over the top.

"With the way that me and Drew Brees worked together and the way we operated together," he says, "you can't even tell me those games would've been that close."

He departed as the franchise's all-time leader at tight end in receptions (386), yards (4,752), and touchdowns (51), despite playing only 78 games. Yet, off to Seattle, those old whispers about being too soft bubbled back to the surface. After the trade, the New Orleans *Times-Picayune* reported that the Saints were concerned about Graham's mental and physical toughness. This was also the same Seahawks team that had publicly ridiculed Graham. Before the Saints' 2013 divisional playoff loss in Seattle—at the height of the Legion of Boom's powers—Graham got into it with defensive tackle Michael Bennett and edge rusher Bruce Irvin. During pregame, he always enjoyed strolling on over to the other team's side of the field to catch balls in the red zone. To intimidate. To throw down a dunk or two as a gentle preview. "So they could see how big I was," Graham says, "and see that I'll be here all day, and I could do this whenever I want to." This day, Irvin was not pleased. He took the football and punted it. Graham snatched his hat off, and a Miami-like skirmish burst out.

After Seattle won, Bennett called Graham "one of the softest players in the NFL" and "overrated" and added, for good measure, "I really don't like him as a person or as a player." When all three became team-mates, they didn't exactly kiss and make up. Bennett told 710 ESPN in Seattle that he still felt the same way, and Irvin tweeted that he wanted to "fade" Graham or, in other words, fight him.

These Seahawks were a gnarly team straight out of a bygone era, skeptical of a former basketball player entering their world. Offensively, the Seahawks preferred to hammer away with Marshawn Lynch. Quarterback Russell Wilson, while talented, wasn't much of a "TDB"-inclined passer. Nor did he have the thousands of built-in reps with Graham. With the Seahawks, Graham would be expected to block. Bennett was likely speaking for many players in that Seattle locker room when he all but insinuated Graham would fall flat on his face.

One year later, nobody could question Graham's toughness.

On November 29, 2015, against the Pittsburgh Steelers, Graham ran a go route to the end zone and, as the ball fell incomplete, landed awkwardly on his right leg. He completely tore the patellar tendon in his right knee, and Dr. James Andrews was blunt. Graham remembers the renowned surgeon telling him that this was one of the worst tears he had ever seen and he wasn't sure Graham would be able to play football again. Three months postsurgery, still on crutches, Graham started to worry himself: "Why can't I walk!?" Panic consumed him daily. After doing rehab at home, alone, the simple process of showering could take a full hour. He remembers getting his clothes and crutches set up preshower and needing to literally army-crawl out of the bathroom postshower.

The Seahawks could've released Graham at any point. All along, he promised the team he'd be ready to play in Week 1.

It took him five months to learn how to walk again. Six months to jog. Eight months to cut. Seattle drafted tight end Nick Vannett out of Ohio State in the third round to be safe and—after missing all OTAs, minicamp, training camp—Graham didn't even take his first hit until Week 1 of that 2016 season against the Miami Dolphins. From afar,

Dr. Andrews called the tight end after the game to ask why he was even playing. He was stunned. "Shook," Graham recalls. At best, his knee returned to 70 percent strength that season. Whatever. He hurdled and stiff-armed and one-handed his way back to the Pro Bowl with 65 catches for 923 yards.

"With a knee they said would never work again," he points out, his tone changing. "I don't think people realize how dark that time was for me in Seattle. When I blew my knee out, I was traded for a first-round pick and the highest-paid to ever live. And I can't even walk? I mean, it was dark."

One year later, he caught ten touchdowns and was on the move again. Graham signed a three-year, $30 million deal to play with Aaron Rodgers and the Green Bay Packers but still couldn't replicate that success he had with Brees. While Rodgers's talent was "mind-boggling," this was also a quarterback more apt to throw toward the sidelines to mitigate the risk of interceptions than give a tight end 50/50 targets over the middle of the field. Graham had two OK seasons in Green Bay, was released, and signed with the rival Chicago Bears. More than all of his dazzling highlights in New Orleans, what Jimmy Graham seems most proud of are the sit-down meetings he had with the team doctors in Green Bay and Chicago. If only anyone who ever called him "soft" was right there to hear each doctor ask him about all his injuries.

By his count, Graham suffered seven high ankle sprains, a Grade 3 AC sprain in his shoulder, shattered his thumb, dislocated his fingers "thirty times," broke his ribs and, in 2012, battled through a wrist injury all season that would require surgery. All this sidelined Graham for a grand total of one game. Few ever knew what he was dealing with because Graham never wanted opponents targeting his injuries. Graham always played on because he believed anything less would be an insult to himself and his teammates. "And that," he adds, "all comes from my childhood. I wasn't going to let my boys down." Father Time chipped away at his athleticism, but he still lived for these brotherhood moments. As a miserable 2021 season eked to its conclusion, ahead of a meaningless game back in Seattle, his locker mate found out he'd be the team's starting quarterback late in the week. Nick Foles hadn't started a game in 405 days. Game day arrived and he was blunt. "Jimmy," he said, "I'm going to need you." With one minute left, on third-and-fourteen, Foles lobbed a jump ball to the tight end. Like old times, the thirty-five-year-old Graham stuck an arm into cornerback D. J. Reed's chest, boxed him out, and caught the game-winning score.

He was reunited with Irvin in Chicago, too. By then, they had become close friends. Once Irvin learned that Graham had a rough upbringing similar to his, he had to respect him. They've shared countless chats about life and business in the sauna.

Pulling through for a friend. Challenging other grown-ass men in the heat of competition. All of this is a high Graham cannot describe. He shakes his head and says he genuinely hasn't found anything in life that can replace this feeling. There's been roughly "five hundred times," Graham estimates, that he stepped up to the line of scrimmage and told himself that he's willing to blow every joint, break every bone, suffer any injury necessary on this one play.

He was willing to sacrifice everything for a game he once knew nothing about.

"I'll cut as humanly hard as I can," Graham says. "I'm willing to blow my knee out. I'm willing to sacrifice it all to get this ball. I do not care what happens. These moments, you only have these moments for a short period of time."

Speaking over the 2022 off-season, Jimmy Graham sounds like a man who'll need to be pried off the football field. He still wonders what would've happened if New Orleans didn't trade him or even if he stayed with Wilson in Seattle. "Am I satisfied?" he asks himself, in a deep state of reflection. "No." He cannot begin to imagine the feeling he'd have atop a podium as a Super Bowl champ. He wants, no *needs*, to get to this game. Only then will he be satisfied. Because Jimmy Graham actually feels empty inside. He hasn't only sacrificed ligaments and bones for this sport. The man hasn't even been on a real vacation for six years. Just this morning, at 5:30 a.m., Graham snuck in a "quick thirty-miler" on his bike. Considering how much energy he has poured into football, Graham believes he has actually underperformed.

There's nothing he hates more than a person telling him how special of a player he's been.

"When people tell me that, it pisses me off. I feel like a disappointment at times. Sometimes, I genuinely feel like I have failed myself."

The clear sense here is that Graham wants to ride this high as long as he can. Maybe because he lived the opposite his entire childhood. Until he met Vinson, he lived a nightmare. Certainly there are "three or four" events in his life he could've done without. But Graham also knows that, like Dallas Clark, he is a direct product of his darkness. He sees the same cause-and-effect in his life. Genetics wouldn't have been enough. Without his grandmother telling him at seven years old that he better learn how to beg for quarters because that was all he'd be doing one day, without those terrifying nights at Kennedy Home, without *everything*, Jimmy Graham is not in the NFL. He wouldn't go back and smooth out his traumatic childhood too much because it forced him to become a man at eleven years old. He learned survival skills that so many of his peers didn't until their twenties and thirties. If at all. Several tight end greats dug themselves out of rock bottoms—it doesn't get much worse than the back of that van.

Graham learned to rely on one person. Himself.

"There's no one to whine to. There's no one to cry to. You're alone," Graham says. "No one cares about you. You have to grow up real quick, and you realize life is tough. Nothing's given. You have to go take it. No one's going to sit here and listen to your sob stories. When you have that notion when you're that young? It grows into something. It builds you into a man very quickly, so when you do become a man, you don't have to learn through all these hardships that young men have to.

"I was forced to become a man at a very young age and realize just how to operate and deal with issues and anger and hate, honestly, because I wasn't spoon-fed."

And, like Clark, he was destined to pour his life experiences into this glorious position. The kid who went from getting straight Fs to graduating as a valedictorian cannot stress enough how intellectually demanding tight end is in the pros. And the reason Graham wasn't afraid to rumble with Irvin in Seattle or obliterate *any* body part before *any* play was that he was fighting for his life as a kid.

Once Vinson got Graham to believe in himself, he was consumed by an all-or-nothing mentality. He gave himself no out. Graham needed to capitalize on his athleticism.

"I said I was going to change my life. I was going to be different than everybody. When people said I couldn't, I was going to do it."

As a result, he gave hope to an entirely different type of athlete. Talented threes and fours on the basketball court who happen to be three or four inches too short for the NBA can now think about an entirely new profession in sports. This athletic body type is now the rule, not the exception, because the skills required on the hardwood translate so, so beautifully to tight end. Graham has spoken to at least fifty basketball players about the transition. Just as he was glued to clips of Gonzalez and Shockey, teens now replay his reels on YouTube. He helped a niche enterprise explode into the mainstream, taking pride in that "Jimmy Graham Rule" and the fact that the richest tight end, George Kittle, is making $15 million per year. If a team doesn't employ an athletic tight end with a basketball background, they'd better start searching for one.

On a deeper level, Graham opened doors beyond football. He knows there are orphans just like him crying themselves to sleep. That's why, in 2015, Graham shared his chilling story at the White House for a "Youth Champions of Change" event. That day, Graham thanked all mentors listening for showing kids like him—kids who think they're worth only $98—that there's hope.

He's only getting started, too. Everyone can count on Graham supplying more detail to his remarkable story. If he makes it to Canton, that person who told Graham football is for grown men better be tuning in.

He'll be using your name.

"Grown men do play this sport," Graham says. "I guess I'm a grown man, too."

Chapter 14

YO SOY FIESTA

Rob is dead!

The thought absolutely crossed his big brother's mind.

Chris was ten years old. Rob was eight. And there Rob Gronkowski laid motionless in their bathtub. Chris couldn't even hear him breathing. He was terrified.

This all started innocently enough. The two were playing a game of Pogs, all the rage in the mid-1990s, in their big brothers' bedroom. They placed candy on top of the circular cardboard milk caps and tried flipping them over with "slammers." Whoever could successfully flip a Pog got to keep that piece of candy. The only problem was that Rob was still seeking revenge for losing a brawl to Chris earlier in the day during a game of Mini Sticks. So, mid-Pogs, he couldn't help but take that twenty-four-inch hockey stick and wail Chris over the back five times.

His back on fire, Chris jolted to his feet and chased after Rob who, as always, sped directly to the bathroom. This was the go-to move for all five Gronk boys. After attacking a brother, you sought shelter.

This time, however, Chris got to the door before Rob could fully shut it and his rageful momentum launched Rob airborne. Rob's head smashed violently against the bathtub and he crumped into a heap of flesh and bones—out cold. Chris froze. He wasn't sure what to do and, after heading back to the bedroom, his mind started to wander: *What*

271

if Rob is seriously dead? Should I call for help? For a good thirty seconds, he was scared shitless. Then, in stormed Rob at full blast wielding that hockey stick. He wailed Chris four more times across the back—*Whack! Whack Whack! Whack!*—before then racing back to the bathroom and, this time, shutting that door in time.

Rob locked it. Rob laughed his ass off.

Such was day-to-day life for the Gronkowski boys.

"Growing up was craziness," Rob Gronkowski says. "Maniac times. It was like WWE back in the heyday—every single day."

That's no exaggeration. A brawl broke out every single day inside their home, just outside Buffalo, New York. And all those brawls created a tight end who certainly can stake his claim as the greatest ever. Rob Gronkowski has always been a wild man straight out of the Paleolithic Age. Long before he was slugging beers, scoring chicks, and spiking footballs in the NFL, he was just the fourth of five boys trying to survive in an environment unlike any other. Gordie Jr. was six years older, Dan was four years older, Chris was two years older. The youngest, Glenn, was born four years after Rob.

There are sibling rivalries. Then there's these five boys.

The best way Gordy Sr., Father of the Gronks, can put it? "Chaotic" and "outrageous." Dad only had two rules: (1) No punches to the face; (2) No punches to the family jewels. Everything else was fair game, which meant the boys usually pinned each other down and unloaded charley horses. That is, hard punches to the thigh. One Gronk would punch another Gronk again…and again…and again… "until," Chris says, "you couldn't even walk anymore." If your victim was too squirmy that day—and you couldn't get a clean shot in—the other maneuver was to simply pin a brother down with both hands until they screamed for mercy.

The Gronks abided by standard WWE rules, meaning you could tap out. Of course, all this afforded you was approximately 3.5 seconds to catch your breath before being pounded again.

One game Gordy created was "Zoom Zoom," in which he cleared

out the family room and had one son start in one corner of the room with another in the opposite corner. Each held pillows and rammed into each other at full speed. "Boom!" says Gordy, smacking his hands together to reenact the epic collisions. Most blood was shed playing Mini Sticks, which is exactly what the name implies. With those miniature hockey sticks, goals, and a ball—playing on their knees—the Gronks went to war one check, one slap shot, at a time. Dad made the arena as safe as he could with legit "boards" along the sides. But that didn't stop Rob from giving Glenn six stitches in his chin at the tender age of three years old. On Christmas Eve of 1996, Rob checked his younger brother so hard into the one part of the basement that was not carpeted that "Goose" started gushing blood and needed to be rushed to the emergency room.

All toughness everyone sees on a football field started right here. With Mini Sticks. Before doing anything else—before homework, before chores, before dinner—they'd sneak a quick game in. And it never truly was a game until someone suffered a deep bruise, a cut to the lip, a damaged ego. Years later, Rob remains damn proud of the collision that sent his little bro to the ER. "He got *cremated* by me." Their mother, Diane, captured it all on VHS camera. They still watch it.

"We laugh our butts off every single time," Rob says. "It just brings us down that memory lane of the great times we had growing up and how much craziness it was growing up, too, with the five of us boys always competing and going at it every day. I just remember those hits. They were epic. Those were the best times growing up. You had to be tough growing up, and that led to where I am today. Installing that toughness into me at that age to where you can take a hit and get right back up and go at it again."

There was a safe alternative in the form of Bubble Hockey, another Western New York staple. With rods, you control small figurine hockey players inside a bubbled dome. Typically, a SuperChexx product like this goes for a cool $3,500. An investment that went up in smoke when one Gronk threw another Gronk off the couch...right through the bubble. Memories blur. Dan is fairly confident Rob and Chris were the culprits.

Adds Gordy: "It was a nice bubble. It went in the garbage, though."

All chaos had one common denominator: Rob serving as the primary instigator. He'd jump atop one brother, chuck a fork at another. "Anything," Dan says, "to start a fight." Everyone tried to tame him. The stern Gordy could usually control all boys with a dad classic, the dramatic "3...2...1..." countdown. He never needed to lay a finger on them. The nebulous fear of Dad kicking their ass usually worked. Except, of course, with Rob. He was unrelenting. On one family vacation to Myrtle Beach, with Rob standing outside at a rest stop, Gordy told him he couldn't put up with him anymore. "I'm just going to leave ya." He then tapped the gas pedal and slowly drove away. A decade before he was knifing through NFL secondaries for 107 touchdowns in 165 games, there was Rob lumbering toward the van. Diane usually busted out the wooden spoon. When Rob was thirteen, she took off after him and Rob tripped over his JNCO jeans, which had been a point of contention. Dad had shut down Rob's nonstop requests for a pair of the absurd wide-legged pants. These were a pair borrowed from a friend down the street. So when he tripped, Mom caught up, Mom wailed away, and there was Dad supplying the commentary: "You deserve it! I told you not to wear those stupid pants!"

Dad even took the mythical "Father Baker" threat to a whole new level. Whenever kids act up in the Buffalo area, parents often warn that they'll ship 'em off to Father Baker, a Roman Catholic priest who took in orphans up to his death in 1936. That was no different at the Gronk household until, one day, Gordy told Rob to pack up his belongings and Rob did. Rob stuffed his jockstrap, his baseball glove, his clothes into a suitcase and off the two went. As they drove down the street, Rob stuck his head out the window and yelled to strangers on the sidewalk, "I'll be back! I was bad just for a little while." And as Gordy cruised down

Sheridan Drive through Amherst, New York, he spotted a random building to serve as his imaginary home of Father Baker.

He pulled up and set the car in park before offering his son a few final words.

"You can't listen to your mother. That's it. It's over. You've got to go away for a little while. This is where all the bad kids are. He'll give me a call when you're better."

With that, Gordy walked around to the passenger side of the vehicle. Rob finally cracked. Tears streamed down his face and he refused to get out. With his hands clutching the steering wheel, Dad pulled his feet. Rob was rendered completely horizontal.

"Let's go, Rob! You gotta go!"

Rob sobbed and sobbed and promised his dad he'd start behaving.

"You promise?!"

"Yeah!"

The two drove home. The next day, Rob was back to wreaking havoc.

Through it all, however, one redeeming quality became clear. A quality that'd separate Rob Gronkowski from all his peers in the NFL. As he absorbed bruise after bruise, he didn't whine and cry and beg for mercy. No, his reaction was different...he giggled. He wasn't simply numb to the pain—he appeared to *enjoy* it. And once he shook free, Rob was a punch-drunk boxer begging for more. He couldn't compute fear. As if he utterly lacked the amygdala, the part of the brain that assesses risk and steers humans away from danger. A large part of this was nurture. At a young age, Dad had all five boys catching tennis balls he threw high into the sky. After this, they'd field ground balls. The first time he tried to ski? Forget the bunny hill. At Holiday Valley Ski Resort, an hour south of Buffalo in Ellicottville, New York, Gronkowski popped on skis, eyeballed a steep slope, got on the chairlift, and recklessly flew right down.

"I'm like, 'Oh shit. I've got skis on. Here's a hill. I've got to go full speed. Right down it, baby,'" Rob says. "I've always been like that. I just never thought about the risk—ever. I only thought about the thrill."

Bring on all charley horses. Bring on that T-bone collision in the secondary. To his core, he's always been a human being who lives like there is no tomorrow. Rob needs the world to know one thing, too: His brothers never knocked him down for good.

"I went full speed back at them. They didn't know how to handle that."

This mentality was inherently in him. Before Gordy Gronkowski was sending four of his five sons to the NFL (with the other drafted into the MLB), he was a high school senior from West Seneca, New York, that no Division I team wanted. He was going to head to the Marines but first figured he'd do everything in his power to get a look. His own coach didn't believe he could play college football, which he says lit a "Fuck you, I'll prove you wrong" fire under his ass. He broke into the coach's office to steal 8 mm game film, packed them into an Adidas bag, and purchased a $240 bus ticket to travel across the country and sell himself to schools in California. The beaches, the girls, the weather, it all served as the "big illusion" in his head. The dream. His bus would pull into a city, and he'd then hitchhike his way to campus to explain to a coach why he deserved a scholarship. Gordy visited UCLA, Berkeley, USC, Los Angeles, San Diego State, and the lone school to offer him a full-time scholarship: Long Beach State.

When Gordy returned home that spring, no one believed him. Nor did he have much support from his own father. Then another door opened. A coach from nearby Syracuse University was in town to watch one of his recruits, future Orangeman running back Dennis Hartman, play baseball. Gordy just so happened to hit the snot out of the ball that game, and the next thing he knew, he was unlocking his car to retrieve that 8 mm game film. SU offered him a scholarship. He chose SU.

"So, here's a kid who got zip. Nothing. Nothing. No Division III, nothing. Now, I have two Division I scholarships on the table."

Yes, it's in the Gronkowski blood to take matters into your own hands.

When one kid was bullying Dan on the school bus, Mom instructed him to tell the bus driver. Dad? He told both Dan and Gordie to bypass the bus driver and confront the bully—to both "kick the fucking shit out of him." Dad knows Rob is wired like him most because Rob was always the most animalistic of the lot. In that basement, he cleared room for five huge trophy cases (one for each son). The message was clear. He wanted all five competing like madmen for the most hardware. At one point, Gordy counted more than six hundred trophies in all. None of the boys were allowed to play tackle football until seventh grade, so until then, Rob had no choice but to unleash all aggression in hockey. Real hockey. This Mini Sticks legend flattened kids and, once, even scored eight goals in a game.

Next came a rite of passage. Into eighth grade, each Gronk boy received a heart-to-heart chat with Dad. If they wanted to play video games like their buddies, fine. Go ahead. Good luck. "Don't waste my time," he'd say, "and don't waste your time." But if they wanted to be an athlete? If they wanted to try to play a sport in college? He promised to do everything in his power to help get them there with a disciplined weight-training program. Gordy sold fitness equipment in Western New York and still does. His company, G&G Fitness, is now an empire with fourteen stores across four states.

Son to son, working out became contagious. Mom spent $600 per week on groceries with the Gronkowskis guzzling two and a half gallons of milk per day. Knowing his kids would be eating all day long, Dad started posting motivational nuggets on the refrigerator. If a pro athlete did something good (like donate to charity) or something bad (like get arrested), for example, he'd pin the newspaper clipping to the fridge.

Dad's life advice always circled back to one theme: "Live every day to the fullest."

Rob needed no coaxing. He wanted to get jacked like his older brothers.

"I was looking at them and saying, 'Man, I can't wait to be as strong as my brothers.' Having arms like that. Biceps like that. When they're in high school, I'm in eighth grade, they look extremely jacked to me. Huge. And muscular. So at that time—my dad did this with all of us— he said, 'If you want to get to the next level, if you want to be the strongest, you have to get in the weight room, you have to work out.' He showed us the way. He didn't really push us. He said, 'This is the way to do it. If you want to do it, you can do it. You need to be stronger if you get to the next level.' That's where it started. My brothers and I fell in love with it. We were pushing each other to work out. We fell in love with it. To this day, we all work out together."

There was one other motivating factor, too. This is the same kid whose AOL screen name was "chickmagnet4life." As a *fourth* grader. Hang around any Gronk lifting session and in no time you'd hear one bellow, "Do it for the chicks!" Dad's plan worked. All five boys earned college scholarships, saving the family approximately $750,000 in tuition. Rob started believing in himself as a football player early. Very early. Elevated to the Williamsville North High School varsity team for the playoffs as a freshman, his confidence soared on kickoffs when he was able to tee off on tenth, eleventh, and twelfth graders.

"From there on out," Rob says, "it was domination. At all levels."

To put it mildly.

In basketball, he once dunked and shattered a backboard during warmups. The game was canceled. Williamsville East sent Williamsville North the bill. Football games were pure comedy. Playing defensive end, Gronkowski once chased down a toss sweep toward the opposite sideline with eyes, head coach Mike Mammoliti recalls, "big as Coke bottles." He caught the poor chap from Clarence High School about two yards behind the line of scrimmage and hurled him, like a trash bag, roughly ten yards into the bench on the sideline. Rob laughed the whole time.

The only way anyone could stop Gronkowski was by hacking him in basketball or giving him the ol' high-low in football. One

kid would shove him high with another chopping his legs low...
and, by God, did that piss Gronkowski off. Released into the public, he couldn't exactly ball up a fist and punch an opponent in the
thigh or wield a hockey stick. Football and basketball coaches alike
would sense his blood boiling and sub Rob out to cool down. Sure,
Mammoliti was protecting Rob. He was protecting everyone else on
the field, too.

"He would've just killed somebody," Mammoliti said. "Everybody
wanted a piece of him. Until they actually tried to get a piece of him.
And then they're going, 'Eh. Nah.' What's that old saying? 'Be careful
how you poke the bear'?"

He was too ruthless and too dominant for anyone he'd face from
any school, so Gronkowski started asking a Division I–bound, 275-
pound offensive guard Will North to stay on after practice and rough
him up at the line of scrimmage to work on his releases. As a fan, he
couldn't take his eyes off of one player: Jeremy Shockey. The way he
ran people over. The partying. This became his favorite tight end of
all time. Gronkowski watched Shockey steamroll defensive backs and
tried to do the exact same thing. He wrote him that letter, too.

"Jeremy Shockey put that position on the map," Gronkowski says,
"with the way I wanted to play the game and live life."

One by one, the Gronks went pro. Dan, Chris, and Glenn all were
able to hang around on the NFL's fringes for a few years. Yet something
about Rob was different. He combined the barbarity of Shockey with
the playmaking of Tony Gonzalez. Dad realized Rob had a shot at being
an all-time great simply by the way he could bend and twist and contort
his body at bizarre angles. Rob was beyond flexible—"like Gumby," he
says.

As a high school junior, Rob had sixty college scholarships. After his
parents separated and his dad moved to the Pittsburgh area to expand
G&G, Rob went with him and attended Woodland Hills (Pennsylvania) as a senior. A major step up. Here, Rob recalls ten players on his
team running a 4.5 in the 40 and eight going Division I, yet the circus

acts only got wilder. New friends soon dubbed him "Drago," after Ivan Drago in *Rocky IV*. Gronkowski would set the JUGS machine at 75 mph and catch passes ten yards away. In one game, he drove a defensive end twenty yards downfield on a perfectly legal block, prompting the officials to tell the coach to calm him down. In another, he toted four players on his back into the end zone. And another, he ejected a running back into a fence along the sideline. As the fourth-ranked tight end in the nation, per Rivals.com, Gronkowski chose Arizona University.

One reason? The pool parties. He liked what he saw on his visit.

Of course, Gronkowski knew he'd need to get bigger. From that February to July, he bulked up from 230 to 260 pounds by feasting on footlongs at Subway. He'd pour every possible dressing on each sandwich and top each one off with two cookies because, on to college, Gronkowski fully planned for his cartoonish dominance to continue.

"I knew I had to level up. Running over people in high school? I should be. I'm faster. I'm stronger. I'm bigger than everyone. So that's expected. But getting to the next level in college, I was like, 'Man, what am I going to do?' I kept the same mentality that it's going to happen. No doubt about that. That's a mental side you've got to keep: 'No matter who's in front of me, I'm going to rock him.' Obviously, I wasn't moving guys like I was in high school, compared to college. But you can still move guys and run people over. I just had that mentality going into college still of, 'Man, nothing's going to change. I'm going to come in and dominate.'"

The play that turned this into reality occurred the night of September 29, 2007. In the midst of a 48–20 rout of Washington State, Gronkowski caught a pass deep down the middle of the field and was simultaneously drilled with a hard right shoulder from No. 18 in white, a blow that renders 99.9 percent of tight ends a carcass on the side of a highway. But not Gronk. He absorbed the blow, spun, staggered, and sprinted into the end zone for the touchdown. His memory of this breakthrough moment remains vivid.

He knows that No. 18 was a DB named Alfonso Jackson, and that he never even saw him coming.

What Gronkowski did not know is that he essentially ended Jackson's football career.

Initially, the science of this all doesn't make sense. *Jackson* brought the boom to Gronkowski, not the other way around. *Jackson* had the bad intentions. But in that millisecond before impact, Gronkowski tensed up those muscles honed back home and basically shape-shifted into a brick wall. Jackson's ears rang. He blacked out. He suffered a concussion and didn't wake up from that concussion until he was in the emergency room. Jackson took one week off and tried to play against Oregon, but his brain was in a haze the entire game. He told the trainers to take him out. Jackson missed two more games and tried to play in Washington State's final three contests, but his vision remained blurry. Into the off-season, he cycled through a string of concussion tests and the symptoms persisted. Something as innocent as high-fiving a teammate could make him see double.

Still, Jackson loved the game and harbored NFL dreams. He tried to play on as a senior.

After suffering another concussion that made his left arm go numb, Jackson told doctors he was fine. Unfortunately, in the rematch with Arizona, he caught a cleat to the chin while tackling a returner. His head rang, his arm was on fire and—finally—he conceded his career was over. A decade later, Jackson told me for a story at Bleacher Report that he still experienced double vision and needed to squint to see objects in the distance. Not surprisingly, as a high school coach, he'd warn his defensive backs not to beeline toward pass catchers like he did because you never know what you're running into.

When I fill Gronkowski in on this scary aftermath, he cannot believe it. He's genuinely empathetic with a loud, "Send him my love!"

Of course, Gronkowski was only getting started. From afar, Mammoliti loved watching how Gronkowski so jubilantly washed everything down as an in-line blocker. He knew blocking had become cathartic for the kid he was once saving from himself. This was a chance to legally unleash his pent-up aggression. Granted, there was collateral damage. After injuring his own back, Gronkowski missed the entire 2009 season. From afar, however, Bill Belichick realized how dangerous this specimen could be in his offense and selected Gronkowski with the forty-second overall pick.

Inside the green room at Radio City Music Hall in New York City—in a pinstriped suit, with his hair gelled—Gronk held the phone to his ear, received the news, and wasted zero time living like there's no tomorrow.

———

Most of America met Rob Gronkowski for the first time that night on national television and realized instantly this was a different species.

Because in this habitat, the green room, it gets lonely.

Players get drafted, families clear out, you can hear a pin drop. This was where a pale, sad Aaron Rodgers spent an eternity in 2005. Yet the second after Gronkowski stuffed the phone back in his pocket, all Gronks popped to their feet and huddled around the table. Faces inches apart, in a pseudo rugby scrum, they shouted in unison "Woo! Woo! Woo!" while jumping up and down. Rob hugged Dad to his right and Mom to his left, and dapped up his brothers.

Off to the main stage he went to meet commissioner Roger Goodell, clutching a New England Patriots helmet. Even the way he held hands with Goodell was different. Gronkowski locked the commish's knuckles in a death grip, appearing to more so flex the guns for a Facebook profile pic. On ESPN, Mel Kiper Jr. pooh-poohed the pick, calling Gronkowski "stiff." He was surprised the Patriots didn't select a linebacker like Sergio Kindle or Daryl Washington. On NFL Network, Mike Mayock compared him to the top tight end taken the year prior, Brandon Pettigrew. Gronkowski was greeted by Deion Sanders for his first-ever TV interview as a pro and Sanders began by joking that Gronkowski nearly dislocated his shoulder bringing him in for a hug.

"Man, I'm so fired up, man," Gronkowski said. "This is a great organization. I love all the coaches, all the players, it's awesome. I'm going to have one of the best quarterbacks ever in the league throwing me the ball. This is the greatest moment of my life, man. It's unbelievable."

The rest of the Gronks soon appeared for pictures. Rob leapt into the air to chest-bump Dad, popped that helmet on and—with all the brothers chanting "Gronk Gronk! Gronk!"—screamed a rebel yell into a camera that served as a warning to the entire league.

Rob Gronkowski was coming for blood.

Year 1 was solid. He caught 42 balls, 10 of them for touchdowns. On Thanksgiving Day, he motioned down the line and, with one blinding crackback, sent Detroit Lions defensive end Kyle Vanden Bosch crumbling to the turf with a bulging disc in his neck. "He didn't even mean to do it," wide receiver Julian Edelman recalls. "He was just having fun and was being a beast. It was pretty gnarly." But Year 2? That was when Gronkowski took a blow torch to pro football. He was Shockey 2.0. Off the field, Gronkowski partied like a rock star, posing for one shirtless Twitter photo with porn star Bibi Jones. On the field, he disemboweled defenses. There was no scurrying out of bounds and no surrender in catching 90 passes for 1,327 yards with an NFL-high 17 touchdowns. There were tight ends before him who were too athletic for linebackers and too strong for defensive backs, but Gronkowski was more mutation than hybrid. He clowned any chump who tried tackling him high.

The man known by all simply as "Gronk" pulled off stunts the position had never seen. He was now a shredded six foot six, 260 pounds and also happened to have the greatest player ever throwing him the ball.

This was the perfect storm Gonzalez could only dream of.

No play boggled the mind more than his forty-nine-yarder against the Washington Redskins on December 11, 2011. First, he made a diving catch and barrel-rolled 360 degrees. When Gronk popped to his feet, he was greeted by defensive backs DeJon Gomes and Reed

Doughty. Their combined 414 pounds dragged him toward the sideline with all momentum for an obvious stop. So obvious that veteran cornerback DeAngelo Hall outright quit on the play and began walking in the opposite direction. Gronk shook free, raced up the right sideline, and only went down when cornerback Josh Wilson hurled himself into the tight end's legs. Such self-sacrifice proved to be the only hope any tackler had. Gronk scored one play later and spiked the pigskin. More accurately, it appears he's drilling for oil. People had been spiking for a half century, but never like this. He revolutionized the celebration. He'd go on to publicly spike everything from a bridal bouquet at a wedding to a puck at a Boston Bruins game to Steve Harvey's Lego sculpture on New Year's Eve.

He didn't seem to be human, to both opponents and teammates. Inside the locker room after the Washington stunt, Wilson described Gronkowski as a "human gargoyle" to reporters. Other times, Edelman remembers sprinting next to Gronkowski midplay and thinking he was keeping pace with a Clydesdale horse.

"A Clydesdale," he specifies, "that was *giggling*. He'd be laughing, 'Hee-hee-hee!' in the middle of running. You could hear the force because of how big he was and how strong he was. He sounded like a fucking horse. Gronk was in a world of his own. In his prime, it was unfair. In those 2010, '11, '12, '13, '14 years, it was like watching an eighth grader play against third graders."

In the 2011 divisional round of the playoffs, he supplied one of the greatest tight end games ever against the Denver Broncos with 10 receptions for 145 yards with 3 touchdowns. On one fade to the corner of the end zone, Gronkowski dove and tipped the ball with his right hand before cupping both hands underneath on his descent for the catch. This wasn't some clumsy linebacker he toasted, either. It was veteran cornerback André Goodman. The only thing that slowed Gronk down that season was a grisly high-ankle sprain the following week in New England's AFC Championship win over Baltimore. Despite wearing a walking boot one week before Super Bowl XLVI in Indianapolis,

Gronkowski played. He nearly topped off this epic season with a scene straight out of Hollywood, too. On the final Hail Mary heave against the New York Giants, he lunged horizontally—like he had done so many times that season—and came within inches of cradling the deflection.

The Patriots lost. The confetti fell. What happened next seemed to captivate the nation as much as any play in the game.

During an invite-only Patriots postgame party at nearby (and ironically named) "Victory Field," videos captured Gronk celebrating as if he won. He flailed all over the dance floor and, per family custom, tore his shirt off. The public wasn't sure how to process this raw footage because the public had never seen this before. After such a crushing loss, Gronkowski should've been sulking in throbbing pain, right? Certainly not party-rocking with the band LMFAO and his brothers at 2:30 a.m. Yet this was zero shock to those who knew the man best. Gronk always lives in the moment, so Gronk was able to move on—quickly.

"What are you going to do? Mope about it?" Gordy Sr. says. "He went out and had a good freakin' time."

When Edelman saw the video, he laughed and chalked it up to "Rob being Rob." The teammates who saw how insanely difficult it was for Gronkowski to gut through that game, he says, did not have a problem with it. The backlash from ex-Patriots was nonetheless deafening. Former Patriots safety Rodney Harrison said that if he or fellow ex-Patriots Willie McGinest, Tedy Bruschi, Larry Izzo, or Richard Seymour were at the party, Gronkowski "probably would have got his head rung." At that very moment, Gronk himself faced quite a dilemma: Was it time to acquiesce to how all stars were supposed to conduct themselves in such a moment? To huddle up with PR handlers and map out an apology tour? To change who he is?

No. No. And, uh, *hell no.*

Gronkowski lived the rock star life he'd always dreamt of, kicking off the "Summer of Gronk." He posed nude for ESPN's The Body Issue. He joked that he'd like to take Tim Tebow's virginity. He participated in a reality dating show on Fox. He won a celebrity home run derby contest back in Buffalo. With three years left on his rookie deal, he became the richest tight end ever with a $54 million, six-year deal. The greatest house party ever happened that off-season, too. Gronkowski estimates about fifteen teammates were present at what they dubbed "Ratio," a likely reference to the number of men and women present. He refuses to provide any details from that night. He only giggles. The next off-season, with a broken forearm, TMZ revealed a shirtless Gronk body-slamming someone at a Las Vegas nightclub that the gossip site described as a friend. "They never said who the guy was that he dropped on his head," Gordy Sr. points out. "It was his brother. They're always doing stupid stuff."

Partying defined Gronkowski those early years in New England as much as any catch, any touchdown, any spike. A period of time that fullback James Develin confirms was genuinely "*nuts.*" After the Patriots clobbered the Colts in the 2014 AFC Championship, players packed Gronkowski's Foxborough home. His place resembled a nightclub, right down to the DJ and strobe lights and drinks. And, perhaps, scantily clad women? "I won't say if there were or weren't," Develin says. He actually brought his wife to the party and, within no time, one random dude in a thong started dancing all over her like "Party Boy" from *Jackass*. Develin had no choice but to step in. He thinks it was one of Gronk's pals from Buffalo.

"I mean-mugged him," Develin says. "He's like, 'No, man! I'm just having a good time! Playing around!' It wasn't a big deal but that was the type of scene it was—people having fun, people letting loose."

The Gronk Cruise, in February 2016, was the stuff of legend. Rapper Waka Flocka Flame, who calls Gronk the white version of himself, had never partied like this before. He described it as kids going to school without a principal, a teacher, laws of any sort. There were free drinks and loud music everywhere. "Like being in Willy Wonka's Chocolate Factory," he said, "with strobe lights and bass." Through the first four years of his career, Gronkowski admits he'd go hard on Friday and

Sunday nights during the season. He speaks today in an ultra-nostalgic tone. He believes he caught the last wave of real partying in the NFL—*house parties*—and is thrilled he took full advantage, too.

"You're partying. You're drinking. You're throwing some back. You're running people over," Gronkowski says. "That's just how you picture it, man. Just living it up like we were in a movie. Living that party life in the NFL, and also going out and playing in the games and dominating. I would definitely say in my younger twenties we were rocking out big time.

"Lived it all to a T. Partying with musicians. Other athletes. I mean, I kind of got into the last phase of athletes partying. Before all this social media took over. That last phase of people in the NFL all living it up like you're in the '90s. I caught a couple veterans in New England who loved to do that stuff, too. My young twenties was like the last era of it. And I'm glad I got it in, man. I didn't want to sit here like, 'Man, I didn't live how I wanted to live in the NFL.' I did it. That's how I thought the NFL should be. Rocking out like a rock star off the field and on the field. There's no regrets. I lived it up."

If anything, all the partying helped him as a tight end. For starters, Gronkowski would usually force himself to work out the next morning. Like Shockey, he'd feel guilty. He'd pop in an *INSANITY* DVD and plow through the piercing hangover with his brothers. The party cruise was total debauchery—Gronkowski was dead to the world for a full three days afterward. But it wasn't like he even needed to train those three days. At one point, Gronk, Waka, and WWE star Mojo Rawley all decided to wrestle. And whenever he partied those early years, he danced nonstop. Vodka-waters helped him stay hydrated while also avoiding the beer gut, and if the party was five hours? He danced for five hours. He turned a night of partying into a workout.

"Burning that many calories while partying, that kept my football game going. No lie. Hands down. No doubt about it."

Not that his dance moves were derived from a Michael Jackson video.

He'd shake his whole body without any semblance of a plan.

"Everyone said it looked like I was having a seizure and I thought I was killing it. I'd say, 'At least my whole body was shaking! It was warming up. It was loosening everything up!' "

And if anyone had a problem with Gronk's lifestyle? Too damn bad. "They were just jealous," Develin says. There was nothing the New England Patriots could say. They weren't thrilled initially, but Gronkowski wasn't causing any trouble. Like Shockey, he was never arrested. "He's in Vegas," Dad says, "dropping his brother on his head. They understand that." Gordy was always cognizant of the fact that his own father was an alcoholic, too. Back when Rob and the gang were in high school, he made sure they understood what abusing alcohol could do. Waka was stunned by how controlled Gronk was in chaos. It also didn't hurt that Gronkowski was simultaneously emerging as one of the best players in league history. Edelman admits that Belichick gave Gronkowski a different set of rules from everyone else. Teammates didn't care, either. They saw how hard he worked.

A player doesn't get to Tom Brady's level by accident.

The same tight end telling ESPN Deportes "Yo Soy Fiesta!" earned the ironclad trust of his legendary quarterback. Not easy. Years prior, Brady simply shut out receivers he couldn't trust like Joey Galloway and Chad Ochocinco. Anyone running an option route needs to see the same thing he does. From Year 1 to Year 3, every day, Gronkowski stayed after practice to drill down up to twenty different routes with Brady. The same obsession with detail that floored Gonzalez at that sale's pitch of a workout was something Gronkowski experienced non-stop. "Now it's instilled in us," Gronkowski says. "He knows where I'll be. I know when the ball will be there."

The number of routes decreased, but the two continued the ritual through all their years together. This element of Gronkowski's game unfortunately got lost through all the viral videos, but that's OK.

To him, it was simple: To *play* hard, he needed to *work* harder.

"There's a lot of people out there that come up with a great invention and say, 'Why isn't anybody praising me for all the work I did to create this great invention?' No, you get the credit when the credit's due. When you bring out the final project. In order to get what you want, you've got to work for it. I knew I had to put the work in day in and day out on the field with Tom. . . . I only partied and had fun when I knew I took care of my business. Let me get everything done. Let me make sure I'm in shape and I worked out, I studied up *so* I can go out."

His brothers always kept him humble, too. They could deliver a charley horse at any moment and, as Dad always reminded them, "We all piss and shit in the same pot." Still, even Dad's jaw tended to drop at what Rob was accomplishing. When he wasn't slashing through secondaries, Rob relished the opportunity to physically punish in the trenches. This was his chance to step into a time machine and travel back to his childhood home. Pro football essentially became Gronkowski's personal game of Mini Sticks. Only instead of getting revenge on a brother for smashing him into a bathtub, he was kicking his enemies out of the club.

Nothing on the field defines the essence of Gronk's rise quite like his feud with NFL safety Sergio Brown.

It all began when the two were rookies in 2010. Gronkowski was the second-rounder and Brown was the undrafted free agent fighting for his football life, so naturally, Brown tried to face the hulking tight end in every practice drill possible. "I'm not going to lie," Brown says. "Rob used to fucking kick kids' asses. No one could guard him other than myself. No one." To Brown, the only comparison in all of sports is Shaquille O'Neal. With this humongous catch radius, brute strength, and athleticism, the only way to defend Gronkowski at all was to undercut routes. Sort of how the only chance opposing NBA centers had at stopping Shaq was to front him in the paint.

Full tackling was obviously off limits. He hated the fact that he couldn't even hit this tight end taking over the NFL, so Brown resorted to the next best thing: talking copious amounts of shit. This was how he fueled his own game back to childhood. Once Brown could get another player riled up, he played better. Always. In New England, Brown's go-to line was a high-pitched "Sunday Funday!" which annoyed Gronkowski to no end. After two years of Grade-A trolling, Brown was released, signed with the Indianapolis Colts and *finally* got the opportunity to hit Gronk on November 18, 2012.

The Patriots shellacked the Colts that day in Foxborough, 59–24, but the final score became irrelevant on that fifty-ninth point. With 3:55 remaining, Gronkowski couldn't help himself. He lined up for the extra point, spotted Brown across the line of scrimmage and mocked his ex-teammate with an exaggerated, baritone "Suhhn-dehh Fuhhhn-dehhh! Suhhn-dehh Fuhhhn-dehhh!" that Brown imitates here in his finest caveman voice. Hearing this filled him with an adrenaline rush Brown had never experienced in his life. "I'm about to fuck you up!" he screamed back. Brown exploded out of his three-point stance, rushed inside of Gronkowski and came within inches of blocking the kick. Gronkowski wasn't able to get his hands up in time, so he threw a last-ditch, old-school, chicken-wing-like block with his left arm at Brown that broke his forearm and ended his season.

"When I sat back and thought about it," Brown says, "I was like, 'Wow. He literally chose a broken arm over letting me block a kick.' I have no choice but to respect the shit out of that as a football player."

Those Gronk-less Patriots lost in the AFC Championship. One week later, at a Super Bowl party in Las Vegas, Brown spotted Gronkowski across the room and went over to say hello with an outstretched hand. He wanted to make amends.

"He just looks like he saw a ghost. I'm like, 'Oh, OK. Well, I'll try again next year.'"

Brown laughed, returned to his side of the room and the two would eventually meet again. A torn ACL ended Gronkowski's 2013 season, but into 2014, he was to back to pure domination. Back to making plays like his one-handed catch against Denver. Visually, he was imposing.

A massive black brace around his arm made Gronkowski look like a transformer. On November 16, 2014, the Patriots and Colts squared off on *Sunday Night Football*. All game, the Colts swapped Brown and LaRon Landry in and out for each other at safety. Belichick knew to run when Brown was in and pass when Landry was in. Which drove Brown mad. Whenever he was within earshot of Gronkowski, of course, he reminded Gronkowski how he got that massive brace on his left arm and told him that Tom Brady wasn't even looking his way.

Gronkowski's blood boiled. That temper returned. No coach would be pulling him from this game.

From the 1-yard line—with the Patriots leading, 28–20—Gronkowski lined up as the left flanker across from Brown. And as running back Jonas Gray pranced in for a touchdown off his butt, Gronkowski grabbed ahold of Brown and piledrove him directly into NBC's roving television truck. On the sideline, the cameras caught Gronk flapping his fingers to indicate Brown couldn't keep his mouth shut, and nobody—especially the head coach—cared about the flag. Edelman remembers Belichick loving the play because this is what gave his entire team an edge.

"When you see a guy get driven back fifteen, sixteen yards," Edelman says, "and then tossed into the back of the end zone? That makes your whole team say, 'Well, if he's going to go that hard, we want to go that hard.'"

Afterward, Gronkowski famously said that Brown was yapping all game, so he "threw him out of the club." What Brown didn't do remains the greatest regret of his playing career. After the back of his head bounced off that truck, instantly, Brown thought about the future. All game, his coach was telling him to keep his cool. Since he was in a contract year, he feared retaliating could be costly. Looking back? Brown wishes he declared war on Gronk then and there. For a moment, he imagines an alternate universe. Brown would have grabbed Gronkowski by the facemask, ripped his helmet off, and gotten in as many haymakers as possible.

His voice raises. His adrenaline pumps. Seven years later, the scar's still fresh.

"I should've chosen to be the villain that day," he says, "and just went West Side Chicago on that motherfucker."

Alas, the beef ended with Brown getting embarrassed on national television. He wasn't even on the field for Gronkowski's epic twenty-six-yard touchdown the next drive—a spinning, stiff-arming, leaping work of art. He played all of two defensive snaps when these two teams met again in the AFC Championship. A 45–7 Patriots romp. The ensuing house party at Gronk's proved to be nothing but an appetizer, with the tight end exacting some Super Bowl revenge in a 28–24 thriller over the Seattle Seahawks.

This time, he partied so hard in Hollywood that he tore his pants.

Such is the theme of his football life: Gronk gets the last word, Gronk trudges right along. As passionate as players like Jackson and Brown are reliving plays that truly did change their lives, to Gronk, it's like asking what he had for dinner that evening. He has rampaged through so many humans his entire life that the wreckage blurs together. The damage isn't only physical—it's *emotional*. In 2017, Gronkowski humiliated Pittsburgh Steelers safety Sean Davis on a game-winning drive and, after topping it off with a two-point catch over Davis, he literally laughed in his face. Develin can still see Gronk's beaming expression when he returned to the sideline. "You could put a string of light bulbs on him," he says, "and they'd go off." Davis told reporters afterward that he had no clue how anyone could cover a tight end like this.

Granted, it's not always hee-haws and fiestas. Belichick tried to adopt the same strategy as Mammoliti, pulling Angry Gronk off the field before it was too late. Unfortunately, he didn't always get to him in time. Gronkowski became a villain in his own hometown for his cheap shot of cornerback Tre'Davious White. He believed White held him at the top of his route and retaliated. A good two Mississippis after the play, Gronkowski concussed White with a WWE-style body slam. Mammoliti was up in a suite with the Gronk family for that game and, when he caught up with Rob in the tunnel afterward, he got the sense that Rob "lost his consciousness" for a moment. Gronk apologized. Gronk was suspended. Gronk admitted years later he actually enjoyed his one-game suspension and didn't care at all that he lost a $300,000 game check.

And he gronked right along because, always, Rob Gronkowski forced the NFL to adjust to him. Not the other way around.

Right when the overall tenor of the sport was softening, Gronkowski reminded everyone what they truly love about football. Much of the league's proactive measures were needed, of course. Concussion awareness exploded with the release of the bombshell book and documentary *League of Denial*. But the all-encompassing overcorrection on violence proved extreme. The league's search for a magical middle ground that does not exist started to eliminate the badasses that defined the sport for so long. The headhunting safety. The quarterback crusher. The kamikaze special-teamer. Viewers became conditioned to expect flags after whistles and, no, it's not hyperbole to suggest the NFL becomes flag football one day.

Yet there's also zero denying that what makes football king among all major pro sports leagues is its inherent violence. The tight end position best preserves that violence, and no era was more crucial to this preservation than the 2010s. Gronkowski's unapologetic, live-like-there-is-no-tomorrow play style became a guilty pleasure for all.

He is confident football will remain *football*.

"Who doesn't love big hits?" Gronkowski asks. "You can't get it in any other sport: Every single play, monster guys that are so fast and so strong just running into each other. I would say I definitely contributed to keeping that legacy of what football really is going. Big hits. Getting smacked. Getting back up. Breaking tackles. That's what brings joy to football fans."

The same kid who'd laugh as his brothers whacked him over the back enjoyed getting hit by NFL safeties—no matter the cost—but those hits did add up. As the years passed, it started to get a lot harder to lift himself up off the canvas. In a Super Bowl rematch with the Seahawks, in 2016, Gronkowski ran up the seam and absorbed a hard right shoulder from safety Earl Thomas that felt more like a harpoon through the sternum. This time, he didn't spin and stagger into the end zone like he did back at Arizona. Seattle's Kam Chancellor, in coverage, swatted the ball away incomplete. Gronkowski gingerly ambled to his feet.

He played on, albeit while bleeding from his mouth the rest of the game. While he had no clue at the time, he had punctured his lung. His next game, against the Jets, Gronkowski herniated a disc in his back and was placed on IR. An injury he knows was collateral damage from the Thomas hit. As much as Gronkowski cherishes a one-handed catch or a pancake of a block, *this* is what he's most proud of when he reflects on his career.

This was the biggest hit he took in his life, but he kept going.

"It was like when I was a kid. I'd get smacked so much. All the charley horses would hurt so much. But guess what? I had no choice but to keep going.

"You're never going to win all of them. Because everyone's going to get smacked in the NFL at one point. When I get smacked people are going to remember that, too. But they'll say, 'Hey, he gets up every single time.' I'll take that any day."

In other words, Gronkowski never did practice how to *avoid* contact like Gonzalez. Whereas Gonzalez played in 277 of a possible 279 games, Gronkowski played in 143 of a possible 183 games through the 2021 season. There was no practicing how to fall here. At twenty-one and twenty-two, Gronk remembers thinking "Everyone hit me!" with the ball in his hands. Not surprisingly, injuries accumulated. To Gronkowski, it's simple. Some require a couple of weeks, some require eight months, and he always finds a way to come back stronger.

Without one shred, one split second of hesitation whatsoever. The football field forever served as that ski slope at Holiday Valley in his mind—he's going straight down.

Says Gronkowski: "I don't even think about the risks."

Having a fitness expert for a father helps. So does having Brady for a QB, and his famed "TB12" method. Gronkowski learned new forms of injury prevention, but most of his injuries were also the result of simply "getting rocked." There wasn't much to do about that, and he always tried bouncing back as fast as possible because like so many tight ends before him Gronkowski feared being replaced. "Then," he adds, "you're nothing." The best decision he made when it comes to his health, to last so long, was cutting back on the partying. Into his late twenties, Gronkowski saw how his self-described "dangerous" lifestyle was making his body ache more than it used to the next day. That's why he believes it's impossible for any player past the age of twenty-eight to play in the NFL if they're throwing back drinks in such "insane amounts."

"I love the game," he says, "and the game was starting to get taken away from me because of the off-the-field stuff. I wanted to keep playing, so I had to change things up. If you're drinking too many beers, and you're trying to go out there and run the next day, the next day your muscles get fatigued. You feel like you'll pull a muscle. You can't be doing that type of stuff. I was getting to that point where I thought my muscles were going to tear. I was like, 'Oh man. I've got to do things right.'"

Hence, the sharp decline in TMZ cameos.

In 2017, he posted his fourth 1,000-yard season and exploded for 116 yards with 2 scores in a Super Bowl loss to Philadelphia. The following year, he catapulted the Patriots into yet another Super Bowl with yet another clutch catch. On third-and-five, from the Chiefs' 29-yard line with fifty-four seconds left, Brady lofted a prayer to Gronkowski in one-on-one coverage, and he hauled it in for twenty-five. The Patriots then took down the Los Angeles Rams in the Super Bowl, and it appeared Gronkowski had finally taken one hit too many.

He retired on top and sat out the entire 2019 season. The Gronkowskis were even close to signing a deal with the WWE for a new project. Wrestling mogul Vince McMahon was prepared to pay the family a large sum of money. Enough, Dad says, to make all Gronks "happier than a pig in shit." Rob himself was satisfied with being finished. The year off allowed his punching bag of a body a full year to recover. By lifting weights and going for runs, he simply left a fraction of his mind open to a return. You know the rest. His pal Brady signed with the Tampa Bay Buccaneers in the spring of 2020, Brady delivered a phenomenal sales pitch and, considering Mom lived a short two-hour drive away, the opportunity to head south for a reunion felt like destiny.

Rob told his dad to hold off on that wrestling deal. He wasn't done yet.

"You've gotta be kidding me," Gordy said. "You *really* wanna go back? You really wanna do this?"

Gronkowski told Brady "yes" in 2020 where Gonzalez said "no" in 2014…and Gonzalez has every reason to be jealous. The Bucs won the Super Bowl that season with Gronk catching a pair of touchdowns. "Two tuddies!" Brady shrieked when they celebrated on the confetti-covered field. The next year ended with a loss in the divisional playoff round. But it should be noted that the final regular season game in 2021—at the same site, Raymond James Stadium—was essentially the exact opposite of what Gonzalez experienced at Catch No. 999 with Mike Mularkey and the Falcons. Late in this win over Carolina, Gronkowski gave Brady a heads-up that he was one catch away from a $1 million bonus. Brady quickly got his tight end the incentive with a short pass and, instead of wanting to fight someone, there was Gronk dancing and singing "I got a milli!" on the sideline with tackle Donovan Smith.

With Brady's help, Gronkowski's legacy only grows. And grows.

"He's going to be remembered as the greatest tight end of all time. The most dominant tight end of all time," Edelman said. "He helped evolve the position to what it is now. The thing about Gronk was Gronk could also block like a tackle. Nowadays, you're getting tight ends who are just receiver tight ends. They don't put their head in the mix. Gronk was an elite—an *elite*—blocker the first six, seven years of his career. He still does it now. Also, he's a guy who's a big character for the

National Football League. Just a big teddy bear that loved to have fun and went out and had a bash-brother mentality combined with like a care bear."

A career of pain is now haunting the tight end who donned No. 87 a generation prior, Ben Coates, so Gonzalez shudders to think how Gronkowski will feel fifteen years from now. He tells tight ends today, "Don't *Jeremy Shockey* this shit. You can't run over everybody." To which, Gronkowski says that he did adjust his play style in Tampa Bay. He's not breaking necks or throwing defenders out of the club or toting three players on his back for three more yards anymore. The toll he took, however, is undeniable.

Every single injury is scary to his dad. He was not in favor of Rob coming out of retirement—"at all."

"You hate being a dad and watching your son not get up after a play," Gordy Sr. said. "It's the worst feeling. Your gut, everything, just *drops*. 'Ah shit, here we go again.' "

Inside G&G Fitness headquarters in Western New York, Dad steps into his office and gazes at walls scattered with pictures and newspaper clips of his sons and Rob. At the time of this chat, he still has the edge on his son: twelve surgeries to eleven. He was also reckless with his body. But in his sixties, Gordy works out every morning, has no arthritis, and is confident Rob's rehab is so intense and so detailed that he'll avoid the issues that affect other retired greats.

True, the worst thing anyone can do is doubt Rob Gronkowski. He's been defying logic his entire life and was never the Neanderthal caricature he often portrays. His senior year of high school, he pulled a 4.0 GPA. Edelman, for one, was blown away by how good he was with numbers. To date, Gronkowski has lived solely off his endorsement deals. He hasn't spent one penny from his NFL contracts and never splurged on high-end purchases like a Mercedes or a pair of diamond earrings. Even Gonzalez wonders if Gronkowski played up the frat-boy angle to fool people, joking that Gronkowski is probably deciphering codes at night for the CIA.

There's a method to his "Yo Soy Fiesta" madness. Gordy expects us all to see his son starring in movies when he's done playing. Whenever that is. Seconds after Rob retired a second time, in June 2022, his own agent insinuated that the break may be temporary. Drew Rosenhaus told ESPN that he wouldn't be surprised if one call from Brady coaxed Gronk back.

These days, Gronkowski isn't swiveling his hips at too many parties. He's settling down with his longtime girlfriend. It'd also be impossible for Gronkowski to do anything too outlandish in public with social media capturing every celebrity's every move. Dad glares down at his phone and curls his lip. These stupid things turn any citizen into a paparazzi hound. Those who know Gronkowski best insist that every step of the way—Amherst to Arizona to Foxborough to Tampa—he has managed to stay his authentic self. He's still a big kid with a big heart who donated a park to Boston worth $1.2 million.

At his core, he's still his father's son.

"We're basic people," Gordy says. "I grew up as a blue-collar guy. They have that mentality, too. He's the same old 'Every Joe.' Nothing that comes out of him is hurting people. It just makes him look goofy. Like a meathead. But he's harmless."

Not only did Gronkowski change the tight end position and keep real football alive, he preserved a sense of true self in what's exponentially become a dehumanizing sport. He took what Jeremy Shockey started in 2002, shoved it into a cannon, and lit the fuse. He danced. He partied. He showed off those six-pack abs smack-dab in a culture that supposedly treated such behavior with an iron fist. In Foxborough, thou must "do your job" because this is the "Patriot Way" and oh, by the way, we're "on to Cincinnati." As Bill Belichick collected championships, this cold approach spread throughout the league. Fun was extinguished right out of so many NFL locker rooms.

And in swooped Rob Gronkowski. Playing for a coach who set this trend into motion, the tight end never changed. He played hard and worked harder, so Belichick didn't sweat it. Gronkowski is full proof that any professional football player can still have the time of their life.

"Bill has this very stoic portrayal in the media," Develin said. "But he's much more personable and approachable for these things when the cameras are off. He, more than anybody, understood Rob Gronkowski. Bill didn't need to step in and get involved with Rob because Rob wasn't hurting anybody."

Other tight ends noticed, too. Gronk's rise paved the way for more personalities at the position to flourish.

The tight end position—the sport itself, really—is in fantastic hands.

Good thing Rob Gronkowski got out of that bathtub.

Chapter 15

THE NEW STANDARD

This is how a human being is born into the sport.

On a "Football Saturday," October 9, 1993, a mother's water breaks and the father is sent driving through game-day traffic in Madison, Wisconsin. This was baby number two, so everything was packed and ready to go. But the timing couldn't have been worse with the hospital kitty-corner from Camp Randall Stadium. As his wife had a contraction, Bruce Kittle weaved through the maze of cars on Monroe Street, cut over the double yellow lines and...dammit.

A police siren blared. An officer pulled his Subaru over.

Bruce told the gentleman that his wife was having contractions and they were hustling to deliver a baby. The way the officer was standing he couldn't see Jan Krieger, in pain, fifty pounds heavier this pregnancy, leaned back in the passenger seat. So he scoffed. He told Bruce that he has heard every excuse in the book. And, oh boy, did that set Jan off. She made it *very* clear she was *very* pregnant, dropping an F-bomb when she almost never curses.

The officer couldn't believe his eyes and told Bruce to follow him. They'd get a police escort to University of Wisconsin Hospitals and Clinics.

If Jan had a girl, the plan was to name her "Georgia." If it was a boy, "George." And when they could see the full stadium from a massive window in the hallway—just outside their room—Bruce knew. He told Jan to absolutely expect a baby boy. To the soundtrack of the Badgers

300

blistering Northwestern, 53–14, Jan went into labor and gave birth to a ten-pound, ten-ounce football messiah. One year later, George joined Dad right inside that stadium. Bruce was a season ticketholder to home games and usually had George wrapped up in his lap. When George needed to sleep, he'd tuck him inside a makeshift "bed" right underneath the seats. Forget "Twinkle Twinkle Little Star." Kittle's lullaby was the roar of seventy-seven thousand fans at a Big Ten football game.

"The crowd would be cheering and yelling," Bruce says, "and he'd never make a peep. He'd wake up. I'd grab him and he'd be sitting on my lap the rest of the time. I'll probably get charged with abuse now."

This baptism changed football. Two decades later, George Kittle became the game's greatest tight end. One determined to save the sanctity of the sport. His gregarious, toothy smile takes up half his face. Greasy blond hair pours from the back of his helmet. A bushy beard is unkempt, implying that this is a mountain man who's clearly hunting black bear with nothing but a spear when he's not stiff-arming cornerbacks.

In every way, Kittle was born and raised for a profession unlike any in America.

"You can beat the shit out of somebody," George says, "and not get arrested for it."

Not quite the scene inside the break room at most nine-to-fives. Human anatomy is not designed to play football, nor is the brain neurologically wired to make sense of such a workday. If what happened on a practice field broke out at the office, all involved would receive court dates. Where else do coworkers bludgeon each other for two hours, shout expletives, throw a punch or two, shed blood, then pretend like it didn't even happen inside the facility?

"You go from head-butting somebody," Kittle continues, "to twenty minutes later you're in the ice tub with them having conversations about their kids and what he's doing for the week. Yeah, it's different. And then it's 'Hey, you're going to be by yourself for three months. Make sure you come back in shape. Otherwise, you have a high likelihood of getting injured. Also, if you get injured, we'll cut you and you won't have a chance to provide for your family.' "

The glue to the sport's existence itself is that pressure. It takes a powerful mind to thrive in such a bizarro world. For all of the surreal physical stunts he pulls on Sundays, Kittle is adamant that success in this sport is 80 to 90 percent mental. Particularly at tight end. Some bend with more fluidity. Some are faster. Physical gifts, he's certain, take a tight end only so far. The players who excel are the ones who sustain their confidence through the sport's daily mayhem. Football is not normal, yet that's why the best of the very best find it so irresistible. This drug supplies the highest of highs you cannot quit. The best athletes on the planet collide at warp speed in what Kittle describes as the purest form of "art." His oft-imitated, never-duplicated colorful play style is classic Picasso.

And it all starts with his mind.

Specimens come. Specimens go. What's driving the tight end position more than anything into the future is *mental* fortitude. That's how the thundering Kittle became an inexorable mash-up of the greats who preceded him. He slayed inner fear, like Tony Gonzalez. He's still a big kid, like Rob Gronkowski. He mastered the concept that he doesn't *have* to work, he *gets* to work, like his favorite tight end growing up, Dallas Clark. He has Jeremy Shockey's authenticity. He faced the man in the mirror, like Jackie Smith. He welcomes all one-on-ones with the sport's best pass rushers, like Ben Coates. He's no trash talker but, like Shannon Sharpe, finds a way to piss off defensive linemen.

George Kittle understood and appreciated the dangerous world that Mike Ditka created six decades prior and has sought to preserve that world every Sunday. The tight end evolves. Football evolves. But the blood and guts of the sport? That will never change.

The year after those naps under the seat, at age two, little George Kittle became the source of entertainment at Camp Randall. He'd shuffle down in front of his family's section in the stands to do a dance while the student band played, and fans would throw him quarters.

As soon as Kittle could make sense of the action, at age five and six, he wasted no time identifying his first football hero: Ron Dayne. He went nuts from his seat in the end zone for this runaway ice-cream truck of a running back. Watching Dayne set the NCAA's all-time rushing record against Iowa remains one of his all-time sports moments. The bruising rushing style obviously appealed to him, but Kittle remembers schools nationwide telling Dayne he couldn't play running back at his size. Wisconsin gave him a chance and, Kittle notes, "he was able to kick ass."

With each long run, the PA announcer would boom, "Raaaaaaaaahn!" with the rest of the crowd answering "Dayne!" Kittle loved it. After Dayne was drafted by the New York Giants eleventh overall in 2000, he purchased No. 27 jerseys in home and away. The Kittle clan moved to Iowa, where they became season ticketholders to the Hawkeyes and, soon, George had a new crush. The bare hands. The taped knuckles. Those watermelons for shoulder pads. The inspiring walk-on backstory. Kittle witnessed Dallas Clark's rise firsthand at Kinnick Stadium. And considering his dad was once a captain on Iowa's 1982 Rose Bowl team as an offensive lineman, he decided at a very young age he'd play college ball himself at either Wisconsin or Iowa.

There was only one problem. Kittle was a self-described "toothpick." At eighth grade, he basically stopped growing. When Bruce then moved the family to Oklahoma in 2010 after he took a job on Bob Stoops's staff at the University of Oklahoma, George excelled at wide receiver, strong safety, and outside linebacker through high school. He took only two snaps as a tight end, as Division I programs universally dismissed him as too frail at six foot three, 190 pounds. Kittle was only five miles from the Sooners' stadium. But unless Kittle was a four- or five-star recruit, OU wasn't a realistic option. Even as a walk-on, Dad knew it'd be too strange for his son with himself on staff and the family so close to Stoops. Early on, Bruce says he "popped the bubble" in a chat with the head coach to eliminate any potential awkwardness. Kittle considered accepting his scholarship offer from Weber State before then aiming to grayshirt at Iowa. Like Clark.

A spot opened up on Signing Day and Iowa offered a scholarship. By then, head coach Kirk Ferentz had built a Big Ten power on the strength of gangly projects exactly like this. Kittle didn't care that he was the eleventh-hour prom date—Iowa it was. A wise choice, too, considering the school was established as the Midwest's preeminent tight end manufacturer. Ferentz jokes that his affinity for the position actually dates back to the 1980s when he was a young offensive line coach at Iowa. After losses, the first thing his wife would tell him was that they didn't throw the ball to the tight end enough. "It'd piss me off," Ferentz says, "but she was usually right." That early, he learned the value of moving players to tight end. A high school quarterback who played baseball and track twelve miles from the stadium named Marv Cook generated basically no excitement among coaches on both sides of the ball. The person recruiting Cook banged the table with such passion that head coach Hayden Fry relented, agreed to give Cook a scholarship, and Cook starred.

After working with Ozzie Newsome in Cleveland and Baltimore, Ferentz took over as the head man in Iowa and helped turn Clark into one of the sport's best tight ends. Initially, he wasn't quite sure what to do with Kittle. Was he an outside linebacker or a tight end? The bloodlines were rich. He knew that much. Ferentz coached Bruce during that Rose Bowl season and was well aware that George's mother was an All-American basketball player at Drake University. Jan led Drake to the Elite Eight in '82, scored 1,846 career points, and also played softball.

"You have to have flexibility in evaluation," Ferentz says, "and realize a lot of high schools don't play with tight ends. So, you project, too. That's the one thing about being here as opposed to Ohio State or

Alabama or Georgia. We don't have a 'look test' here. You don't have to fit a certain category to play a position."

Upon arrival, Kittle was told he'd be a tight end. Next, coaches stressed that if he didn't learn how to block, he'd never sniff the field. The nature of practices in Iowa City had a way of weeding out those who didn't belong. Down in Coral Gables, daily fisticuffs toughened up tight ends. Here, it was that rip-snortin' nine-on-seven run drill. Iowa fit in as many blocking drills as the day allowed. Anyone who was not physical in this setting was exposed.

To Kittle, the decision was binary: He'd either enjoy this reality or hate it. He chose to *enjoy* run blocking.

"Enjoy pancaking guys and enjoy moving a guy from Point A to Point B against his will. Once I took in that mindset—'Hey, enjoy run blocking'—it made that whole transition a lot easier for me."

Running routes and catching balls came second nature and required no adherence to a moral code. This did. He was all-in. Kittle didn't sneer at the idea of being a run-blocking tight end. Instead, this felt more like his calling. Instead, tight end felt like "the coolest position in sports" because Kittle had the opportunity to do everything imaginable on the field. Like Clark, this future All-Pro barely played his first three years. But unlike Clark, Kittle was not sacrificing his mind, body, and soul for the game. He redshirted in 2012 and caught six passes the next two seasons with only one person to blame: himself. Into his redshirt junior year, 2015, Kittle was the fourth tight end listed on the depth chart. And that's when one conversation helped get him in line. Ferentz often told his team the story of Pat Angerer. How the linebacker didn't even crack the lineup until his junior year and ended up getting drafted in the second round by the Indianapolis Colts. When Angerer visited that winter, Kittle needed to know how. "What changed?" he asked. Angerer told him that he stopped fighting people, stopped drinking so heavily, and embraced football like never before.

A light bulb went off. Kittle was not busting anyone's nose off the field. But he sure loved to party.

"If he can do that," Kittle told himself, "why the hell can't I?"

He looked at himself in the mirror, asked point-blank questions— *Do you want to play football? Do you just want to party?*—and reoriented his life. OK, so Kittle didn't swear off alcohol completely. He's quite talented in that department. "Still am," he assures. "I will toot my own horn." Yet Kittle did realize he needed to pick his spots and that drinking on weekdays was perhaps not the best idea. He slept more. He practiced better. He chugged more protein shakes and less cheap beer. As one of many Ferentz projects beefing up, Kittle set eight alarms per day on his cell phone to drink shakes. They'd start ringing at 2 a.m. and continue right on through the whole day. Granted, when Bruce hears his son open up on his partying lifestyle, he wants to slap him. From Day 1, Dad stressed how crucial it was to watch film with his quarterback and put the work in.

"It's true with anything," Bruce says. "You can't change a person unless that person chooses to change."

Kittle saw younger tight ends threatening to render him useless and churned out an excellent spring. A stroke of luck helped. Injuries launched Kittle into the starting lineup of Iowa's spring game that year, and he took advantage. By fall camp, Kittle could hold his own and even drive All-Big Ten defensive end Drew Ott five yards downfield. The same Ott who used to "hip-toss" him to the dirt like he didn't belong on a D-I field years past.

Then came the first game of that 2015 season.

Heading into the opener against Illinois State, Kittle knew he wouldn't be utilized as a receiver. The Hawkeyes had a healthy diet of outside-zone run plays scripted. Yet this did mean he'd likely get a shot to block the team's sarsen stone of a defensive end. The six-foot-five, 265-pound Teddy Corwin had 98 tackles with a team-high 12.5 for loss the prior season. For any conference, he was a load. On the sixth play of the game, Iowa called an outside run for running back LeShun Daniels. The left tackle pulled wide, which meant it was Kittle's job to set the edge. It was his time to shine. He got his hands inside Corwin and drove him nine yards downfield before defiantly slamming him onto his back. "Folded the guy in half," he says proudly.

Kittle was giving up three inches and thirty-five pounds. Minor details. He uprooted him nonetheless.

Corwin? He was stunned. His entire football life, *he* was the one flattening players. He almost didn't play with a bad back this game but, after taking a cortisone needle to the butt fifteen minutes before kick-off, said he he felt "incredible." The tight end on his mind wasn't Kittle, rather the team's starter (Henry Krieger-Coble) and when the left tackle pulled, he knew it was his job to beat the tight end over the top with a swim move. Instead, Kittle latched on and six words crossed his mind: *This is going to be bad.*

No one ever moved him like this before. Iowa won, 31–14.

"That had never happened," Corwin says. "I'd get tripped up or taken out, but to be literally driven back and then planted on your back? You don't forget those ones. I didn't even realize it was him until he blew up in the NFL. I said, 'Wait a second. He played at Iowa. I got destroyed at Iowa.' I look back on the roster and said, 'Sure enough. That was him.' "

The following Tuesday, Corwin broke his foot and missed five games total through an injury-plagued senior season. He got a shot as a tryout player during the Washington Redskins' rookie camp but didn't make it. After one year of pro ball in France, he hung up the cleats.

Kittle was only heating up. This was the first pancake of his collegiate career, and that day forward, he made it his mission to stack as many pancakes as he possibly could. He loved everything about such a block. The bench-press-like exertion of force. The lift. The WWE slam. And, above all, the "exhale." When you're stuffing another grown man into the dirt, that victim's sudden thud of a breath is the universal language of a perfect block.

That exhale cannot be forgotten by either player. It lingers. It affects the rest of the game.

"That flips my switch," Kittle says. "That's what gets me in the zone. Because after that, you're just in their head. No matter how hard they try, there's nothing that's going to eliminate the thought that you just whupped their ass on camera."

Infinite variables go into a pass play. A defender could take a bad step, a receiver could simply be faster, a quarterback could inexplicably throw an out route into the tenth row. The mano-a-mano essence of the sport cannot be captured in the passing game. But if it's a run play? If it's all on you and you take a giant like Corwin for a ride? "That shit's awesome," Kittle says. "That's electric."

That is the sport itself.

Quite ironic, too. Kittle was never a violent person. Kittle was always the goofy, fun-loving, free spirit and it wasn't by accident. Instead of shooting him down with "no" as a kid, Dad says he and Jan would give George "conditional yeses" to foster creativity. Kittle dressed then like he does now—in flamboyant colors. And in his hands, he was always clutching a T. rex or one of his "Street Shark" figurines, half men, half sharks who wore Rollerblades. He was exceptionally creative, curious. There was nothing George loved more than posting up in a sandbox to build things. For years, he was homeschooled. The father-son bond ran deep. When it was time for George to head to school, Bruce was so heartbroken he took two days off of work to grieve. He just missed having his buddy around.

Bruce viewed parenting as the "boundaries" on a football field. As long as George stayed within the field of play, he could call whatever plays he wanted. The lessons on a football field were concurrently, uh, different. Bruce also raised George as an offensive lineman. That was what he expected him to play as a former lineman himself.

Every morsel of advice was delivered through this spectrum. To play violently. To dominate physically. To, as Dad says, "take no prisoners."

"We believe you win in the fourth because you pound the shit out of people in the first three quarters," Bruce adds. "Unless you are punishing that person, you don't win in the fourth. That's how the run game works. We want to win in the fourth when that dude surrenders, because you've hit him in the mouth so many times. That's a choice. That's a choice that he made and I'm proud of him for that choice. There's nothing greater on third- or fourth-and-one and drilling your dude. A lot of people don't feel that way, but we always have."

George sounds like his father's echo.

"Football is a violent sport," son says. "You need to be violent to play it. There are violent things that need to happen for you to move the football down the field."

As Kittle turned the corner at Iowa, one keynote lesson started to make all the sense in the world.

Football, Dad always said, was its own living and breathing organism. Football was a sport that needed to be played with a very specific temperament because there are no shortcuts in this one-on-one setting. Skate by with an effort less than 100 percent and *you* will be the one blasted onto your backside. Rarely unleashed in the passing game, Kittle leaned on this philosophy up front. That '15 season, he caught 20 passes for 290 yards with 6 touchdowns. As a senior, in '16, his production increased to all of 22 receptions for 314 yards and 4 scores. Basically, he was half the receiver Clark was in college.

Yet when it was time to go pro, George Kittle had grown far more as a person than any metric could reveal. He turned his brain into his greatest weapon.

Letters from Dad helped. Into his redshirt freshman year, Kittle started receiving handwritten notes from Bruce, who viewed this as a way to stay in touch. George got into the habit of reading each week's letter on game day, as the team bus rolled toward the stadium. What began as short life updates grew into a multipage blend of stories, tips, scouting reports, and movie references. Growing up, the two were big into sci-fi movies, *Star Wars*, and Harry Potter. Bruce even read *Lord of the Rings* to his boy as a bedtime story. All the adversity those characters face along a quest always hits home. Bruce, a phenomenal writer, incorporated it all to create his own entertaining stories. He'd tie in

The Matrix or the video game *Halo* or comic book characters such as Spider-Man, Iron Man, and the Joker.

Alcohol wasn't the only deterrent those first three years, either. Kittle dealt with a serious case of sports anxiety—he was terrified of screwing up. Every practice, raw fear suffocated all thoughts. When coaches called for that nine-on-seven drill, that ultimate test of manhood, he puked. Every single time. It didn't get much better when Iowa moved to full eleven-on-eleven because the team's playbook might as well have been written in hieroglyphics. Kittle would step up to the line of scrimmage, ask himself "Do I even know what I'm doing?" and screw up.

Overthinking the play itself zapped all explosion, all spontaneity from his game.

"You just have to *know* what the play is," Kittle explains, "and then you think about the things that are important, like 'Where's the defensive end? Where's the linebacker? Where's the strong safety?' You have to have a plan going into every play...I changed the way I approached thinking about football. It wasn't an 'Oh no, this is going to happen.' It was, 'I *get* to do this.'"

He truly turned the corner his final season at Iowa. Kittle saw a sports psychologist who gave him the idea of drawing a big red button on his wrist tape so the tight end could manually hit "reset" after every play. He decided to go all out and if he failed, so what? He could slam that button and attack the next play. This instilled what he calls his "fuck-it mentality" as a blocker.

A visit from Clark, his idol, helped. The two hit it off when Clark returned to campus, and they still keep in touch to this day. Their interpretation of the Iowa grind is quite different, though. Whereas Clark describes Chris Doyle as a fatherly figure, a man who helped save his life, Kittle admits he clashed repeatedly with the team's strength coach and criticizes the program as "militaristic." All those protein shakes actually tore up his insides because he was lactose intolerant. Bruce doesn't recall Iowa having any dairy-free products, so his son would often meet Doyle's weight requirements and then puke it out. Adding those final eight pounds was a maddening struggle and Bruce didn't understand why his son needed to be 255 when twitchiness was his greatest asset. George's face was noticeably puffy.

The same winter lifting sessions that Clark savored more than game day itself were soul-sucking to Kittle.

Dad stressed to his son that nobody could take his joy away unless he let them.

"And George," he says, "never let him take his joy."

All while staying accountable, too. Kittle knows coaches viewed him as a dumb player those first three years. So when he looked at his reflection in the mirror, he blamed himself. He vowed to respect the "eye in the sky"—the camera capturing every play, every practice—and go all out every snap. An old piece of advice from a grad assistant finally clicked, too. When Kittle was a true freshman, David Raih told him the window to play football is so minuscule in relation to your entire life. Five years of college ball. Three or so in the pros, if you're lucky, and then it's gone.

He refused to waste one second on a football field.

When the 49ers drafted him 146th overall in 2017, that line of thinking became his edge.

"You don't see reps where George Kittle is taking the play off," he says. "I'm trying to bury somebody as much as I possibly can."

The rest of the world was stunned by the sight of a nobody from Iowa bullying small and large men alike from every inch of the field. In Year 2, Kittle's 1,377 receiving yards set a new tight end record. To the naked eye, this number was inconceivable for a player hardly featured in college. He was a henchman of a blocker, too. Kittle? He was not surprised because of how much he had built up his mental toughness. Schematically, it helped that Kyle Shanahan's X's and O's were similar to everything he saw at Iowa. When the 49ers installed their dizzying outside and inside zone plays, Kittle felt five years ahead of schedule. Dominating as a blocker has a dynamite effect as a receiver, too. He's proof that it pays to embrace the dreary elements of the position. Kittle would see everyone on defense "tighten up" to stop the run, linebackers tilting forward and... *see ya*. On a quarterback bootleg the next play, Kittle would sneak right past a linebacker for a seventy-yard touchdown.

He was a goofball. OK. But Kittle also created an internal switch to become that same player who smeared Corwin whenever he damn well pleased.

Through the use of alter egos, he figured out how to turn his feral violence on and off. "Because in football," he adds, "if you have the flip switched on all the time, you'll get burnt out." Specific characters give him specific energies. Back to the classic Batman cartoons in the '90s, Kittle always saw part of himself in the Joker and still keeps those old-school episodes saved on his phone to binge on his team's road trips. He is fascinated by the Joker's devotion to spreading mass chaos. That became his goal on the field. In the Joker's eyes, his cause was justified—however ill-advised—and Kittle found such passion "inspiring." So inspiring that the night before his wedding, in 2019, Kittle had the Heath Ledger version of the character tatted on his forearm in all black and white with red lips that became his new reset button.

His wife wasn't thrilled. Kittle thought she was going to stab him when he told her about the ink plans. He explained how he needed this tattoo for this mental switch, and though she didn't exactly give him her blessing, she said to go ahead. Kittle spent eight hours in a tattoo chair the day before getting hitched and wrapped his forearm in Saran Wrap the day of. When he took it off, his arm was bleeding terribly.

Of course, it was all worth it. He has channeled the Joker many times over by hammering defenders and cackling atop their bodies. In 2019, Kittle drove Ricardo Allen into the end zone for one soul-snatching pancake. A camera captured Kittle busting into hysterical laughter after somersaulting over the Falcons safety. In 2021, he picked off Philadelphia Eagles linebacker Eric Wilson five yards off the line and, once more, planted a grown man into the grass. Again, he laughed his ass off.

On his right forearm, Kittle tatted a closeup image of the Master Chief, the protagonist in *Halo*. This alter ego brings a different energy because the Master Chief is strictly a leader who always finds a way to complete the job. "No matter the odds," Kittle adds. He's been fascinated by the full *Halo* story line, and has read the entire book series because it runs much deeper than anything the video game depicts. The Master Chief could have zero weapons at his disposal and still destroy anything in his path, exactly as any tight end can feel battered and defeated late in the fourth quarter of a tied game.

After climbing one "14er"—a mountain that exceeds 14,000 feet—together in Colorado, father and son got matching tattoos of Longs Peak. That one's inscribed on George's left bicep.

And to ensure he's always on a seek-and-destroy warpath, Kittle also had Godzilla tattooed on the outside of his right forearm.

"I've always envisioned myself as a thirteen-year-old kid who's living his best life," Kittle says, "and I try to live my life like thirteen-year-old me would always be proud of me."

The receiving record was nice, but the following season was so much sweeter. San Francisco went 13-3 and advanced to the Super Bowl. To get there, Kittle added to the reel of best plays in tight end history. In a late-season NFC showdown against the New Orleans Saints, his offense faced a fourth-and-two on its own 33 with thirty-nine seconds left. Lined up in a bunch formation to the left side, Kittle caught the ball on a short out route, broke a DB's tackle and went full Godzilla. Safety Marcus Williams tried to tackle him high (bad decision), gripped ahold of the tight end's facemask (good try), and was taken on an epic joyride. It took two more Saints defenders to arrive on scene to finally bring him down. The play gained thirty-nine yards in all and, two snaps later, San Francisco kicked a game-winning field goal.

Quite literally, Kittle carried his team to victory. But what most didn't know was that he had visualized this play the night before. Kittle tried to imagine the craziest play possible. A one-handed catch... leaping over a dude... getting his legs cut out... sticking the landing...

running into the end zone with another dude on his back. What actually transpired was pretty close. Kittle wore a six-foot-one, 195-pound adult around his neck like a new fashion statement. As the play unfolded in real time, Kittle was not surprised because he has always manifested plays into reality.

The night before games, he sits in an Epsom salt bath, studies the playbook, then visualizes those exact plays he'll be running.

"If you visualize it enough times," he says, "when the opportunity arises, it won't be foreign to you."

The letters only got better over time, too. Ahead of the 2019 NFC Championship, Bruce sent his son a fourteen-pager. George always waits until he's sitting in his locker at the stadium to read them, too. Many read like a movie script. Bruce once wrote his own Master Chief–themed story that was explicitly related to one of George's obstacles that season. Through the 150-plus letters (and counting), Bruce somehow keeps it fresh and finds a new way to flip that switch in his son. Through the college days, Bruce had access to unlimited college film as an Oklahoma assistant, so he'd break film down for George and offer pointers. He'll still detail footwork and hand placement but—in the pros—the letters evolved. Now, it's all about the "mental game" and "relaxation," Bruce says. Meditations. Breath work. So much imagery to ensure his son doesn't try to do too much because Bruce believes too many guys play far too uptight and lose themselves.

It's no coincidence that the bigger the moment, the more relaxed George is. He works at this. He has *learned* how to relax. George has saved all the letters . . . not that they can all see the light of day. So many are spiked with profanity-laced trash talk on various teams—Bruce loved dogging the SEC.

"I say shit in a letter to my kid," Bruce says, "that I would never say publicly. I drop the F-bomb a lot and say, 'Motherfuck these people.'"

Of course, those are the ones George loves most because those flip that switch within. Those help him tap into his alter egos.

There's a twist to his violence, too. This Joker / Godzilla / Master

Chief of a tight end superhero doesn't trash-talk. He isn't researching an opponent's reptile business or memorizing a girlfriend's phone number. Vengeance doesn't leak through his pores like it does Shockey's, either. Kittle may play violently but he doesn't conduct himself violently between plays. Rather, he flips the script. He attempts to disarm opponents with a "cheerful" joy. Anybody can play angry. But in this wacky profession that asks grown men to assault each other, can you play violently 2.3 seconds after chuckling? Kittle forces the nastiest players in the NFL to find out. Against the Los Angeles Rams, in 2018, he told a joke at the line of scrimmage that made star defensive tackle Aaron Donald laugh and jump offsides. This remains one of his personal all-time favorite plays, too.

All talking junk to a guy does, he reasons, is make him want to kill you. He sees no use giving a snarling All-Pro like Donald even more motivation. So, he talks about the weather. He points out the hot dog vendor in the stands. He discusses a new video game. Then he takes a look at one of his tats, harnesses an alter ego, the ball is snapped, and…he kicks your ass. Most games, Kittle starts by even telling the colossus across the line who'd like to tear his head off, "Good luck" with an ultrakind, "Let's stay healthy." Defensive linemen have told him, in so many words, to shut the hell up and that they will eat him for lunch. He can play that game, too. He has no problem playing that game. But Kittle knows there's a benefit to acting like Ned Flanders in the middle of such a violent sport.

"A lot of guys like to play the game angry," Kittle says, "so I try to get the guys to not be so angry and try to make them laugh. That's always been my MO. Because I can play at that level really well and not a lot of other guys can."

The result was a modernized Mike Ditka at the best possible time. Right when the position was getting a tad too reliant on finesse—with collegiate offenses shipping 225-pound athletes to the pros in droves— in came Kittle to sock you with a smile. He applied the same amount of energy to blocking drills with offensive tackles that he did running routes with wide receivers. Specifically, he mastered the separate arts of blocking a 300-pound defensive end, a 245-pound linebacker, and a 190-pound cornerback. All three body types demand strikingly different techniques. He realized that if he learned how to block all eleven players on the field, he'd change the calculus of the entire offense. San Francisco could call plays other teams cannot.

One of his favorite challenges is blocking a 260-pound edge rusher who's paid $20 million per year to drill the quarterback. Most teams don't dare exile their tight end to such an island. That's why so many announcers lambast offensive coordinators on air for having the audacity to block a *defensive end* with a *tight end.* "That's unrealistic!" says Kittle, in his best impression of a color commentator. "Why would you do that?!" His goal is to eliminate such default analysis from the broadcast and make this a very normal thing for tight ends. Even if it's only four or five plays per game, Kittle gains a sense of satisfaction knowing that any elite pass rusher he stonewalls at the line is bound to get an earful from their coach in the film room the next week. Early in his career, ends like Chandler Jones were surprised to get tied up. That didn't last long.

"Now, they know that if they don't bring their A game, I'm going to do everything I can to try to embarrass them."

As NFL offenses took their cue from spreads in college and flexed into three-, four-, and five-receiver sets—throwing more than ever— many stopped requiring starting tight ends to be dominant blockers. A few select offenses continued to value this and, within the tight end fraternity, such yeoman's work is appreciated. As much as Kittle enjoyed watching Gronkowski truck flailing defensive backs in the open field, the footage he treasures most is the New England Patriots' 41–28 win over the Los Angeles Chargers in the 2018 AFC divisional playoff round. Chances are, nobody watching at home even noticed him this day. Gronk caught one pass. But Kittle was in awe. Kittle identified fifteen blocks worthy of being shown at a clinic and made a point to watch this full game multiple times. This performance was precisely why he modeled his game after Gronkowski.

Stars must align to get a complete tight end. The coach who taught Coates how to block in the early '90s, Dante Scarnecchia, shared his wisdom with Gronkowski. And Kittle has worked with the son of the coach who convinced Sharpe to give a lick about blocking. Kyle Shanahan grew up absorbing the intricacies of his father's zone-blocking scheme with the Denver Broncos and, a generation later, found a way to add his own wrinkles as a head coach. The uncoverable six-foot-six seam-splitter of a tight end may keep defensive coordinators awake at night, but so can this threat.

A knifing blocker capable of wiping out any of your eleven defenders any given play. Within the X's and O's of the 49ers' ground game, Kittle is the tip of the spear.

Longtime defensive coach Gregg Williams describes Kittle as a roving third offensive tackle on the field who creates an entirely new cutback lane for the running back. Possibly no coach over the last three decades has revered violence more than Williams. He kindly reminds all this is not badminton, not track, not Ping-Pong, and explains that he gives every one of his teams an entire presentation on how to impose your will, how to look another man in the eye and say "there's nothing you can do to stop me." His firebrand style has always been more psychological than schematic. Williams is incensed at how soft football has become but absolutely believes the primitive nature of the sport has a healthy pulse at tight end. While the wide receiver is mostly cocooned from kill shots, the tight end is bound to crash into linebackers and strong safeties over the course of three hours.

You better be tough to win that matchup and tight ends like Kittle and Kansas City Chiefs star Travis Kelce, the coach insists, turn the table. *They* are the predator. *You* are the prey. Finding a defensive player capable of stepping into this ring can be a grim proposition. Williams has forty-two packages in his defense and has thrown every possible body type at today's hybridized tight end. A linebacker may match their toughness, but lags in coverage. A nickel cornerback may be able to cover them, but...

"You've got to have a nickel who's got some balls—some *nuts*—who can play the physical game against him, too," Williams says, "if you're going to match him up like he's a wide receiver. It's tough. It really is."

Blocking ends have been around since the first pigskin was laced, but this is where we see Kittle's Darwinian impact. Whereas the Mark Bruener types grabbed ahold of defensive ends off the line of scrimmage, a weapon like Kittle—who, again, is operating at one obsessive pace for seventy-five of seventy-five snaps—is on the move. He's in the slot. In tight. In motion. Foaming at the mouth to tee off on players at all three levels. An innovative play designer like Shanahan is able to design the perfect angle for a devastating collision, too.

"Where a receiver is going to be somewhat of a pussy, a tight end is not," Williams says. "And you'll see Kittle and Kelce and Jimmy [Graham]—all those guys, I'm telling ya—they're physical as all get-out on space plays out there vs. bigger people."

This is why no name was brought up unsolicited more than George Kittle through the reporting of this book.

The position's gladiator from the '90s, Coates, believes Kittle's game most echoes his. How Kittle morphs into a linebacker with the ball in his hands. Speaking from experience, he's concerned for Kittle's longevity but doesn't see anyone else dragging three people on their back. Most today crumble on first contact. "I wanted to take people out," Coates says, "and that's what I see in George."

One of the position's chief engineers, the longtime coach Mike Pope, believes Kittle would have dominated in the '60s, '70s, '80s, and '90s. "Because," he says, "he's tough as nails."

The journeyman who could've choked to death if not for Shockey played through the position's great awakening from 2004 to 2013. Ben Hartsock witnessed teams embrace athletic tight ends who "couldn't block a defensive end to save their life." Now, he thinks it's switching back thanks to two players specifically: Gronkowski and Kittle.

The star who forced the NFL to view the position in a completely new way, Tony Gonzalez, rattles off several names of tight ends who despise blocking and then stops in his tracks. "The old-school guy who I fucking love," he says, "is George Kittle." It's no shock that both Gonzalez and Kittle had the same position coach at their peak in Jon Embree. A true tight end whisperer, Embree also helped the likes of Chris Cooley (77-849-3) in 2010, Jordan Cameron (80-917-7) in 2013, and Cameron Brate (57-660-8) in 2016 enjoy career seasons at three separate stops. With average quarterbacks, the coach has a gift for scheming tight ends open.

When the 49ers drafted Kittle in the fifth round, Embree told Gonzalez that he had a feeling the kid would be special.

Now, arguably no player in the sport, period, appeals to a wider audience. Kittle is a throwback who reminds the old guard of the glory days while still a free spirit that Generation Z is replaying on Instagram reels. No player is better miked up during games. On the bench, he sings the "three best friends" song from *The Hangover* with his tight ends, swaying back and forth. On the field, he's liable to go full Ric Flair any given moment with a loud "Woooo!" And with Kelce and Greg Olsen, he launched "TE U" in 2021, an annual three-day summit that allows tight ends to swap secrets in Nashville. There's field work, classroom sessions, and nonstop camaraderie as Kittle drives the position into the next era. The league is full of tight ends posting dazzling numbers. In 2021, the Atlanta Falcons made Florida's Kyle Pitts the fourth overall pick. But Kittle all but pledged to Gronkowski that the position will never stray from its constitution.

His thinking was straightforward. He saw teams employ six-foot-six, 260-pound tight ends who look like they moonlight as bouncers at the dark-alley nightclub. This player will eliminate defensive ends but can hardly run. He'll catch twelve passes all season, and all twelve will be late balls in the flat. Kittle has also seen teams send receivers who are "tight ends" in name only on forty routes per game. They'll catch ten passes for a hundred yards but treat the trenches as a forbidden forest.

And Kittle sought to be the best of these two tight ends rolled into one transcendent player.

When I tell him that many tight ends claim to be such a dual threat when they certainly are not, he agrees. He hears it, too.

"I had to revitalize it a little bit," Kittle says. "To me, there's a specific way football should be played. You should want to be great at all aspects you're asked to be great at. I'm asked to be great at catching the ball, running routes, blocking downfield, blocking defensive ends, blocking linebackers, digging out safeties, pass pro, running the ball, so I'm going to do everything I can to train my body and my mind to set myself up to be great in all of those aspects. And, hey, if guys don't want to do that, they don't have to do that. That's going to be my MO.

"I'm trying to set the standard for how the tight end position is supposed to be played."

No wonder he pushes back on the criticism that the sport's going soft. It's partly true. The days of safeties attempting to remove skulls from the shoulders of receivers over the middle have passed. So is the recent era of a safety, like Pittsburgh's Troy Polamalu, helicoptering over the line of scrimmage the second the ball's snapped. Yet, one arrow points only upward. Players at all positions become bigger, faster, stronger. "The collisions," Kittle stresses, "are harder." Replay footage from the '60s and some of the helpless chaps diving at the ankles of Ditka, John Mackey, and Jackie Smith could be mistaken for children on a playground. No such weaklings even warrant a tryout in today's NFL. On the contrary, Kittle's nemesis of five years in the NFC West, Chandler Jones, is another Marvel character with what he calls "Go-Go Gadget arms" that extend so far he can't even touch him.

He's not concerned with how his body will feel a decade from now. Not while that eye in the sky still glares down. Informed that he may be cutting a deal with a football devil, that his body will undoubtedly face a day of reckoning, and Kittle is undaunted. He politely disagrees that he'll be limping around in his fifties and, like Gronk, cites the technological advancements in rehab. Year-round, he conditions his body for contact and believes the resources available to him today do not compare to what was at the disposal for tight ends past.

This opportunity will not last forever. He still hears the ticking of a clock in his head 24/7. Hell no, he will not step out of bounds or whisk past that pass rusher.

He's still refusing to slow down.

"I want to play as long as my body will let me. It's a violent sport and I will play it violently as long as I can."

Dad certainly knows this and cites his son's unearthly pain threshold. When it comes to the field, Bruce Kittle believes his son's legacy is what he always preached: pure domination. George not only raised the bar when it comes to run blocking but even gave it a little "prestige," Dad says. Out of 75 plays, Shanahan may call 52 runs…and his son brings it all 52 times. Still, it's the personality of Kittle's play style—the high-voltage electricity—that will have the everlasting effect on the position. Says Bruce, "He has helped players realize, 'I can *choose* not to go out of bounds. I can *choose* to put my helmet into somebody's chest. It is a choice.'"

This choice is how this tight end continued to save football. George Kittle never thought twice.

Football was always something biblical in this household. More than a game.

"We believe," Bruce says, "the game of football has its own spirit. There is a field. There are players. But when you put it all together and that whistle blows and that kickoff goes, the game knows which players honor the game and who disrespects it. And if you disrespect the game, the game comes back. This will sound crazy to a lot of people. When you step on that field, when you walk from off to on, and you cross that white line, you're entering sacred ground."

Father and son have discussed the "many heroes" who walked before him. Guys like Ditka who built this game. And Bruce tells his son that he carries that lineage with him, that he must honor the game and its legends.

"That means something to us. It doesn't mean that much to everybody else."

I tell Bruce that all of us who cherish the sport should be thanking him. More tight ends will view the sport this way because of his son and how he mentally attacked it. One day, maybe Kittle is able to lounge at his own golf course with a stogie. He's not done yet.

Like those before him, era to era, Kittle keeps this sport alive.

"Let's be safe," Bruce begins, with a slight pause.

"But it's about knocking the shit out of each other, too."

WORK CITED

Unless otherwise noted, all direct quotes are from interviews conducted by the author. Statistics derived from Pro Football Reference and College Football Reference.

Chapter 1

Ditka: An Autobiography, by Mike Ditka with Don Pierson, Bonus Books, July 1, 1986.

"NFL 100: At No. 96, Mike Ditka 'Put the Fear of God' in NFL Defenses," The Athletic, July 10, 2021.

"America's Game: The Epic Story of How Pro Football Captured a Nation," by Michael MacCambridge.

"The Chicago Tribune Book of the Chicago Bears: A Decade-by-Decade History," by Chicago Tribune staff.

"Hail to Pitt: A Sports History of the University of Pittsburgh," by Jim O'Brien.

"Cowboys Have Always Been My Heroes: The Definitive Oral History of America's Team," by Peter Golenbock.

"Monsters: The 1985 Chicago Bears and the Wild Heart of Football," by Rich Cohen.

"The Town That Forged Iron Mike," *Chicago Tribune*, Nov. 13, 1989.

"Bears Can Thank Dallas for 'Da Coach,'" ESPN.com, Dec. 5, 2013.

"#4 Mike Ditka | Top 10 Tight Ends of All Time | NFL," NFL Films YouTube channel, Nov. 11, 2016.

"#59: Mike Ditka | The Top 100: NFL's Greatest Players (2010)," NFL Films YouTube channel, July 6, 2016 (includes Roger Staubach quote).

Chapter 2

Blazing Trails: Coming of Age in Football's Golden Era, by John Mackey with Thom Loverro, Triumph Books, Sept. 1, 2003.

"A Player Defined by Greatness and Illness," *New York Times,* July 9, 2011.

"Steelers Trade Jefferson to Colts for Richardson and a High Draft Choice," *New York Times,* Aug. 21, 1970.

"#42: John Mackey | The Top 100: NFL's Greatest Players (2010)," NFL Films YouTube channel, Aug. 16, 2016.

"#2 John Mackey | Top 10 Tight Ends of All Time," NFL Films YouTube channel, Nov. 11, 2016.

"Ranking the 100 Best Bears Players Ever: No. 37, Ken Kavanaugh," *Chicago Tribune,* July 31, 2019.

"The Greatest Game Ever Played! (Colts vs. Giants, 1958 NFL Championship)," NFL Throwback YouTube channel, Feb. 21, 2019.

"1970 Baltimore Colts Team Season Highlights 'Super Bowl Champions,'" NFL Films via Sports Odyssey YouTube channel, July 5, 2019.

Chapter 3

"Jackie Smith Talks Extensively about the Drop That Almost Ruined His Life," *Sports Illustrated,* Jan. 19, 2016.

"1964 Week 10: Mud Bowl: New York Giants at St. Louis Cardinals Highlights," St. Louis Football Cardinals YouTube channel, Aug. 3, 2017.

"1978 NFC Playoffs—Atlanta Falcons at Dallas Cowboys," CBS Sports/ NFL via Classic Sports YouTube channel, Sept. 29, 2019.

"Jackie Smith Highlight Video," St. Louis Sports Hall of Fame YouTube channel, Feb. 10, 2013.

"Top 50 Sound FX | #39: 'Bless His Heart, He's Got to Be the Sickest Man in America,'" NFL YouTube channel, Oct. 23, 2015.

Chapter 4

"Oz the Great and Powerful," *Sports Illustrated*, Sept. 12, 2013.

"Happy 20th Birthday, Ravens: City Selected Nickname 20 Years Ago," ESPN.com, March 29, 2016.

"Cleveland Browns History," by Frank M. Henkel.

"Memories from Club 46: Brian Sipe Says Kardiac Kids Era 'Was Just a Riot,'" ClevelandBrowns.com, Sept. 24, 2019.

"How Selma's 'Bloody Sunday' Became a Turning Point in the Civil Rights Movement," History.com, July 18, 2020.

"Montgomery Bus Boycott," the Martin Luther King, Jr. Research and Education Institute.

"No. 97: Ozzie Newsome, The Football 101," *JoeBlogs*, Sept. 13, 2021.

"Ozzie Newsome on His Journey from Alabama to NFL History," The Undefeated, April 25, 2018.

"The Best Bear Bryant Quotes," Tide 100.9, Jan. 26, 2015.

"How Bear Bryant Became the Branch Rickey of Alabama Football," Bleacher Report, Apr. 24, 2013.

"Wizard, Pro Football Hall of Fame Class of 1999," *Coffin Corner*, Vol. 21, No. 4 (1999).

"Too Easy to Say Bear Bryant Was Too Slow to Integrate Alabama Football," AL.com, Oct. 30, 2013.

"A Strange Scouting Trip and Draft Deals Bring Ozzie Newsome to Cleveland," Cleveland.com, June 3, 2021.

"Inaugural Address of Governor George Wallace," Alabama Department of Archives and History, Jan. 14, 1963.

"1980 Week 15—Browns vs. Vikings," NBC Sports via 80s Football Cards YouTube channel, Aug. 15, 2018.

"Ozzie Newsome Full Episode | Episode 19 | Club Shay Shay," Club Shay Shay YouTube channel, Feb. 2, 2021.

Chapter 5

"NFL 100: No. 71 Mel Blount, the Physical Steelers DB Who Made the League Change Its Rules," The Athletic, July 23, 2021.

"Pass-Block Rule Change Aids Offense," *Washington Post*, Aug. 1, 1978.

"From the Archives: Sept. 25, 1978: The Crash of PSA Flight 182," *San Diego Union-Tribune*, Sept. 25, 2020.

"Kellen Winslow," *Coffin Corner*, Vol. 17, No. 1 (1995).

"Coryell Has Hall of Fame Numbers but No Hall of Fame Spot," *Orange County Register*, July 5, 2010.

"America's Game Missing Rings: 1981 San Diego Chargers," NFL Network, Sept. 18, 2008.

"A Matter of Life and Sudden Death," *Sports Illustrated*, Oct. 25, 1999.

"Epic in Miami/Kellen Winslow Game Chargers vs. Dolphins 1981 Divisional Playoffs," NFL YouTube channel, Nov. 11, 2016.

Chapter 6

"Mouths of Miami," *Baltimore Sun*, Jan. 27, 1999.

"Sharpe Takes the 5th As the Broncos Pursue Their 13th," Associated Press via *Free Lance–Star*, Dec. 6, 1998.

"Trash Talk: All about Finding an edge," ESPN.com, Jan. 29, 2014.

"NFL Brothers Shannon & Sterling Sharpe," Club Shay Shay YouTube channel, Sept. 22, 2020.

"Shannon Sharpe," *All the Smoke* podcast, Ep. 21, YouTube channel, Mar. 26, 2020.

"Top 10 Tight Ends of All Time, No. 5 Shannon Sharpe," NFL Films YouTube channel, Nov. 11, 2016.

"Top 50 Sound FX, No. 46 Shannon Sharpe Calls Mr. President," NFL YouTube channel, Oct. 9, 2015.

"1998 Broncos at Chiefs (Monday Night Football)," ABC Sports via Dillon Murway YouTube channel, May 9, 2020.

"Shannon Sharpe," Hall of Fame, College Biography on Savannah State Athletics website.

"Super Bowl XXXII Elway's 1st Super Bowl Win | Green Bay Packers vs. Denver Broncos | NFL Full Game," NFL's YouTube channel, Nov. 15, 2016.

Chapter 7

"Ben Coates," CIAA Hall of Fame members on CIAA website.

"Drew Bledsoe, Unfiltered," *Go Long*, Jan. 7, 2021.

"Coates Catches Passes and Praise," *New York Times*, Dec. 4, 1994.

"Sold! Time to Call Them New England Permanents," *New York Times*, Jan. 22, 1994.

"The Parcells Factor: The Day When Patriots Fortunes Changed Forever," *Eagle-Tribune*, Jan. 21, 2018.

"1993 WK 1 New England Patriots vs. Buffalo Bills," NBC via Max Speedster YouTube channel, Oct. 11, 2015.

"Bledsoe & Marino Epic Opening Day Duel," NFL Throwback YouTube channel, Sept. 10, 2019.

"Top Ben Coates Touchdowns | Ben Coates Highlights," Official JaguarGator9 YouTube channel, Aug. 16, 2019.

"Brett Favre's First Super Bowl Win! | Packers vs. Patriots Super Bowl XXXI | NFL Full Game," NFL's YouTube channel, Aug. 5, 2016.

"A Dominant Defense Makes History Super Bowl 35 Ravens vs. Giants," NFL's YouTube channel, May 31, 2020.

Chapter 8

"The Last Badass," *Go Long*, Jan. 8, 2021.

"WCW Monday Nitro 6-22-98 The Giant vs. Kevin Greene," WCWArchive YouTube channel, Jan. 18, 2010.

"Back in Black: Lloyd Takes His Tae Kwon Do to Higher Degree," *Pittsburgh Post-Gazette*, May 16, 1999.

"1997 NFL Week 6: Steelers at Ravens," CBS Sports via F1 Nut YouTube channel, Feb. 17, 2021.

Chapter 9

"From Chicken to GOAT," CantonRep.com, July 29, 2019.
"Cracked Code," *ESPN The Magazine*, Aug. 15, 2005.
"A Football Life: Tony Gonzalez," NFL Network, Sept. 19, 2019.
"The Norwegian Way," *Real Sports with Bryant Gumbel*, HBO, May 2019.
Falcons-Buccaneers, 2009 Week 17 Full Game, NFL Rewind.

Chapter 10

"The Revenge of Jeremy Shockey," *Sports Illustrated*, July 28, 2003.
"Shockey Watches His Mouth, But a Pattern Remains," *New York Times*, July 31, 2006.
"Vioxx Taken Out of Locker Rooms," ESPN.com, Oct. 4, 2004.
"Timeline: The Rise and Fall of Vioxx," NPR.org, Nov. 10, 2007.
"Jeremy Shockey Trucks Colts Defenders in 2002 for Giants," Fox Sports via Angry Mut Guy YouTube channel, May 22, 2014.
"Saints Tight End Shockey Hospitalized," ESPN.com, May 27, 2010.
"Seminoles Miss FG in Final Seconds," Associated Press via ESPN.com, Oct. 7, 2000.
"Shockey Looking to Erase Pain of Giants' Title Run," Yahoo! Sports, Jan. 22, 2010.
"Giants Try to Put Fight at Team Dinner Behind Them," *New York Times*, Aug. 2, 2002.
"Shockey Debut a Stunner," *New York Post*, Aug. 7, 2002.
"Giants Dealing with Ugly Side of Super Bowl Glory," ESPN.com, July 12, 2008.

Chapter 11

"Greg Olsen's Twins Are Born; T.J. Will Have Surgery Thursday," WCNC Charlotte, Oct. 11, 2012.

"Panthers' Greg Olsen—An NJ Champ with His Dad—Keeps Family First," *New York Post*, Jan. 28, 2016.

"How the Hospital Former Carolina Panthers TE Greg Olsen Helped Build Saved His Son TJ's Life," ESPN.com, July 10, 2021.

"Greg Olsen—TJ Olsen the HEARTest YARD Feature on FOX," Fox Sports via ThePLfog YouTube channel, Oct. 12, 2014.

"Falcons vs. Panthers | NFL Week 16 Game Highlights," NFL YouTube channel, Dec. 24, 2016.

T.J.'s videos from the hospital from Greg Olsen's Instagram page @gregolsen88.

Chapter 12

"Dallas Clark Retirement Press Conference," Colts.com, June 18, 2014.

"Colts to Cut Stokley, Reagor after Players Fail Physicals," *Tribune-Star*, Mar. 2, 2007.

"Indianapolis Colts at Baltimore Ravens (AFC Divisional, 2006)," CBS Sports via CT Archives YouTube channel, Nov. 3, 2020.

"Dallas Clark 2009 Colts Highlights," CBS/ESPN/NBC/Fox Sports via Collin Telesz YouTube channel, June 16, 2017.

"Tom Brady vs. Peyton Manning: 2006 AFC Championship | Patriots vs Colts | NFL Full Game," NFL YouTube channel, Sept. 9, 2016.

"2003 11-30-03 Patriots at Colts Pt 1," CBS via Larry's Classic Sports Videos YouTube channel, Sept. 25, 2021.

"2002 Iowa vs. Purdue—95 Yard Dallas Clark TD," ESPN via HawkeyeTV YouTube channel, July 24, 2010.

"The Legend of Brandon Scherff," *Sports Illustrated*, Mar. 11, 2015.

Work Cited

Chapter 13

"Jimmy Graham Ruled a Tight End," ESPN.com, July 2, 2014.

"Jimmy Graham Speaks at White House Champions of Change," Seahawks.com, May 2015.

"Jimmy Graham Fined $30,000 for Goal-Post Dunks," NFL.com, Aug. 22, 2014.

"New Orleans Saints Rookie Jimmy Graham Appreciates Life's Lessons," NOLA.com, May 17, 2010.

"Jimmy Graham's Unlikely Path," ESPN YouTube channel, Oct. 23, 2011.

"Michael Bennett: I Still Feel the Same Way about Jimmy Graham," Pro Football Talk, Apr. 9, 2015.

"Saints vs. Ravens 2010 Week 15," NFL Network via All Highlights YouTube channel, May 23, 2019.

"Saints vs. 49ers 2011 NFC Divisional," NFL Network via All Highlights YouTube channel, Oct. 28, 2018.

"Steelers vs. Seahawks | Week 12 Highlights | NFL," NFL YouTube channel, Nov. 30, 2015.

"Jimmy Graham University of Miami Basketball Highlights Full Video," Official Jimmy Graham YouTube channel, Mar. 24, 2016.

Chapter 14

"It's Time for the NFL to Remember What It Means to Get Gronked," Bleacher Report, Aug. 2, 2017, https://bleacherreport.com/articles/2353607-rob-gronkowski-finally-partied-hard-enough-to-rip-his-pants-apart.

"Rob Gronkowski Explains Why He Was Happy to Serve a Suspension in 2017," PatriotsWire, Jan. 5, 2022.

"The Last Happy Man," *Sports Illustrated*, Sept. 3, 2012.

"Rob Gronkowski—Vegas WRESTLING with Broken Forearm," TMZ.com, Feb. 5, 2013.

"'YO SOY FIESTA'—Gronk," ESPN Deportes via Flick It Cards You-Tube channel, Jan. 24, 2012.

2010 NFL draft coverage, via NFL Network, on Mansion Pro Vimeo channel, https://vimeo.com/17411360.

"2010 New England Patriots 2nd Round Pick-Rob Gronkowski," ESPN via xXPatsManXx93 YouTube channel, Apr. 23, 2010.

"The Majesty of the Gronk Spike: How It Began and Why It's So Awesome," ESPN.com, Apr. 21, 2020.

"Rob Gronkowski, Shirtless Matt Light Danced Away Their Sorrows after the Super Bowl," *Deadspin*, Feb. 6, 2012.

"It's Good to Be Gronk," ESPN.com, Jan. 11, 2012.

"Rob Gronkowski Drops Tebow-Sized Bomb on Audience," NFL.com, Apr. 13, 2012.

"The 55 Gronkiest Things Rob Gronkowski Said in 2015," Boston.com, Dec. 24, 2015.

"Rob Gronkowski Called Out," ESPNBoston.com, Feb. 8, 2012.

"Steelers S Sean Davis on Rob Gronkowski: 'He Made More Plays Than Me,'" PennLive.com, Dec. 18, 2017.

"NFL Week 18 Mic'd Up 'I Just Got a Milly and We Going to the City,'" NFL YouTube channel, Jan. 12, 2022.

"Gronkowski's Record-Breaking Day! (Patriots vs. Redskins, 2011)," NFL Throwback YouTube channel, Aug. 9, 2018.

"How Rob Gronkowski's Dad Raised America's First Family of Jocks," *Vanity Fair*, Dec. 9, 2015.

Rob Gronkowki's Scouting Profile, Rivals.com, 2007, https://n.rivals.com/content/prospects/2007/rob-gronkowski-7260?guccounter=1.

Chapter 15

"Mic'd Up: Clutch Plays and Sideline Commentary with George Kittle," San Francisco 49ers YouTube channel, Jan. 4, 2022.

"Who Is 49ers TE George Kittle? According to the Kittles," NBC Sports YouTube channel, Jan. 10, 2020.

"Bonded by Football: Inside George Kittle's Unique Relationship with His Dad, KNBR.com, Dec. 7, 2018.

"Illinois State at Iowa—Football Highlights," Big Ten Network You-Tube channel, Sept. 5, 2015.

"George Kittle Discusses Jimmy Garoppolo, the 49ers' NFL Draft, and More," The Ringer YouTube channel, Mar. 31, 2021.

George Kittle block of Ricardo Allen on Fox Sports broadcast, shared via Twitter here: https://twitter.com/Mr_KevinJones/status/1206334852284370944.

"49ers vs. Saints Week 14 Highlights | NFL 2019," NFL YouTube channel, Dec. 8, 2019.

"Inside Tight End University: George Kittle & Co. Are Out to 'Learn from the Best in the Country,'" ESPN.com, June 26, 2021.

Extras

"The Tight End: Version 2.0," *Sports Illustrated*, Sept. 25, 2006.

"The Route You Can't Defend: Inside the Y Option," ESPN.com, Sept. 20, 2018.

"#9 Dave 'The Ghost' Casper | Top 10 Tight Ends of All Time," NFL Films YouTube channel, Nov. 11, 2016.

"Top Controversial Plays: The 'Holy Roller,'" NFL YouTube channel, July 9, 2015.

"Holy Roller at 40: How a Raiders' Fumble-turned-TD Changed the NFL," ESPN.com, Oct. 2, 2018.

ACKNOWLEDGMENTS

Where do you start? I've been writing sports features my entire adult life, but when folks tell you that taking on a book project is a different beast, they are not lying. *The Blood and Guts* would not have been possible without the help of so many different people across so many different walks of life. First, a huge thank-you to my literary agent, Daniel Greenberg, who reached out to me, a total stranger, one day in spring 2021 to help formulate the angle for this book. I owe Daniel immense gratitude. To Sean Desmond, our publisher, I'm forever grateful for the dialogue, the feedback, and the freedom to take on this project.

From the get-go, my hope was for this book to serve as a mere reflection of these tight end greats. That's possible only if the tight ends— and those who knew them best—choose to cooperate, of course. So I owe everyone who took hours upon hours to chat with me the world. Honestly, I didn't know what to expect when I started reaching out to these tight ends. NFL players, past and present, are a busy breed. One by one, they invited me right to their cities and/or dropped everything to chat on the phone, on Zoom. The same goes for so many teammates, opponents, coaches, scouts. You could sense everyone's genuine excitement in the project. They weren't checking off a box—these tight ends, and everyone who knew them, wanted to share their stories with you. The reader.

I was incredibly fortunate for all the people who helped bridge these connections. Sometimes it was a helpful public relations official. Many of my friends in sports media dropped everything they were doing to fetch a number and make a connection—to you all, I am extremely grateful. Also, in many cases, sources for this book had no problem answering a cold call from a stranger. Appreciate you not ignoring that 716 number.

There were several stretches over the ten months of reporting on and writing this book that I didn't talk to some of my closest friends and family. A brother. A college roommate. An uncle. Working on a book, you tend to get lost in an endless cycle of chasing people down...meeting with those people...transcribing...transcribing...transcribing...and writing. Next thing you know, holy heck, months have passed. Thank you to everyone for understanding that I had to be a bit of a maniac.

To Mom and Dad, wow. Your love and support and 24/7/365 willingness to help in every conceivable way means more than you'll ever know. You're the most selfless parents in the world, the most hardworking, the most loving, and I thank God every day you raised me. There's no two people I ever want to make prouder. If I'm able to be half the parent you each were to us three kids, I'll be happy.

And of course we've got to close here at home. Number one, I need to thank my beautiful wife and kids. What a whirlwind this was writing a book and running a business with two kids under two. Each day could feel like a bit of a journey, and there's zero chance this book happens without the best wife imaginable. Gina, you were such a rock. Everyone needs to know how amazing a human being you are. Day in and day out, you take care of our Ella and Sonny—not easy when things heated up with the book. Neither one of us knew what to expect, but there's no doubt about it: This was a team effort in every sense of the word. I love you.

ABOUT THE AUTHOR

Tyler Dunne is the founder of *Go Long*, a newsletter publication dedicated to longform pro football journalism. He has covered the NFL since 2007 for various outlets, including Bleacher Report, the *Buffalo News*, and the *Milwaukee Journal Sentinel*. His writing has been acknowledged by APSE and PFWA, and his story on the Green Bay Packers in 2019 drew the most reads for any story in Bleacher Report history. He graduated from Syracuse's S. I. Newhouse School of Public Communications and now lives in Western New York with his wife, Gina, and two children. This is his first book.